MASTER THE

AP* EUROPEAN HISTORY

T E S T

NATHAN BARBER

TEACHER-TESTED STRATEGIES AND

TECHNIQUES FOR SCORING HIGH

5th Edition

THOMSON

ARCO

Australia • Canada • Mexico • Singapore • Spain • United Kingdom • United States

An ARCO Book
ARCO is a registered trademark of Thomson Learning, Inc., and is used herein under license by Peterson's.

About The Thomson Corporation and Peterson's

With revenues of US$7.2 billion, The Thomson Corporation (www.thomson.com) is a leading global provider of integrated information solutions for business, education, and professional customers. Its Learning businesses and brands (www.thomsonlearning.com) serve the needs of individuals, learning institutions, and corporations with products and services for both traditional and distributed learning.

Peterson's, part of The Thomson Corporation, is one of the nation's most respected providers of lifelong learning online resources, software, reference guides, and books. The Education Supersite[SM] at www.petersons.com—the Internet's most heavily traveled education re-source—has searchable databases and interactive tools for contacting U.S.-accredited institutions and programs. In addition, Peterson's serves more than 105 million education consumers annually.

For more information, contact Peterson's, 2000 Lenox Drive, Lawrenceville, NJ 08648; 800-338-3282; or find us on the World Wide Web at www.petersons.com/about.

Acknowledgements
For Noah and Christy. Thanks to my professors who mentored me, encouraged me, and instilled in me an appreciation and fascination of history.

ISBN 0-7689-0993-7

Printed in the United States of America

10 9 8 7 6 5 4 3 2 1   04 03 02

CONTENTS

PART 1   ABOUT THE TEST

PART 2   REVIEW

Chapter 7 The French Revolution and the Napoleonic Era (1789–1815) 89

Chapter 8 The Agricultural and Industrial Revolutions 105

Chapter 9 Europe from 1815–1900 117

Chapter 10 Europe in the Twentieth Century and Beyond 133

Chapter 11 Enrichment Resources 157

PART 3 PRACTICE TESTS

About the Test

PART

1

PREVIEW

*The Advanced Placement
European History
Course*

*Elements of the
Advanced Exam*

The Advanced Placement European History Course

THE ADVANCED PLACEMENT PROGRAM

The Advanced Placement (AP*) Program is a series of college-level courses and exams in a number of academic fields designed for highly motivated, hardworking secondary students. The AP Program allows secondary students the opportunity to take advanced courses, such as European history, as a part of their high school curriculum and to potentially receive college credit for their work in the courses. Thousands of colleges and universities around the world grant course credit to students who complete AP courses and achieve a satisfactory score on the AP exams (typically a score of 3 or above). Each AP course, designed by a team of college faculty members and AP teachers, seeks to reflect the latest trends and developments in the curricula for the specific field of study.

Participating secondary schools and testing centers administer the AP exams each May. You should consult your AP teacher or school guidance/ placement counselor in January for registration dates, exam fees, and the dates and times of specific AP exams. Additional information about the Advanced Placement Program and Advanced Placement Exams can be found on line at www.collegeboard.org/ap/.

GOALS OF THE ADVANCED PLACEMENT EUROPEAN HISTORY COURSE

According to the College Board, the organization that designs the test, the goals of the Advanced Placement European History course are "for students to gain knowledge of basic chronology and of major events and trends from approximately 1450 to the present and to develop an understanding of some of the principal themes in modern European history, an ability to analyze historical evidence, and an ability to analyze and express historical under-standing in writing." If you break the College Board's requirements down into digestible chunks, you'll better understand the areas in which they expect you to gain proficiency. The College Board expects AP European History students to:

- **Gain knowledge of basic chronology and of major events and trends from approximately 1450 to the present**

  Quite simply, you should have a general understanding of some of the most important events from the last six centuries of European history as well as a sense of when these events occurred, particularly in relation to the other major events from this period of time.

- **Develop an understanding of some of the principal themes in modern European history**

  In other words, you must begin to see how the events and trends of modern European history fall into several categories, such as intellectual and cultural history, political and diplomatic history, or social and economic history. These themes are examined more closely in the following section.

- **Be able to analyze historical evidence**

  Historical evidence comes in a variety of forms, which includes (but is not limited to) journal entries, pamphlets, government documents, books, works of art, political cartoons, and maps. You should be familiar with many of the major pieces of historical evidence. More importantly, though, you must be able to demonstrate your ability to analyze this evidence for such things as bias, point of view, sarcasm, and propaganda value. More simply put, you must read between the lines for the deeper meaning, symbolism, and true nature of historical evidence.

- **Prove your ability to analyze and express historical understanding in writing**

  Restated—by incorporating historical evidence in your writing and by presenting a clear and concise argument, you must demonstrate a deep comprehension and understanding of a given historical topic through proficient writing.

In a nutshell, the College Board expects you to develop a thorough understanding of the chronology, major events, and major themes of the last six centuries of European history and to develop an ability to demonstrate your comprehension of European history through your writing. They determine whether or not you've reached these goals satisfactorily, based upon the results of the AP European History Exam.

THEMES OF THE ADVANCED PLACEMENT EUROPEAN HISTORY COURSE

The AP European History course explores and examines some of the more important areas, or themes, of the last six centuries of European history. All of the major events and trends from the last six centuries fall into at least one of the following categories:

- Intellectual and cultural history

- Political and diplomatic history

- Social and economic history

INTELLECTUAL AND CULTURAL HISTORY

The first major theme category is intellectual and cultural history. *Intellectual* history covers changes in religious thought and institutions and changes in attitude toward religion. Also included in intellectual history are the secularization of learning and developments in literacy, education, and communication as well as developments in social, economic, and political thought. Finally, scientific and technological advances, along with their consequences, are part of the intellectual history of Europe.

Cultural history includes the diffusion of new intellectual concepts among the different social groups. The new intellectual developments and their relationship to social values and political thought also fall under cultural history. Cultural history includes any and all changes in elite and popular culture, the family, work, and ritual. Changes and trends in literature and the arts are part of cultural history. Finally, cultural history includes the impact of global expansion on European culture.

POLITICAL AND DIPLOMATIC HISTORY

The second major theme category is political and diplomatic history, which, simply put, explores politics and diplomacy throughout European history. *Political* history includes the growth of nationalism and the rise and functioning of the modern state. Also included within political history is the evolution of political parties and ideologies. The extension and limitation of rights and liberties, along with political persecution, falls within the realm of political history. Finally, going hand in hand with rights, liberties, and political liberties, are forms of protest, reform, and revolution, all important aspects of political history.

The *diplomatic* history of Europe, as you well know, can be quite complicated. Diplomatic history covers not only foreign policy but also the relationship between foreign policy and domestic policy. Much of the diplomatic history focuses on the efforts to restrain conflict by way of treaties, balance-of-power diplomacy, and international organizations. When those efforts fail, we are left with war and civil conflict; diplomatic history explores the origins, developments, consequences, and technology involved in those conflicts. Finally, the relations between Europe and the rest of the world, as manifested in colonialism, imperialism, decolonization, and the ever-developing global interdependence, are included in diplomatic history.

SOCIAL AND ECONOMIC HISTORY

The third major theme category is social and economic history, or the history of society and the economy. The *social* history of Europe explores the growth and development of social classes, racial and ethnic groups, mainstream and nonmainstream groups, and demographics. Social history also includes social structure, family structure, and interest groups, especially as influenced by gender roles. The influence of urbanization, sanitation and healthcare, food supply, diet, famine, and disease on society also falls under the category of social history.

Economic history includes both private and state economic activity. The changing distribution of wealth and poverty is an important aspect of economic history. Economic history also includes the development of commercial practices, industrialization, the growth of competition, and the interdependence of national and world markets. Finally, economic history examines the social impact of each of these economic phenomena.

Many of the questions on the AP exam, particularly within the multiple-choice section, will be limited to only one of the three major themes. However, some of the multiple-choice questions will require you to draw on your knowledge from the perspective of more than one theme. The thematic essay questions will almost *certainly* require you to address specific topics as they relate to at least two, if not all three, of the themes of the AP European History course.

As you work through the course, don't limit your study to just one, or even two, of the three major themes, as all three themes will be tested on the AP European History Exam. In addition, try to develop a sense of how all of the major events and themes are not independent, but rather, interconnected. After all, one of the major purposes of the course is for you to see the big picture of European history.

THE EXAM FORMAT

The AP European History Exam is 3 hours and 55 minutes in length. The exam is divided into two sections, each comprising 50 percent of the total score. The first section is a 55-minute multiple-choice section, which is used to test your knowledge of the three major themes, and the second is a 130-minute free-response section, which tests your historical comprehension and historical writing abilities. The free-response section is divided into two smaller sections—Part A, the Document Based Question, and Part B, the thematic essays. The exam questions span the period from 1450 to the present and test the three major themes outlined in this chapter (intellectual and cultural history, political and diplomatic history, social and economic history).

SCORING THE EXAM

The exam is scored on a five-point scale as follows:

> 5 - Extremely Well Qualified
>
> 4 - Well Qualified
>
> 3 - Qualified
>
> 2 - Possibly Qualified
>
> 1 - No Recommendation

Before you take the exam, set a goal for yourself concerning the score you want to earn on the exam. If you want to score a 5 on the exam, you will need a different strategy than if you simply want to score a 3 on the exam.

COLLEGE QUALIFYING SCORES

Colleges and universities that offer credit for AP courses usually accept a minimum score of 3. However, this is not the case for all institutions. AP students who wish to receive college credit for their score should contact the college or university where the test score will be sent to determine the minimum score that will be accepted by that institution.

Elements of the Advanced Placement Exam

WHAT TO EXPECT

In this chapter, we will examine each of the three types of questions you will encounter on the exam: multiple-choice questions, document-based questions, and thematic essays. We will take you step by step through each type of question and show you not only what to expect, but also what the graders of the exam will expect from you. In addition, we will you show you exactly how to attack each type of question successfully.

THE MULTIPLE-CHOICE SECTION

The first section of the AP European History Exam consists of 80 multiple-choice questions that test the entire period of European History that is covered in the AP course (from 1450 to the present). The multiple-choice section counts as 50 percent of your exam grade, and you are allowed 55 minutes to complete the section.

The questions on this section of the exam have been carefully designed and organized by the test-making team at the College Board. Questions aren't scattered haphazardly throughout the exam, they're presented in a precise order that is based on chronology and level of difficulty.

CHRONOLOGY

The multiple-choice questions are placed together in small groups. Within each group, the questions are arranged roughly in chronological order. For example, the first question in a given group may cover the Reformation, while one of the questions in the middle of the group may address the Industrial Revolution. The final question in the group may ask about the post–Cold War Soviet Union. You should be aware that a new group of questions has begun when the the questions change from a more modern subject to one from the very earliest part of the AP European History course.

The multiple-choice section covers the period of time from 1450 to the present and does not only deal with particular topics within that time period. You can count on the questions to be rather consistent in at least one respect. Approximately half of the multiple-choice questions will focus on the time period from the Renaissance through the French Revolution/Napoleonic Era. Therefore, approximately one half of the questions will focus on the time period from the French Revolution/Napoleonic Era to the present. Not all of the multiple-choice questions will focus on one era or time period. Some questions will require you to draw on your knowledge of a topic or an issue that spans several periods of history.

LEVEL OF DIFFICULTY

The multiple-choice section of the AP exam has been designed so that the first questions in the section are relatively easy, with an increasing level of difficulty as you proceed. Don't be lulled into a false sense of security by the simplicity of the first few questions. Because the questions toward the end of the multiple-choice section will be difficult and complex, concentrate on making good decisions in the early stages of the multiple-choice section in order to bolster your score. In other words, take advantage of the less difficult questions up front to compensate for questions you may not know toward the end of the section.

You must also remember that you will most certainly encounter questions about a topic or a subject with which you are not familiar. THAT IS OK. The test makers designed the questions in the multiple-choice section to test the limits of your knowledge. The test is not designed to trick, frustrate, or overwhelm you, but to find out what you know and what you don't. If you need a score of 3 on the exam, you only need to focus on the first 60 questions and try to correctly answer as many of those as you possibly can. If you want a 4, focus on the first 70 questions, and if you want a 5, try to get as many correct as you can on the entire section. In other words, you can miss several questions and leave several questions unanswered without really hurting your chances for a good score.

THEMES TESTED BY MULTIPLE-CHOICE QUESTIONS

The questions in the multiple-choice section test knowledge in all three themes of AP European History (intellectual and cultural history, political and diplomatic history, social and economic history) and the number of questions that deal with each theme is fairly predictable. Between 20 and 30 percent—16 to 24 questions—of the multiple-choice section will deal with cultural and intellectual topics or subjects. Between 30 and 40 percent, or 24 to 32 questions, will test political and diplomatic topics or subjects. The remaining 30 to 40 percent of the questions will address social and economic topics or subjects. Remember that some questions require knowledge of a topic from the perspective of more than one theme. Also remember that the themes will not appear in any particular order throughout the section, so don't read anything extra into the questions based on the themes you see.

TYPES OF MULTIPLE-CHOICE QUESTIONS

The AP European History exam contains several different types of multiple-choice questions. You should understand, though, that the types of questions are very predictable. In other words, you can expect to see several of each of the following types of multiple-choice questions: identification, analysis, reading-based, EXCEPT, and illustration-based. This section will break down each and provide a strategy for answering each type of question.

IDENTIFICATION QUESTIONS

The most common type of multiple-choice question is one that asks you to identify something. You could be asked to identify a person and his ideas, an invention or development and its historical period, a group of people and their actions, or any other person, place, thing, or event that has particular historical importance. A basic knowledge of the topic is all that is required to correctly answer an identification question. Detailed analysis is not necessary to choose the correct answer or to eliminate possible wrong answers. Here is a good example:

The writings of Mary Wollstonecraft argued

- (A) that Christian women should devote themselves to the proper maintenance of the household.
- (B) for equality among the sexes.
- (C) against women in the workplace and institutions of higher learning.
- (D) that France should restore the rights of the *ancien regime*.
- (E) that women of the lower classes should serve the women of the upper classes.

The correct answer is (B). To answer the question, you must know that Mary Wollstonecraft was a women's rights advocate. Even without knowledge of Wollstonecraft's specific political agenda or the names of any of her writings, you can answer this correctly by knowing that she was a champion of women's rights.

ANALYSIS QUESTIONS

Another common type of multiple-choice question, the analysis question, is one that requires you to break down a larger topic into more basic elements. The analysis question tests your ability to draw conclusions and determine causation. A question of this nature may require you to analyze an event for cause and/or effect or to analyze a treaty to determine its results or effects. You can answer this type of question if you have less specific knowledge of a topic and a broader understanding of trends, relationships, or the big picture. By using context clues, knowledge of the topic, and knowledge of the chronology of the question and the answer choices, you can eliminate wrong answers and choose the correct answer. Below is an example of this type of question:

The Treaty of Versailles (1919)

- (A)   convinced the United States to join the League of Nations.
- (B)   placed blame on several major European countries for the outbreak of war.
- (C)   never really settled the issues that originally led to the war.
- (D)   allowed Germany to keep all of its territories and colonies.
- (E)   created the United Nations.

The correct answer is (C). The example above requires you to examine each answer choice and determine its validity. By analyzing the provisions of the Treaty of Versailles (1919), you can determine that the treaty never settled the issues that caused World War I, resulting in the outbreak of World War II only twenty years later. If you don't know the answer immediately, you can use the process of elimination to disqualify some—if not all—of the incorrect answers. For example: The Treaty of Versailles (1919) actually *deterred* the United States from joining the League of Nations, so if you know about the treaty and the League of Nations, you can eliminate choice (A). If you remember that Germany shouldered all the blame for World War I and that Germany lost much of its territory, choices (B) and (D) can be eliminated as well. If you use your knowledge of twentieth-century chronology and remember that the United Nations came into existence after World War II, which obviously ended many years after 1919, choice (E) can be eliminated, leaving choice (C), the correct answer.

READING-BASED QUESTIONS

Several questions on the AP exam will require you to read a quote or a passage from a piece of literature and identify the author, the religion, or the philosophical school of thought to which it is attributed. If you recognize the quote or the passage, the correct answer should be easy to find. If the quote or passage seems unfamiliar, you should look for key words or clues within the passage that might indicate authorship or the ideology represented. Questions of this nature are generally very answerable. This is a typical question involving a quote or reading sample:

> "The modern bourgeois society that has sprouted from the ruins of feudal society has not done away with class antagonisms. It has but established new classes, new conditions of oppression, new forms of struggle in place of old ones."

The quotation is from

- (A) the writings of Machiavelli.
- (B) the writings of Sartre.
- (C) the writings of Darwin.
- (D) the writings of Locke.
- (E) the writings of Marx and Engels.

The correct answer is (E). This question uses a passage that may not be immediately recognizable to you. However, the theme of the passage is clearly that of class struggles. You should be able to associate the theme of class struggles with Marx and Engels to correctly select choice (E) as the answer, but if you did not recognize the passage as that of Marx and Engels, you could, again, use the process of elimination to narrow down the choices. You should be able to identify Machiavelli with style of government or behavior of a ruler, Sartre with twentieth-century philosophy, Darwin with natural selection, and Locke with natural rights. By eliminating all of these as wrong answers, you are left with choice (E).

EXCEPT QUESTIONS

There is one question type that can really catch you off-guard if you're not prepared: the EXCEPT question. EXCEPT questions are tricky because they ask you to throw traditional test-taking logic out the window. Rather than looking for a correct answer choice, you're supposed to choose one that *doesn't* fit the statement or question. Fortunately, these questions will all end with the word EXCEPT, but they can still be a little confusing. When you encounter an EXCEPT question, circle the word EXCEPT in the test booklet to remind you of what you're really being asked. An example of the EXCEPT question type:

Martin Luther believed all of the following EXCEPT

- (A) each man's eternal fate has been predestined.
- (B) salvation is granted by the grace of God.
- (C) women should be good wives and mothers.
- (D) indulgences had no place in the church.
- (E) the Catholic church was in need of reform.

The correct answer is (A). Be careful! If you're not paying close attention, you may read the name "Martin Luther" and hastily choose the first right answer you see. Recognize that this is an EXCEPT question and start looking for the answer choice that is *not* a belief of Martin Luther's. All of the answers are in line with Luther's conservative, protestant beliefs *except* choice (A), which you should recognize as the theology of Calvin. It is extremely important when you come across an EXCEPT question to read all of the possible answers before choosing one, even if the first answer appears to be correct.

ILLUSTRATION-BASED QUESTIONS

The final type of question that the College Board includes on the AP exam requires the interpretation of an illustration. Illustrations that may appear on the multiple-choice section of the AP European History exam include maps, graphs, charts, political cartoons, posters, photographs, and works of art, such as paintings and sculptures. These questions are usually very straight-forward, so avoid trying to read too much into the illustrations. Here is an example of a question that uses an illustration:

The poster on the previous page reflects the idea that

    (A) Hitler controlled all of Europe.

    (B) German citizens should be on the look-out for spies.

    (C) indiscriminate conversation may allow Hitler to learn valuable secret information.

    (D) prisoners of war should avoid confessions so as not to give information to the enemy.

    (E) Hitler has the power to solve the problems of Europe.

The correct answer is (C). By carefully studying the poster and then carefully reading each answer, you should be able to glean the information you need to make the correct choice. Let's examine the poster. Notice the way the poster depicts the German hand, signified by the Nazi ring, as dark and menacing. The hand is putting together a puzzle which, when complete, reveals a message. By putting this message in historical context, you should see that a message such as the one in the puzzle might aid Hitler's efforts and harm the efforts of the Allies. The text at the top of the poster serves as a warning to citizens not to carelessly reveal any information about the Allied war efforts. The enemy, Hitler and his forces, might be able to piece together a large amount of information from small pieces of information (the pieces of the puzzle). Based on these observations of the poster and your historical knowledge of World War II, you should be able to identify choice (C) as the correct answer. Choice (A) is incorrect because the hand is putting together a puzzle with a message, not moving about puzzle pieces that represent European countries. Choice (B) is incorrect because a poster meant for German citizens would be written in German. Choice (D) is incorrect because propaganda posters were used to send messages to citizens on the home front, not prisoners of war. Choice (E) is incorrect for the same reason choice (A) is incorrect. You might also use the process of elimination to discard all the incorrect answers. Either way, by taking your time and thinking about each answer, you can choose the right answer—not only on this example but also on any question like this you may encounter.

SCORING THE MULTIPLE-CHOICE SECTION

The multiple-choice section contains 80 questions and counts as one half of the exam grade. Each question answered correctly will earn you one point; therefore, the highest possible score on the section is 80 points. You earn no points for questions that are not answered at all, and you are penalized one fourth of a point for each incorrect answer. The penalty is to correct the score for random guessing. Basically, if you hope to make a 3 on the exam, you need to correctly answer 50 percent of the multiple-choice questions (in addition to demonstrating competency on the free-response section).

GUESSING ON THE MULTIPLE-CHOICE SECTION

Because the scoring system for the multiple-choice section of the AP European History exam penalizes for incorrect answers, some people think that guessing is a foolish thing to do. Granted, blind, random, shot-in-the-dark guessing is probably not the most advisable approach to take if you want a high score, BUT educated, calculated guesses can prove to be valuable on this section of the exam.

If you can't eliminate any of the choices by identifying them as incorrect, skip the question altogether. On most questions, however, you will probably be able to eliminate at least one or two of the potential answers. If you guess after two of the incorrect answers have been eliminated, the chances of guessing the correct answer have been improved from a shaky one-in-five chance to a much better one-in-three chance. If you can eliminate three wrong answers, which is a very good possibility on many questions, the chances of guessing the correct answer improves to one-in-two—you've got a 50-50 shot.

Consider this scenario. If you were to eliminate three wrong answers on four different questions and then guess on each of those four questions, the odds are that you would answer two questions correctly and two questions incorrectly. You would get two points for the two correct answers and would be penalized one-half of a point for the two incorrect answers. Instead of receiving no points for leaving the four questions blank or guessing randomly on all four questions and possibly receiving a penalty of minus 2 points, you would net one and one-half points. You can see from this example that it is beneficial to be aggressive and attack the multiple-choice section instead of being intimidated by it. Just remember not to guess blindly; instead, try to eliminate incorrect answers and make an educated guess from the remaining answers.

HINTS AND STRATEGIES FOR MASTERING THE MULTIPLE-CHOICE SECTION

1. Read the question carefully. Make sure you know exactly what the question is asking. Sometimes you can even pick up clues by the other words in the sentence.

2. Read each answer choice carefully. Read all the answers before making your final choice. Some wrong answer choices may contain words or phrases that make the answer appear correct at first glance. Only by slowing down to get the full meaning can you be sure to choose the best answer.

3. As you read each question, underline or circle the key ideas or key words in the question. This will help to reinforce the ideas in your mind before you read the answer choices.

4. When you come to an EXCEPT question, circle the word EXCEPT to reinforce what the question is asking you to find among the answer choices.

5. As you eliminate incorrect answers, mark through them. Do this on every question except for the easiest questions. (The answers to the easiest questions should be obvious to you.)

6. Go with your first instinct. Your first choice is usually the correct choice. Be confident in your ability to answer the question correctly.

7. Make educated guesses only after you have eliminated some of the incorrect answers. Don't guess blindly.

8. Choose the best answer. Sometimes two or more answers may seem as if they could answer the same question, but each question will have one answer that is better than the others.

9. Don't spend too much time on one question. You do not have to answer every question and you will not be penalized for questions left unanswered. Circle any question you leave unanswered and come back to it later if you have time.

THE FREE-RESPONSE SECTION

The second section of the exam is the 2 hour and 10 minute free-response section, which includes a Document Based Question (DBQ) and two thematic essay questions. As with the multiple-choice section, the free-response section counts as 50 percent of your exam grade. This section begins with a MANDATORY 15-minute reading period. After the 15-minute reading period, you will begin Part A, the Document Based Question, for which you will be allotted 45 minutes to write your essay. You will have 70 minutes in Part B to write two thematic essays. We will examine in detail each part of the free-response section in the following sections of this book.

ORGANIZATION OF YOUR THOUGHTS

Before we get to each part of the free-response section, let's consider the writing strategy you will need to be successful on the exam. First, before you start writing on your exam, use the 15-minute reading period to organize your thoughts. After all, the 15-minute reading period is mandatory! Use this time to read through the directions, the background information and the question in the DBQ, the DBQ documents, and the thematic essay questions. Start thinking about how you want to organize your thoughts on the DBQ.

In the following sections, we'll show you how to interpret the different types of essay questions you will see and how to develop your thesis. We'll also show you how to use a chart or grid to organize your thoughts on the DBQ and how to use an outline for the DBQ and the thematic essays. Don't underestimate the power or value of organization on this part of the exam! One of the secrets to quality writing is being clear, concise, and *organized*.

INTERPRETING THE QUESTIONS

To write a great essay that answers the question, you first must know what the question is asking. In other words, it is important for you to know exactly what types of questions the exam will ask you as well as the vocabulary the questions will contain. The secret to correctly interpreting questions is actually not a secret at all. To correctly interpret questions, you simply need to be familiar with the vocabulary found in typical AP essay questions. Let's look at the most common essay question vocabulary, in no particular order, and see what each means.

Describe Questions

The word *describe* requires you tell about, or give an account of, something. In other words, when asked to describe something, you should paint a picture using words. Example: "Describe the economic and social conditions of the French urban poor and rural peasants in the months and weeks prior to the French Revolution."

Explain Questions

The word *explain* is your signal to discuss the meaning of or clarify something. Another option would be to give greater detail. Example: "Explain the effects of the printing press on the spread of religion and literacy throughout western Europe in the late fifteenth century."

Compare and *Contrast* Questions

In everyday usage, many people use the words *compare* and *contrast* interchangeably. However, that usage is erroneous. Remember that the two words have two very different meanings. *Compare* means identify the similarities between two or more things, while *contrast* means find the dissimilarities, or differences, between two or more things. The test makers and readers know the difference between the two words and they expect you to, as well. These words are frequently used together in the same question, but that does not change the meanings. Example: "Compare and contrast the extent to which Louis XIV and Peter the Great were absolute monarchs."

Discuss Questions

When asked to *discuss* a topic, you should write about the topic and include a treatment of more than one point of view. When you *discuss* a subject, you should address the pros and cons or different sides of the subject. Example: "Discuss the Marshall Plan and its effects on Western Europe, particularly Germany."

Assess Questions

When you are asked to *assess* something, frequently a statement or generalization, you must evaluate, or appraise the value of, that statement. In other words, you should judge the character, validity, or reliability of a statement or generalization. Example: "'The Scientific Revolution was not a scientific revolution but an intellectual revolution.' Assess the validity of this statement. Include facts in your assessment that support your argument."

Analyze Questions

Some of the most common essay questions are those that require you to *analyze.* When you *analyze* something, be it an event, a trend, or something else, you are to break it down to its most basic elements or components. You should also examine the relationship between the elements or between the components and the whole. Quite often you will be asked to examine a cause and effect relationship. Example: "Analyze the key developments of the Industrial Revolution that occurred in Europe in the early nineteenth century."

DEVELOPING YOUR THESIS

To write a good essay in the free-response section, you must include a good thesis. Your thesis may be the most important part of any essay you write on the exam. Your thesis should set the tone for the rest of the essay and, more importantly, your thesis should tell the reader exactly what you are about to say in your essay.

When writing your thesis, answer the question that is being asked. Do not simply restate the question. This may seem simplistic, but AP readers report that the most common mistake made by test takers is the use of a thesis that does not answer the question. The readers are looking for an original thought, argument, or a statement based on facts or evidence. Without a good thesis, your essay will be mediocre, at best. With a good thesis, your essay will be well on its way to a great score!

Now that you have an idea about how to organize your thoughts for the essays, let's move on to each of the types of questions in the free-response section, the DBQ, and the thematic essays.

PART A: THE DBQ

Part A of the free-response section is the Document Based Question, or the DBQ. The DBQ counts as 45 percent of your free-response score. After a mandatory 15-minute reading period, you are given 45 minutes in which to write your answer.

WHAT IS A DBQ?

The DBQ is a unique question that requires both analysis and synthesis. Basically, a DBQ presents a question followed by some historical background information and several historical documents. In the past few years, the number of documents has been between ten and twelve. You are to read these documents, analyze the information provided by the documents, and then answer the question based upon your analysis. The purpose of the DBQ is not to test your knowledge of the subject of the documents. Rather, the DBQ tests your ability to work with historical evidence and formulate an answer to the question based upon that evidence. In other words, the DBQ requires you to act as a historian who must piece together information to shed light upon a particular topic. And, just like with the work of a historian, there will be no single right or wrong answer to a DBQ. Instead, your answer will be graded according to a rubric, which we will explain later in this section.

SAMPLE DBQ

Let's look at a good example of a DBQ. We'll use the following DBQ throughout the rest of this section to show you how to interpret the question, organize your thoughts with a chart, develop a thesis, and write the essay. Part A of the free-response section will look very much like the following DBQ, including the directions, structure of the question, and the types of documents. Carefully read the following Document Based Question and pay close attention to the directions, the question, and the documents.

Directions: The following question is based on the accompanying Documents 1–12. (Some of the documents have been edited for the purpose of this exercise.)

This question is designed to test your ability to work with historical documents. As you analyze the documents, take into account both the sources of the documents and the authors' points of view. Write an essay on the following topic that integrates your analysis of the documents. **Do not simply summarize the documents individually.** You may refer to relevant historical facts and developments not mentioned in the documents.

1. Analyze and discuss how the issue of child labor in factories was perceived by different groups during the Industrial Revolution in Great Britain.

Historical Background: In the early nineteenth century, Great Britain found herself in the midst of sweeping industrial change. Machines were replacing workers and workers were needed to operate new machines. Many factory owners turned to children, instead of adult laborers, to fill their factories.

Document 1

From a speech by Henry Thomas Pope to the House of Commons, 1832

It is obvious that, if you limit the hours of labour, you will, to nearly the same extent, reduce the profits of the capital on which the labour is employed. Under these circumstances, the manufacturers must either raise the price of the manufactured article or diminish the wages of their workmen. If they raise the price of the article the foreigner gains an advantage. I am informed that the foreign cotton-manufacturers, and particularly the Americans, tread closely upon the heels of our manufacturers.

Document 2

An advertisement that appeared in *The Derby Mercury* on September 20, 1781.

Wanted at Cromford. Forging & Filing Smiths, Joiners and Carpenters, Framework-Knitters and Weavers with large families. Likewise children of all ages may have constant employment. Boys and young men may have trades taught them, which will enable them to maintain a family in a short time.

Document 3

From a speech by Lord Francis Egerton to the House of Commons, 1836

I perceive that the growth of the cotton manufacture in America has proceeded with a rapidity almost equal to our own, and that of France, although the progress has not been so great, it is still but little short, and quite sufficient to make me deeply apprehensive. I therefore think that any legislation by which our manufactures are likely to be effected, we should keep the increased production of foreign countries closely in view.

Document 4

From a speech by William Bolling to the House of Commons, 1836

I mistrust interference on behalf of the poor which the poor are themselves to pay for. Let the question be presented honestly and fairly. Let the parents of factory children know that the diminishing of the hours of daily toil must diminish the amount of weekly pay. Certainly, there are cases of hardship and oppression, but I dislike all cases of legislative interference between master and man—between parent and child. And, moreover, all such interference would be unsuccessful. Your laws to regulate wages, and hours of labour, and conditions of contract for work—they are merely cobwebs broken through at will—because it is the interest of master and servant that they should be broken. Cultivate commerce with all the nations of the world; this will raise wages and will prevent the necessity for exhausting labour.

Document 5

From The Philosophy of Manufactures by Andrew Ure, 1835

I have visited many factories, both in Manchester and the surrounding districts, during a period of several months and I never saw a single instance of corporal punishment inflicted on a child. The children seemed to be always cheerful and alert, taking pleasure in using their muscles. The work of these lively elves seemed to resemble a sport. Conscious of their skill, they were delighted to show it off to any stranger. At the end of the day's work they showed no sign of being exhausted.

On my recent tour through the manufacturing districts, I have seen tens of thousands of old, young and middle-aged of both sexes earning abundant food, raiment, and domestic accommodation, without perspiring at a single pore, screened meanwhile from the summer's sun and the winter's frost, in apartments more airy and salubrious than those of the metropolis in which our legislature and fashionable aristocracies assemble.

Document 6

A chart showing the weights of children factory workers and children not working in factories.

Age	Average Weight of Males in Factories	Average Weight of Males Not in Factories	Age	Average Weight of Females in Factories	Average Weight of Females Not in Factories
9	51.76	53.26	9	51.13	53.44
10	57.00	60.28	10	54.80	54.44
11	61.84	58.36	11	59.69	61.13
12	65.97	67.25	12	66.08	66.07
13	72.11	75.36	13	73.25	72.72
14	77.09	78.68	14	83.41	83.43
15	88.35	88.83	15	87.86	93.61

Document 7

Resolution passed by the Leeds Short Time Committee, 1831

The ten hour day would equalise labour by calling into employment many male adults, who are a burden on the public, who, though willing and ready to work, are obliged to spend their time in idleness, whilst children are compelled to labour from twelve to sixteen hours per day.

Document 8

A letter by Richard Oastler published in the *Bradford Observer*, July 17, 1834

The mill-owners obtained their wealth by overworking and by defrauding the factory children. They were praying people, but took care their work people should neither have time nor strength to pray. These hypocrites pretended it was necessary to keep these poor infant slaves at this excruciating labour just to preserve them from "bad company" and to prevent them learning "bad habits".

Document 9

From a report by Leonard Horner, Inspector of Factories, 1850

On the 4th May, Mr. Jones and I visited the factory of Christopher Bracewell & Brothers at Earby. It stands apart from the village, in an open field, and as we came near, one of the brothers was seen running with considerable speed from the house to the mill. This looked very suspicious, but we did not discover anything wrong. A few days afterwards I received an anonymous letter stating that when Mr. Bracewell saw the factory inspector he went to the mill, and got those under age into the privies. He also said that the children worked from 13 to 14 hours a day. In a few days, Mr. Jones went again to the mill, taking the superintendent of police at Colne along with him. After having made his first examination, he directed the constable to search the privies, and there were found in them thirteen children. All of them were found to be illegally employed in the mill.

Document 10

An illustration of boys working in a factory.

Document 11

Submission by a group of factory working children from Manchester's Factory Children Committee which was sent to the House of Commons, 1836

We respect our masters, and are willing to work for our support, and that of our parents, but we want time for more rest, a little play, and to learn to read and write. We do not think it right that we should know nothing but work and suffering, from Monday morning to Saturday night, to make others rich. Do, good gentlemen, inquire carefully into our concern.

Document 12

An interview of Robert Owen before Robert Peel's House of Commons Committee, April 26, 1816

Question: At what age do you take children into your mills?

Robert Owen: At ten and upwards.

Question: Why do you not employ children at an earlier age?

Robert Owen: Because I consider it to be injurious to the children, and not beneficial to the proprietors.

Question: What reasons have you to suppose it is injurious to the children to be employed at an earlier age?

Robert Owen: Seventeen years ago, a number of individuals, with myself, purchased the New Lanark establishment from Mr. Dale. I found that there were 500 children, who had been taken from poor-houses, chiefly in Edinburgh, and those children were generally from the age of five and six, to seven to eight. The hours at that time were thirteen. Although these children were well fed their limbs were very generally deformed, their growth was stunted, and although one of the best schoolmasters was engaged to instruct these children regularly every night, in general they made very slow progress, even in learning the common alphabet. I came to the conclusion that the children were injured by being taken into the mills at this early age, and employed for so many hours; therefore, as soon as I had it in my power, I adopted regulations to put an end to a system which appeared to me to be so injurious.

Question: Do you give instruction to any part of your population?

Robert Owen: Yes. To the children from three years old upwards, and to every other part of the population that choose to receive it.

Question: If you do not employ children under ten, what would you do with them?

Robert Owen: Instruct them, and give them exercise.

Question: Would not there be a danger of their acquiring, by that time, vicious habits, for want of regular occupation.

Robert Owen: My own experiences leads me to say, that I found quite the reverse, that their habits have been good in proportion to the extent of their instruction.

INTERPRETING THE QUESTION

Using the sample DBQ, let's look at the question and break it down into its basic elements. The question states:

> Analyze and discuss how the issue of child labor in factories was perceived by different groups during the Industrial Revolution in Great Britain.

First, the question requires that you *analyze* and *discuss*. Remember that *analyze* means to break down into component parts and "discuss" means to provide a treatment of the topic from more than one point of view. Therefore, in your essay, you are to break down the topic into its component parts and write about those parts from more than one point of view. But what should you *analyze* and *discuss*?

The next step is to find the topic or subject of the question to *analyze* and *discuss*. In this question, the subject is the perception of child labor as held by different groups during the Industrial Revolution. How do you write about such a specific topic?

In the DBQ, the information you need is found within the documents provided. Use the documents, along with the historical background information, and find the information needed to answer the question. Now you simply put all the steps together. Based on all that you have learned thus far, you can determine that the question is asking you to identify the different perceptions of child labor during the Industrial Revolution, break those perceptions down into their component parts, and write about those perceptions from different points of view, using the documents as historical evidence upon which you will base your essay.

INTERPRETING THE DOCUMENTS

To use the documents as the basis for your essay, you must understand the types of documents you may encounter and what information to look for in those documents. First, using our sample DBQ as a point of reference, let's look at some of the documents that may appear in a DBQ. A common DBQ document is an excerpt from a book (Document 5). Another very common document is a letter (Document 8). Speeches, or at least excerpts from speeches, are frequently used (Documents 1, 3, and 4). Charts, graphs, and tables are documents that historians use, so they are commonly found in DBQs (Document 6). Government reports provide valuable historical information (Document 9). Advertisements, both written and illustrated, can be valuable, too (Document 2). Many DBQs will include artwork of some kind; this artwork may be a painting, a sculpture, a cartoon, an illustration, or a photograph (Document 10). Resolutions, petitions, legislation, and other statements made to or by a legislative body serve as valuable sources (Documents 7, 11, and 12). Other types of historical documents you may see include journal entries, songs, and excerpts from periodicals.

Now you know the types of documents with which you will be working, but what should you look for within each of those documents? Look for what historical information is offered by the document. Understand, though, that a document is not necessarily true, valid, or accurate just because it is a historical document. You may or may not be able to determine the validity or accuracy of each document, and that is okay.

One of the things that will help you determine the trustworthiness of each document is consideration of the authorship of the document. This involves a few things. First, who wrote or authored the document? Second, why was this document created, and for whom was it created? Did the author have a motive, an agenda, or an axe to grind. All of these factors can affect whether or not you take the document at face value. Third, does the document demonstrate any bias or sarcasm? Bias and sarcasm definitely affect whether or not a document can be taken at face value, and you absolutely must be able to detect either of these in an historical document.

Let's apply this information to a document from our DBQ to get you started. Let's use Document 3 as our example:

Document 3

> From a speech by Lord Francis Egerton to the House of Commons, 1836
>
> I perceive that the growth of the cotton manufacture in America has proceeded with a rapidity almost equal to our own, and that of France, although the progress has not been so great, it is still but little short, and quite sufficient to make me deeply apprehensive. I therefore think that any legislation by which our manufactures are likely to be effected, we should keep the increased production of foreign countries closely in view.

First, let's consider the authorship of this document. This an excerpt from a speech given by Lord Francis Egerton to the House of Commons. From the excerpt, Egerton appears to be trying to dissuade Parliament from changing any laws that might affect the manufacturing industry. By putting this document in historical context and by looking for bias, it is safe to say that Egerton is using the national economy as a reason why new legislation should not be introduced when, in fact, Egerton is concerned that the elimination or restriction of child labor would hurt his business. Therefore, you should not take this document at face value but in the manner in which it was intended—to be persuasive.

By practicing with this sample DBQ and on the DBQs found in the practice exams, you will get better and better at analyzing the documents like we did in the preceding paragraph. As you read each of the documents, make notes about the documents concerning the things we mentioned (authorship, bias, sarcasm, etc.). This will help tremendously when you start to use your chart to organize the information.

ORGANIZING THE INFORMATION IN THE DOCUMENTS

The DBQ will present information to you in the form of historical documents, but these documents, and the information in them, will need to be organized. Usually the documents will be grouped in one of two ways. First, they may be organized chronologically. If this is the case, you may need to deal with the question and the answer over that specific period of time. Second, the documents may be arranged by point of view or some other grouping. If this is the case, the question is likely to ask you to compare and/or contrast in your essay or look at a topic from several points of view, as in our sample DBQ.

To use the information from the documents in an organized manner to support your essay, you should organize the information so that you can look at the information and see it all at one time. Perhaps the best and most efficient way to do this is to create a chart or grid. You can create a chart for any DBQ. To do this, look at what the question is asking. In our sample DBQ, the question is asking about perceptions of child labor during the Industrial Revolution and different points of view. Therefore, your chart might look similar to this:

	Child Labor—Necessary	Child Labor—Unnecessary
Economic Reasons		
Social Reasons		
Medical Reasons		

By creating a chart like this one, you can write the numbers of the documents in the appropriate cells. For example, a document that uses economic reasons to justify child labor, such as Document 3, would be put in the column under "Child Labor—Necessary" and in the row across from "Economic Reasons," like the chart that follows.

	Child Labor—Necessary	Child Labor—Unnecessary
Economic Reasons	3	
Social Reasons		
Medical Reasons		

At this time, read through the documents in the sample DBQ again and fill in the remainder of the chart. This will be good practice for you and it will help you when you write the essay for this DBQ. (You didn't know you would have to practice on this one, did you?) After you have organized all the documents, you will be ready to decide how you want to answer the question. Remember, there is no right or wrong answer on a DBQ. Look at the way the documents are organized in your chart. Do you see a pattern? Reread the question. Now you should be able to formulate an answer for the question.

DEVELOPING YOUR DBQ THESIS

The first and most important thing to remember when writing your DBQ thesis is to answer the question being asked. Do not restate the question. As was mentioned earlier, it is imperative that you answer the question and tell the reader what you are going to say in your essay. Think about how you are going to answer the question and what evidence you are going to use to support your answer; your thesis should be a summary of this. A well-written thesis makes it much easier to write a good essay, so take your time and develop a strong thesis.

DEVELOPING AN OUTLINE

Once you have developed a good, strong thesis, you need to plan a strategy for clearly writing the rest of your essay. One of the best ways to write a clear, concise essay is to use an outline. An outline provides structure and organization for your essay. If you follow an outline, you will stay on task and not get sidetracked. To develop a good outline, follow this simple model:

I.   Introduction—This should be an introductory paragraph that includes your thesis. Tell the reader what you are going to say in your essay.

II. First point or argument that supports your thesis (one to two good paragraphs)

III. Second point or argument that supports your thesis (one to two good paragraphs)

IV. Third point or argument that supports your thesis (one to two good paragraphs)

V. Conclusion—This should be a conclusory paragraph that includes a summation of your arguments. Remind the reader of what you said in the essay. Provide closure.

By using an outline, you can confidently attack the DBQ. By arguing three main points, you will be able to support your thesis, but you won't get bogged down in an endless amount of information. Finally, an outline of this size will keep you on a good time schedule and will not allow you to waste your writing time.

WRITING THE ESSAY

With a clear plan of attack, you are now ready to write your DBQ essay. Let's review the process. First, read the question and make sure you understand exactly what the question is asking. Second, carefully examine each of the documents. Note things about each document (such as bias, sarcasm, point of view, and intended audience) that will help you organize the documents later. Third, organize the documents using a chart. Fourth, based on the evidence before you, develop a thesis that answers the question and tells the reader what you are going to say in the essay. Fifth, create an outline to follow as you write your essay. Finally, put all the steps together and write each of the paragraphs in your essay just as you planned in your outline. Follow this plan and you will be on track to write a good DBQ essay.

SCORING THE DBQ

You will be delighted to know that the readers, who spend countless hours grading exams like yours, do not grade the exams based on whether or not they like your exam or your handwriting or some other arbitrary characteristic. On the contrary, the graders use a *rubric* to evaluate your essay. The scoring scale is from 0–9. In order to score a 7, 8, or 9, you must first receive all six of the Basic Core Points. You can earn Extended Score Points only after you earn the Basic Core Points. Let's look at exactly what the rubric measures.

Each item below, which is included in the basic core, is worth one point toward a total of six Basic Core points:

1. The essay has an acceptable thesis.

2. The essay uses a majority of the documents.

3. The thesis is supported with appropriate evidence from the documents.

4. The writer of the essay understands the basic meaning of each document (the writer may misinterpret one document).

5. The essay demonstrates an analysis of bias or point of view in at least two or three documents.

6. The essay demonstrates analysis of documents by grouping the documents (depending on the DBQ question).

Once the reader awards you the six Basic Core points, he or she can add up to three Expanded Core Points for any of the following:

1. The essay has a "clear, analytical, and comprehensive" thesis.

2. The essay uses all or almost all of the documents.

3. The essay uses the documents in a persuasive manner.

4. The essay demonstrates "careful and insightful" analysis of the documents.

5. The essay demonstrates analysis of bias or point of view in at least four documents.

6. The essay demonstrates analysis of documents in additional ways (groupings or other).

7. The essay incorporates relevant outside historical content.

This rubric demystifies the DBQ, because you now know exactly what the readers will be looking for in your DBQ essay. Use this rubric as a checklist when you write your practice DBQ essay and when you write your DBQ essays included in the two practice exams in the last section of this book.

HINTS AND STRATEGIES FOR MASTERING THE DBQ

1. Use the 15-minute reading period to read the DBQ question, historical background and documents. Make notes of anything that will help you organize the documents.

2. Underline or circle any important words in the question that may help you better understand the question or what to look for in the documents.

3. Don't get frustrated trying to find the right answer. These questions are designed so you can argue from different perspectives.

4. Use as many of the documents as you can in your essay. However, do not force documents into your essay just so you have all of them included. It is not necessary to include all of the documents in your essay.

5. Cite documents in your essay by using the author's name and/or using the number of the document. The readers will be familiar with the documents.

6. Incorporate the documents into your essay. Do not simply give a "laundry list" of documents or a summary of the documents.

7. Don't quote long passages from the documents; just cite the documents. Again, the readers will be familiar with all of the documents.

8. Include some "outside" historical information but be careful not to use a wrong date or an inaccurate fact.

PRACTICE DBQ

The time has come for you to put all this information to use. Choose a quiet place, perhaps the library, and set aside one hour in which to write your practice essay using the sample DBQ. When your time begins, use the first 15 minutes as your mandatory reading time, just like the real exam. (You know what to do with this time!) After fifteen minutes, begin writing your essay. Stop writing after 45 minutes and take a break. You deserve it! After your break, check your essay against the rubric to make sure that you have included at least all of the six elements listed under basic core points. If you have earned all six basic core points, check your essay to see if you are eligible for any of the expanded core points. You should read the sample DBQ essay and see how your essay compares. If your essay is not just like the sample essay, don't worry! No two essays will be exactly like. Are you ready to write?

SAMPLE DBQ ESSAY

In Great Britain during the nineteenth century, in the midst of the Industrial Revolution, the issues of child labor and the length of the children's work day became topics for much debate. During this time, social activists lobbied heavily against the evils of child labor and the exploitation of children, while businessmen and industrialists countered those efforts by arguing the importance of the children workers to the economy. These debates took place in the factories, in books, in periodicals, and even in houses of Parliament. The two sides in this debate differed for economic, social, and medical reasons.

Defenders of both child labor and the longer than ten-hour work day argued that the children employed by factories and mills learned valuable trades, as noted in Document 2. In addition, the document contends that boys and young men were able to maintain a state of constant employment in the factories, thus enabling them to have the means to support families. Other supporters, such as Lord Egerton in his speech to Parliament, added that a reduction of work hours for the children would logically result in a reduction of wages for them as well, putting them in an economically disadvantageous position.

Henry Thomas Pope and William Bolling, in Documents 1 and 4, respectively, went even further in their arguments. They both insisted that the national economy depended on the production of goods by factories that employed children. Both speakers warned that any legislation that affected child labor and the work day also affected the national economy, which happened to be in fierce competition with America.

Anti–child labor activists countered these statements with economic arguments of their own. A shortened work day, argued the Leeds Short Time Committee, would create opportunities for unemployed adult males to find jobs, thereby reducing the burden on the public. This economic situation was unacceptable to the children's rights advocates.

In Ure's *The Philosophy of Manufactures*, Ure argued that, based upon his own travels and experiences, the children who worked in factories earned both food and housing. Occasionally, he pointed out, the housing conditions were quite favorable. Additionally, he claimed that the children seemed to be enjoying themselves, both during and after work. Ure saw no evidence of substandard social conditions among the children he witnessed.

The children's rights advocates painted a different picture of the children's social condition. Richard Oastler, in his letter, claimed that many children were being employed to keep them away from "bad company," and yet the children were worked to the point where they had neither the "time nor strength to pray." In an interview before Parliament, Robert Owen argued that children did not need to be employed at a young age to keep them away from bad influences. Owen went on to say that children actually did better at an early age with instruction and exercise than with employment. The children's social condition was thought to be so poor that a group of children were actually brought before a committee that then sent a report to Parliament. In Document 11, the children pleaded for legislation that would give them relief from their suffering.

Finally, child labor advocates offered evidence that no real harm was done to the children who worked in the factories. Ure explained that the children he witnessed had not once been abused. He added that the children were constantly screened from the sun and the cold and they often worked without even sweating. Document 6 shows that there was no significant difference between the weights of children who worked in factories and children who did not. Document 10 is an illustration showing boys working in a clean, well-lit environment. These offered validation to the argument that factory labor was not necessarily bad for children.

Opponents of child labor disagreed. In Owen's interview, Owen argued that factory work caused not only injury to children but also disfigurement in some cases. The unsanitary, unhealthy conditions, according to many children's rights advocates of the day, were quite common at factories and mills.

People on both sides of the debate over child labor and the length of the work day offered volumes of evidence to support their arguments, evidence that was economic, social, and medical in nature. Ultimately, though, Parliament sided with the children's rights advocates. During the nineteenth century, Great Britain passed numerous pieces of legislation, such as the English Factory Act and the Ten Hour Act, that sought to end the exploitation of British children by factories and mills.

PART B: THE THEMATIC ESSAYS

Part B of the free-response section consists of the thematic essay questions. The thematic essay questions count as 55 percent of your free-response score. You will have 70 minutes to answer two essay questions, one each from two groups of three questions. In other words, you will choose one question from Group 1 and one question from Group 2; each group contains three questions. It is recommended that you use 5 minutes as planning time for each question and 30 minutes for writing. In the paragraphs ahead, we will explore the essay topics and types of questions that may appear and show you how to decide which question is the best question for you to answer. Finally, we'll help you develop a strategy for writing good essays.

The Most Common Essay Questions

Although no one can predict the exact questions you will see on the exam, we can tell you which types of questions have appeared the most on past AP exams. Based on the released exams and free-response questions from 1994 to 1999, the most common type of thematic essay question is one that requires analysis. Coming in at a close second is the compare and contrast question. With almost the exact same frequency, describe and discuss questions are third and fourth. The remaining types of questions appear intermittently from year to year.

What does this mean? This information tells us that you can almost count on seeing an analyze question or a compare and contrast or maybe both. You are also likely to see a describe or a discuss question. Knowing what types of questions you probably will encounter should help you go in to take the exam with some added confidence.

POSSIBLE ESSAY TOPICS

When it comes to the types of questions that may appear, no one can predict which topics will be on this year's exam. But, just like before, we can tell you what topics have been used before and how often. Some of the most common topics have been women's issues, the Reformation, the Cold War, family life and structure, the French Revolution, art interpretation, and economic issues and the nineteenth century. The three themes (intellectual and cultural, political and diplomatic, social and economic) are pretty well balanced in this section. Each theme has been represented more or less equally over the past six exams.

CHOOSING THE BEST QUESTIONS TO ANSWER

When you get to the thematic essay section, you will need to choose two questions to answer. This decision is important because, naturally, you will be better prepared to answer some questions than others. You will want to find the questions you match up with the best. How do you find the best questions to answer?

First, carefully read each of the questions in Group 1. Make sure you understand exactly what each question is asking. You do not want to try to answer a question if you aren't sure what it's asking! Jot down next to each question some things that come to mind when you read the question. After you have read all of the questions in Group 1 and have made some notes, think about which question you feel the most adequately prepared to answer. Do the same thing for the questions in Group 2.

Is there a question you simply don't understand? If so, mark through it with your pencil and don't go back to it. Remember, no question is worth more than another and there is no secret question that will be graded differently than the others. The readers, the professionals who grade the AP exams, are not going to penalize you for choosing one question instead of another.

Is there a topic in one of the questions on which you did a paper or report? Is there a topic in one of the questions on which you focused in your course? If so, choose that question to answer. You should answer the question in each group with which you feel the most comfortable. Once you choose the question you want to answer, you are ready to start organizing your thoughts.

YOUR THESIS

After you have read and interpreted the questions and have chosen the question you are going to answer, begin to think about how you want to answer the question. What you want to say in response to the question should be summed up in your thesis. Remember, when writing your thesis, answer the question that is being asked. Do not simply restate the question. The readers are looking for an original thought, an argument, and a statement based on facts or evidence.

USE OF AN OUTLINE

Now that you have chosen a question and developed your thesis, you are ready to finish your plan of attack. One of the best ways to write a clear, concise essay is to use an outline. An outline provides structure and organization for your essay. If you follow an outline, you will stay on task and not get sidetracked. To develop a good outline, follow this simple model:

I.   Introduction—This should be an introductory paragraph that includes your thesis. Tell the reader what you are going to say in your essay.

II.   First point or argument that supports your thesis (one to two good paragraphs)

III. Second point or argument that supports your thesis (one to two good paragraphs)

IV.   Third point or argument that supports your thesis (one to two good paragraphs)

V.   Conclusion—This should be a conclusory paragraph that includes a summation of your arguments. Remind the reader of what you said in the essay.

By using the model above, you can sufficiently address most any essay question on the exam or elsewhere. By arguing three main points, you will be able to support your thesis, but you won't get bogged down in an endless amount of information. In conclusion, you will be able to manage your time well if you stick to the outline.

WRITING THE ESSAY

Now you have a very clear strategy for attacking and answering a thematic essay question. All that is left to do is put the steps together. Let's review the process. First, read each of the questions and make sure that you understand what each is asking. Second, consider the topic of each question and choose the question you feel the most adequately prepared to answer. Third, think about how you want to answer the question and develop a good thesis that answers the question. Fourth, devise an outline that supports your thesis and answers the question. Finally, put all the steps together and write each of the paragraphs in your essay just as you planned in your outline. If you use this recipe and provide good, solid information, you will have a clear, concise, and solid thematic essay.

HINTS AND STRATEGIES FOR MASTERING THE THEMATIC ESSAYS

1. Write legibly. The exam readers spend hour after hour reading essay after essay. They probably won't be very excited about trying to decipher handwriting that looks like a secret code. The readers will not deduct points for poor handwriting, but they certainly won't look favorably upon an essay that requires a translator. In addition, you may make a brilliant argument in your essay but if they can't read it, then it doesn't matter.

2. Use good sentence structure. Your sentences don't have to be long and complicated to make a good point. In fact, if you try to make your sentences complicated, you are very likely to make a grammatical or some other type of error.

3. Don't use a word if you don't know what it means. Use *your* vocabulary to write the essay. You will hurt your credibility if you misuse a word in an effort to impress the reader.

4. Clarify terms that may have multiple meanings. If you use a word like *conservative* or *liberal*, explain to the reader what you mean when you use that word.

5. Don't include a fact if you aren't sure of its accuracy. Again, you may damage your credibility by misusing or misquoting a fact, a date, or some other information in an attempt to score some extra points with the reader.

6. Be confident in your essay. Your writing should convey confidence to the reader, confidence that shows you know the subject. Don't be wishy-washy and indecisive—you are trying to prove your point to the reader.

7. Proofread your essay. Check for misspellings, grammar errors, and poor sentences. Also look for factual inconsistencies that may weaken your argument.

Review

The Renaissance (c.1350–c.1550)

OVERVIEW

The word *Renaissance* literally means *rebirth*. To many Italians in the years between 1350 and 1550, they were living in a time of rebirth. Many scholars and artists believed that they were living in a time when, after a thousand years of no progress, the cultures of classical Greece and Rome were being reborn after the intellectually and culturally stagnant Middle Ages. Fourteenth and fifteenth century intellectuals looked back at the Middle Ages, the period of time between the fall of the Roman Empire and the late fourteenth century, with much disdain and contempt. They viewed the Middle Ages as a dark period of history in which man showed little creativity, productivity, or civility. The Renaissance, as they saw it, was a new period in history that appeared to be in stark contrast to the Middle Ages.

Historians have put to rest the notion that the Middle Ages were as the Renaissance scholars described. In fact, Europe, in the thousand years before the Renaissance, did indeed produce art, architecture, literature, and other intellectual developments contrary to the claims of Renaissance Italians. It would be unfair, though, to totally dismiss the Renaissance contemporaries' views of the Middle Ages and of their own times. The concept of rebirth does have some validity. During the late fourteenth century, Europe, and Italy in particular, was trying to recover from the devastating effects of the bubonic plague, or Black Death, which included widespread economic hardship and social and religious upheaval. With that in mind, it is much easier to understand how Renaissance thinkers proclaimed their era one of rebirth.

The Renaissance was, however, if not a rebirth, at least a renewal or rediscovery of interest in and fascination with the cultures and values of classical Greece and Rome. The treasures of Greece and Rome had not been lost for a thousand years. Rather, the language and literature of these cultures had been carefully preserved in the monasteries of Europe by monks and scholars. Accompanying the revival of the classical cultures was a renewed interest in learning, which was fostered by the growth of

NOTE

It is important to remember that history does not fall neatly into categories such as *Middle Ages* or *Renaissance*. A historian can't point to one date and say, "The Middle Ages ends here," or "The Renaissance begins here." Rather, terms such as *Middle Ages* and *Renaissance* are used to categorize trends, ideas, and cultural developments, etc., that share a more or less common time period. The lines between these time periods are blurred at best. Remember to try to see the "big picture" of history.

universities. A new world view developed in the Renaissance, which was a view of marked contrast to that of Europeans during the Middle Ages. Finally, the Renaissance brought with it a new artistic movement influenced by and modeled after the art of Greece and Rome.

THE ITALIAN RENAISSANCE

The Renaissance was largely an urban phenomenon. It was not by accident that the cities that gave rise to the Renaissance were Italian. During the Middle Ages, the towns of Italy began to develop their own identities and economies. Not owing allegiance to one nation or monarch, they developed into powerful, independent city-states that ruled the surrounding areas as well. These city-states, which had long been trade centers, grew into bustling urban areas driven by overseas trade, banking, and commerce. Venice, Genoa, Pisa, Naples, and Florence took advantage of their close proximity to the sea to market their goods such as wool, silk, and other products to countries in Asia and Europe. In addition, bankers in these cities made loans to monarchs and other power-hungry individuals across Europe. These commercial ventures sparked tremendous economic growth for the Italian states and gave rise to such powerful families as the Medici family of Florence, one of the most influential of all the Renaissance families.

From the continued economic success of the Italian states emerged a wealthy class of merchants and bankers who participated in, and many times even controlled, the politics of the city-states. The merchant class discovered the many material pleasures of life that their wealth could provide—fine fashion, fine art, and fine architecture. Therefore, the merchants and bankers of Italy became the patrons, or sponsors, of artists and designers of Italy. They called for these artists and architects to create artistic beauty simply to be appreciated and flaunted. The patrons demanded paintings and sculptures of themselves to be created so they and their wealth might be remembered for generations to follow. This was a break from the medieval tradition in which art was created for the higher purpose of the glorification of God. This new way of thinking ushered in the idea of secularism and began to chip away at the medieval notion of piety in all things, including art. It was these artists who spawned a new era in artistic achievement and are generally referred to as the Renaissance artists.

The newly created merchant class often found conflict with the nobility—those who owned land and whose wealth dated back many generations. In addition, each of these classes found themselves in conflict with the *popolo*, or the lower class that resented the wealth and power of the upper classes. These conflicts erupted in 1378 in Florence in the Ciompi revolt. The revolt brought about the establishment of a republican government in Florence and in Venice. In other states, such as Milan, the conflicts led to rule by the *signori*, or tyrants. At the height of the Renaissance, Italy consisted of several major city-states that dominated the Renaissance era including the

Republic of Florence, the Republic of Genoa, the Venetian Republic, the Duchy of Milan, the Papal states, and the Kingdom of Naples.

HUMANISM

Out of the Italian Renaissance came a few schools of thought that had a profound effect on both Italian and European society for many years to follow. As mentioned before, the concept of secularism flourished during the Renaissance. This idea broke from the medieval tradition of having pious or religious motivations for doing things, whether it is creating art or reading and writing texts. Secularism grew out of the new, more materialistic view of the world by Renaissance society. Likewise, individualism broke with medieval tradition by placing importance and significance on the individual, on man. The celebration of the individual was an important aspect of the Renaissance.

Perhaps the defining concept of the Renaissance, one that developed out of individualism, is that of *Humanism*. Humanism can be defined in a number of ways; the focus on man, his potential, and his achievements is one definition. To some extent, this is part of Renaissance humanism. Perhaps the best way to define humanism within the context of the Renaissance is to say that it was the promotion of education and culture based on the classical models—Greek and Roman.

Often called the Father of Humanism, Francesco Petrarch (1304–1374) learned classical Latin (he already knew medieval Latin) and studied original classical texts by such authors as Cicero. Petrarch developed a following, particularly in Florence, of people who sought the wisdom of the classics on matters of government. These people became known as *Civic Humanists*. One such Civic Humanist, Leonardo Bruni (1370–1444), wrote a biography of Cicero called *New Cicero*. Through such literary works, the Civic Humanists used their powerful rhetoric to inspire humanists to become civic-minded and active in both political and cultural arenas. Soon, Civic Humanism spread to all parts of Italy.

Gradually, humanists began to develop an interest in Greek authors and texts, especially in Plato and his works. The study of Plato not only revived the study of both Greek language and scholarly works but also influenced many Renaissance philosophers. Much of Plato's work dealt with the idea of being and the idea that a truth exists beyond that which man can determine by using his senses alone. Plato pointed out, though, that man can discover this truth through the use of reason, which preexisted the physical world. Renaissance philosophers were fascinated by this concept. Renaissance scholars and philosophers echoed the classical authors by also emphasizing man's amazing and almost unlimited potential. This concept is illustrated better in no document than in Pico della Mirandola's (1463–1494) *Oration on the Dignity of Man*.

NOTE
The modern concept of the Renaissance was first created by Jacob Burckhardt in 1860. In his work *Civilization of the Renaissance in Italy*, he proposed that the Renaissance, being in contrast to the Middle Ages, was the birthplace of the modern world.

NOTE
It was not uncommon for medieval scholars to study ancient texts by studying commentaries, or secondary sources, on the classical texts. Many commentaries presented the classical texts in a new Christian light or provided a Christian interpretation of the texts. Renaissance scholars wanted to glean the original and, in their opinion, the true meaning of the texts by studying the actual texts instead of commentaries.

NOTE

Modern humanities courses and liberal arts courses are based upon the educational ideals of Renaissance Humanism.

Humanism had far-reaching effects throughout Italy and Europe. The church-influenced and Christian-dominated field of historiography, or the recording of history, changed completely with the advent of humanism. Humanism secularized historiography by allowing laymen to write and interpret history and by allowing, even encouraging, the use of secular documents in the study of history.

Perhaps the greatest effect of humanism was on education. Humanists advocated the study of such things as grammar, logic, poetry, mathematics, astronomy, and music. They sought to educate and develop every part of a person intellectually. It is from this approach to developing an individual that we get the idea of the "Renaissance man," the man who is universal, well-rounded, and adept in many fields. *The Courtier* by Conte Baldassare Castiglione (1478–1529) set forth guidelines for the ideal man, thus embracing the notion of the Renaissance man. Castiglione claimed that the ideal man should be skilled in language, literature, and the arts.

Humanism and Women

The humanist movement affected women, too. During the Middle Ages, few women outside of convents could read or write. During the Renaissance, women became increasingly literate, due in no small part to the effort of humanists who argued that women should have access to some of the same educational opportunities as men. In addition to reading and writing, some women also learned the classical languages. An extraordinary example of a classically-educated Renaissance woman is Christine de Pisan (1364-1430). After growing up in the court of Charles V of France, she later wrote his biography. Pisan's most famous, and most influential, work, *The City of Ladies*, documented the great deeds of great women in history.

Humanism and the Printed Word

The texts that were being produced by humanists were being spread across Italy and Europe at an unprecedented rate. With the invention of the movable type printing press around 1450, the German Johann Gutenberg revolutionized the way in which ideas were shared and distributed. While pre-printing press documents were produced either by hand or by block printing at tediously slow speeds, documents printed using the movable type press were produced relatively quickly and they far outnumbered their predecessors in a matter of a few short years. Many of the new documents were Bibles and other religious texts, although a large number of the new documents were reprints of classical works, previously available only as expensive manuscripts.

THE NORTHERN RENAISSANCE

The humanism of the Italian Renaissance began to make its way into the rest of Europe during the second half of the fifteenth century. This movement in the rest of Europe, widely regarded as the Northern Renaissance, manifested itself somewhat differently than in Italy. Whereas Italian humanists focused on secular topics and texts and did not concern themselves very much with the study of Christianity or Christian texts, the humanists of the Northern Renaissance took a much different approach. They studied the early Christian texts along with original Greek and Hebrew. Basically, the difference between the Italian Renaissance and the Northern Renaissance is this: both were humanist movements, but the Northern Renaissance emphasized Christianity and the Italian Renaissance emphasized secularism and individualism

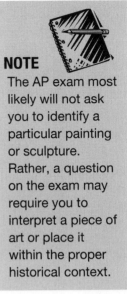

NOTE
The AP exam most likely will not ask you to identify a particular painting or sculpture. Rather, a question on the exam may require you to interpret a piece of art or place it within the proper historical context.

RENAISSANCE ART

Art produced during the Renaissance represented a major break from the art that had come before it. During the Middle Ages, the church was the leading patron of art, and artists worked without ever receiving credit for their creations. The Renaissance changed both of those traditions. Wealthy merchants, bankers, and other individuals offered great wages for artists to create sculptures and paintings—frequently of the wealthy individuals themselves. With the newfound clientele, the artists achieved unprecedented social status and income levels. They no longer worked anonymously but were instead heralded as geniuses. The painters, sculptors, and architects of the Renaissance basked in the glory they received for their work.

The style of Renaissance art varied greatly from that of the Middle Ages. Medieval art—because it was paid for by the church—usually centered on religious themes and exalted the church and God. In addition, medieval art generally appeared to be more abstract than real. Renaissance art, although it sometimes portrayed religious images, tended to glorify the achievements of man. These achievements were often those of the patron but occasionally were those of some heroic figure, either mythical or Biblical. With the development of new techniques and methods, Renaissance art took new forms. Oil painting became popular throughout Italy. The use of contrast and perspective allowed Renaissance artists to create three-dimensional images unlike any seen during the Middle Ages.

Humanism played a major role in the development of the Renaissance art style. Renaissance artists, inspired by the humanist ideals, sought to reproduce the artistic styles found in classical Greece and Rome. In both paintings and sculptures, artists went to great lengths to add intricate details. The artists wanted to glorify and accurately reproduce the human body, just as the Greeks and Romans had done centuries before. As part of their

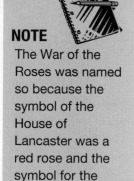

NOTE
The War of the Roses was named so because the symbol of the House of Lancaster was a red rose and the symbol for the House of York was a white rose.

glorification of man and the human body, artists were not afraid or ashamed to show the body in its most natural form. They frequently produced nude figures, both male and female.

The artistic style of the Italian Renaissance pushed its influence north and affected artists across Europe. The Flemish painter Jan van Eyck (1385–1440) included great detail and perspective as in his classic painting *Giovanni Arnolfini and His Bride,* and the German artist Albrecht Durer (1471–1528) added detail, proportion, perspective, and realism to his famous paintings and woodcuts. The artistic influence of the Renaissance reached across Europe and across time, affecting European art and artists for several centuries.

THE NEW MONARCHIES

During the second half of the fifteenth century, Europe saw the rise of a new group of monarchs called the *new monarchs.* These rulers were skilled in diplomacy and were quite crafty, employing new methods of control over their realms. The new monarchs used many of the tactics of the Italian rulers during the Renaissance to try to obtain more power and more territory. For example, these regents often limited the power of the nobility and brought the church under their own control to increase royal authority in their lands. The best examples of these new monarchies were in England, France, and Spain.

After suffering defeat in the Hundred Years' War, England struggled to rebuild its economy. Unfortunately for England, the end of the war brought with it more than just economic hardship. The *War of the Roses* erupted in the 1450s between the House of York and the House of Lancaster. This civil unrest pitted aristocratic families against one another for some thirty years before Henry Tudor (1457–1509, king 1485–1509) defeated Richard III (1452–1485, king 1483–1485) and established what was to become the Tudor dynasty. One of Henry's most famous, if not infamous, accomplishments was the establishment of the Star Chamber. The *Star Chamber* was a court that was established to control the nobles. It used no jury and torture was commonplace.

Although France technically won the Hundred Years' War, it too was left devastated. The economy was in ruins, farmland was destroyed, and many French lives were lost. France did, however, emerge from the war with a new sense of nationalism. King Charles VII (1403–1461, king 1422–1461) took advantage of this new national feeling. He began to take administrative power away from the Estates-General and secured more power for the monarchy by increasing its control over the church in France. His successor, Louis XI (1423–1483, king 1461–1483), also known as the Spider, permanently imposed the *taille,* an annual tax on property, thereby securing an annual source of income for the crown. Many historians give Louis XI credit for establishing the national state.

In 1469, with the marriage of Isabella of Castile (1451–1504) and Ferdinand of Aragon (1452–1516) in Spain, two dynasties were united. Although they worked together, the two kingdoms maintained their own identities. Ferdinand and Isabella worked to strengthen royal authority and the Spanish army. They renewed a system of town-based organizations, called *hermandades*, which were to help control the lawlessness among the aristocracy. One of the major events during the reign of Ferdinand and Isabella was the *Inquisition*. The Inquisition, among other things, served as a political and religious tool to monitor the *conversos*, the Muslims and Jews who had converted to Catholicism. Ultimately, both the Muslims and Jews were driven from Spain. In addition to controlling domestic policy, the royal couple pointed Spain in the right direction by promoting and sponsoring voyages of exploration, which eventually took Spain into its Golden Age.

NOTE

It has been said that the Hundred Years' War began with two kingdoms (England and France) and ended with two nations.

THE MAJOR PLAYERS

Cosimo de'Medici (1389–1464)—A shrewd politician, banker, and statesman of Florence, Cosimo de'Medici held almost total control of the local politics. He held no public office; instead, he stayed behind the scenes, influencing and persuading others. He encouraged industry and favored a balance of power among the Italian states. One of the richest of all Italians of his time, Cosimo sponsored many artists and scholars.

Lorenzo de'Medici (1449–1492)—During the Renaissance, Lorenzo, often known as Lorenzo the Magnificent, continued the Medici tradition of shrewd politics. A banker by trade, Lorenzo inherited the family business and rule over the Florentine republic. After causing the pope, along with Naples, to declare war on Florence, Lorenzo single-handedly avoided warfare through his skilled diplomacy. After that incident, he spent the rest of his life patronizing great artists like Michelangelo and Boticelli.

Giovanni de'Medici (1475–1521)—The son of Lorenzo de'Medici, Giovanni became Pope Leo X and served as pope from 1513–1521. Because of the Medici tradition of an appreciation for the finer things in life, Leo accomplished more as a patron of the arts than as a pope. Leo spent excessive amounts of money on art and architecture and sponsored such geniuses as Raphael. He also financed the rebuilding of St. Peter's Basilica. It was Leo who would eventually excommunicate Luther in 1521.

Niccolo Machiavelli (1469–1527)—Although Machiavelli gained fame primarily with his work *The Prince*, he was originally a historian and statesman. He held a prominent government position in Italy until the Medici family came back into power in 1512. He lost his position and was actually imprisoned for a short while. In an attempt to regain the favor of the government, Machiavelli wrote *The Prince*, a virtual instruction manual for a prince, or ruler, on the manner in which he should rule. The majority of Machiavelli's points are based on actual historical figures and their accomplishments and failures. Machiavelli strikes many people as immoral, but his

NOTE
Machiavelli is often credited with the phrase "the end justifies the means." This Machiavellian philosophy implies that one's purpose for doing things often justifies the things one does; in Machiavelli's mind, this particularly applied to rulers.

political philosophy is actually amoral; he argued that a prince need not be bound by the same code of ethics and morals as citizens. Whether Machiavelli intended for the work to be taken literally, or if he simply used it as a tool to try to regain his governmental position, is a subject that has been debated for some time. His influence on political philosophy both during and after the Renaissance cannot be denied.

Giotto (c.1267–1337)—Giotto was undoubtedly the most important and influential of all fourteenth Century Italian painters. He broke with tradition by portraying human figures in a more natural and real state rather than in the two-dimensional state that was common in the art of the Middle Ages. Although most of his work is either in poor condition or not even attributed to him, his frescos in Padua and Florence and his painting *The Ognissanti Madonna* illustrate his style, which was far ahead of his time.

Donatello (c.1386–1466)—Donatello studied under such masters as Ghiberti and held the company of Brunelleschi. Therefore, it should be no wonder that Donatello became one of the most prominent and influential sculptors of the Renaissance. Donatello created striking sculptures such as *St. Mark* and *St. George*. However, Donatello created a masterpiece in *David*, the first nude statue of the Renaissance, for which he is most often remembered. Donatello made several trips to Rome to study the figures of antiquity. Exemplifying the Renaissance ideals, Donatello based many of his figures on the works of the ancient Romans.

Leonardo da Vinci (1452–1519)—If ever there lived a true Renaissance man, it was Leonardo da Vinci. Leonardo excelled in painting, architectural design, drafting, engineering, and many fields of science including meteorology, geology, and hydraulics. Educated in Florence under the supervision of Verrochio, Leonardo learned painting and sculpting. Leonardo was nearly 30 years old before he began work on his first large piece, *The Adoration of the Magi*. Unfortunately, like many of his works, it was never finished. Some thirteen years later, Leonardo worked experimentally on one of his most famous pieces, *The Last Supper*, which was painted with oil on a plaster wall. Technically, the experiment failed because the plaster began peeling away and only through extensive restoration projects is the work somewhat preserved today. In 1503, Leonardo began painting one of the most famous portraits of all time, the *Mona Lisa*. Also known as *La Gioconda*, this painting must have held special meaning to Leonardo, as he carried it with him wherever he went.

Leonardo devoted much of his time to drafting and engineering as well as painting. Although many of his ideas were never carried out and many of his projects were never completed, his genius is evident in the numerous drawings and sketches of his fantastic contraptions and inventions. He devised many architectural plans, some of which were based on Roman architecture, but never had the opportunity to build all of his structures.

Unlike the other great minds of his time, Leonardo realized the importance of observation of the natural world. He worked on and studied extensively the circulation of the blood, the mechanics of the human eye, and the general

CAUTION
Do not confuse Donatello's *David* with the *David* of Michelangelo. Donatello's sculpture was done in bronze, while Michelangelo's was marble.

anatomy of the human body. Leonardo was fascinated by fluids, and he did much work with hydraulics. He even theorized about the moon's effects on the tides. Leonardo's greatness, however, was not fully realized until his notes and other writings and drawings were discovered and made public after his death.

Michelangelo (1475–1564)—Perhaps one of the greatest artistic talents of all time, Michelangelo created some of the most beloved yet technically superior art man has ever known. Influenced as a young man by Lorenzo the Magnificent, Michelangelo trained to be an artist from the time he was a teenager. Although he created works during his teens, his first great work was the *Pieta*. Finished while he was in his early twenties, the *Pieta* depicts the crucified Christ in the lap of Mary. The detail in the marble sculpture is almost unbelievable. By the time he was thirty, Michelangelo had finished what would become his most famous work, *David*. This fourteen-feet-high statue proved to the world that Michelangelo was a master. Michelangelo combined soft detail, bold expressions, and monumental size in an unprecedented manner.

Michelangelo was more than just a sculptor, though. While on commission in Rome, Michelangelo painted the Sistine Chapel ceiling. He created an incredibly detailed fresco (while lying on his back) that included nine different scenes from the Book of Genesis. Some of the most famous scenes include *The Creation of Adam* and *The Flood*. Michelangelo went on to create other magnificent sculptures, such as the *Moses*, and frescos, such as the *Last Judgment*. In addition, Michelangelo was named the head architect for St. Peter's Basilica for which he designed the famous dome. Michelangelo, along with Leonardo da Vinci, embodied the idea of the Renaissance man.

Raphael (1483–1520)—Among the greatest Italian Renaissance painters was Raphael. Raphael painted a number of Madonnas, mostly during his time in Florence. During his stay in Rome, though, Raphael created one of the true masterpieces of the Italian Renaissance. His fresco *The School of Athens* epitomizes the ideals embodied not only by Renaissance art but also by the Renaissance itself. Raphael's use of proportion, perspective and realistic detail vividly portrays, among others, Plato and Aristotle. His artistic style and his choice of subjects for the painting exemplify the art of the Renaissance.

Giovanni Boccaccio (1313–1375)—An Italian humanist author who grew up in Florence, Boccaccio is best known and remembered for his classic work, *The Decameron. The Decameron* is a collection of 100 stories told by a group of people who have retreated to the country to escape the plague. Boccaccio's work is the first and arguably the best prose work of the Renaissance.

Jan van Eyck (c.1390–1441)—Even into the sixteenth century, Jan van Eyck's fellow painters often referred to him as the King of the Painters. A Flemish painter, van Eyck helped found the *Ars Nova* or "new art" style of painting in northern Europe in the fifteenth century, which is now associated with the Northern Renaissance in Europe. This "new art" followed much of the form of Renaissance art that developed in the Italian tradition though it

NOTE
The *Pieta* is the only sculpture of Michelangelo that he actually signed.

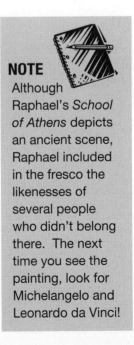

NOTE
Although Raphael's *School of Athens* depicts an ancient scene, Raphael included in the fresco the likenesses of several people who didn't belong there. The next time you see the painting, look for Michelangelo and Leonardo da Vinci!

evolved into its own distinct style. Van Eyck's art is known for its bright and vivid colors, outstanding detail, and three-dimensional appearance. Perhaps the most recognizable van Eyck work is the portrait *Giovanni Arnolfini and his Bride (1434)*, a striking portrait that epitomizes van Eyck's use of color, detail, and three-dimensional effects.

Desiderius Erasmus (c.1466–1536)—Desiderius Erasmus was the greatest of the northern humanists and perhaps the most influential of all Christian humanists. Although his work later contributed to the movement known as the Protestant Reformation, Erasmus did not consider himself a religious reformer. Erasmus believed that Christianity should return to the simple "philosophy of Christ." He sought ways to educate people about the early Christians and about Christ. Erasmus felt that the Vulgate, which was the standard Latin translation of the New Testament, contained errors. Therefore, he edited and published new translations of the New Testament in Greek and then in Latin. The other influential works of Erasmus include *Adages*, a book of classical proverbs, and *The Praise of Folly*, a satirization of contemporary society.

Thomas More (1478–1535)—Having received a good education in his early life, Thomas More originally set out to be a lawyer. However, this English humanist became fascinated by the classics and he learned both Greek and Latin. More translated several works by Greek authors and wrote original works in Latin. His most famous work, *Utopia*, was also his most influential work. *Utopia* describes the ideal society, a community in sharp contrast to the one in which More lived. The work illustrated More's views of the political and social problems of contemporary society. More's devotion to his beliefs later cost him his life. King Henry VIII executed More when he refused to recognize the king as the head of the Church of England.

Michel Montaigne (1533–1592)—Montaigne was a French writer who wrote essays. He introduced the essay as a sincere literary form. The subjects of his essays were usually subjects he had pondered and considered. His *Essays* (1580) cover a variety of subjects ranging from cannibalism to bodily functions to death and dying.

CHRONOLOGY OF THE RENAISSANCE

1337–1453—Hundred Years' War raged on between England and France. The war left both nations crippled. (Actually, the war lasted 116 years!)

1347–1350—The bubonic plague, also known as the Black Death, ravaged Europe and decimated the population. The disease claimed almost one third of the entire population of Europe.

c.1350—Boccaccio's *Decameron* became the first great prose work of the Renaissance.

1378—The Ciompi revolt in Florence won the workers there some representation in government and the right to have guilds.

c.1390—Geoffrey Chaucer's *Canterbury Tales* became one of the first works written in the vernacular, or language of the people of the author's homeland.

1397—The Medici family founded its bank, thus laying the foundation upon which was built one of the greatest ruling families in Italian history.

c.1411—The writings known as *The Imitation of Christ* was first published anonymously. The work has generally been attributed to Thomas à Kempis, a mystic who de-emphasized the sacraments and the dogma of the church.

c.1450—German Johann Gutenberg revolutionized the world of the written word with the introduction of the movable type printing press.

1454–1485—The Northern Italian states experienced a period of relative peace.

1455–1485—The English House of York and House of Lancaster fought each other for political control in the War of the Roses.

1469—Ferdinand and Isabella were married in a dynastic union that eventually led to the unification of Spain.

1479—The Inquisition was introduced into Spain to control the activity of the *conversos*.

1485—The Tudor dynasty was established in England with the end of the War of the Roses.

1487—The English Parliament approved the Star Chamber which was to control the behavior of lawless aristocrats and nobles.

1492—Christopher Columbus "discovered" the New World by landing on Watlings Island.

1492—The Jews were exiled from Spain and all of their property was confiscated by the government.

1503–1506—Leonardo da Vinci labored on his signature piece, the *Mona Lisa*.

1508–1512—Michelangelo painted the Sistine Chapel ceiling.

1513—Niccolo Machiavelli wrote *The Prince* in an attempt to win the favor of the government and win back his prominent position in the government.

1516–1519—Desiderius Erasmus produced his Greek and Latin translations of the New Testament. Both, according to Erasmus, were more accurate than the Vulgate.

1527—The imperial troops of Emperor Charles V sacked the city of Rome.

TIP
Use this chronology to begin to frame the big picture. Chronologies are helpful when you are trying to see how a story unfolds; in this case, the story is that of the Renaissance.

CAUTION
These questions are for review purposes only, not to predict the questions that will be on the actual AP exam.

SAMPLE ESSAY QUESTIONS

Now that you have reviewed the information about the Renaissance, take a few moments to read through the sample essay questions that follow. The questions are intended to get you thinking about some of the ways the AP exam may test your knowledge of the Renaissance. To completely answer the questions, you will need draw upon the knowledge you gained during your own course of study in addition to your review with this book.

1. Analyze and discuss the extent to which the art of the Renaissance exemplifies the values held by the leading thinkers of the time, using examples of specific art and artists.

2. Compare and contrast the humanism of the Italian Renaissance with the humanism of the north.

3. "It was by mere chance that Florence gave birth to such a large number of great minds, great talents, and great works of art during the Renaissance." Assess the validity of the above statement, using historical evidence to support your argument.

4. Analyze the effects geography had on the development of Italian civilization during the fifteenth and sixteenth centuries.

5. Explain what developments led to, and the extent of, the spread of Renaissance ideals across Europe during the late fifteenth and early sixteenth centuries.

6. Compare the administrative tactics used by the "new monarchs" and explain how those tactics enabled the "new monarchs" to extend royal authority in their kingdoms.

7. Historians generally agree that the Renaissance was not an era that sprung forth in reaction to the Middle Ages. Using specific economic, cultural, and societal examples, explain how the contemporaries of the Renaissance might have seen the Renaissance as a genuine "rebirth."

The Reformation (1517–1648)

OVERVIEW

During the early sixteenth century, while Europe was still in the midst of the sweeping cultural, intellectual, and political changes of the Renaissance, a new phenomenon was being born. The humanism of the Italian Renaissance spread across Europe and affected every aspect of life. One of the areas most affected by humanism was that of religion.

Humanists, especially those of northern Europe, were not anti-religious or even anti-Christian. However, there came with humanism a certain desire for a deeper understanding of things. Humanism empowered man to seek God and to seek spiritual truth without an intercessor, like the church. In other words, man no longer needed a priest to talk to God and man no longer needed the pope dictating the will of God. Man was a free being with the ability to ask questions, seek answers, and develop spiritually on his own. According to the church, these notions were heretical.

These ideas about religion sparked a century of turmoil and warfare between the Roman Catholic Church, headed by the pope, and the reformers, who sought a new and different approach to religion. Those reformers became known as *Protestants*, or those who protested against the church. Initially, the people at the heart of this religious revolution had no intentions other than to reform the existing church and change those things within the church that, in their opinions, had gone wrong over the years This movement was known as the *Reformation*.

HISTORICAL BACKGROUND

The Reformation did not begin in the sixteenth century, nor did it arise out of humanist ideas alone. During the fourteenth century, when Europe found itself at the mercy of the bubonic plague, people's faith in the church, and perhaps even in God, was shaken. Both clergy and laymen alike prayed for deliverance, yet one third of all Europeans died from the disease. As Europe began to recover from the plague, problems within the church began to arise. People began to question the practice of *simony*, or the selling of church

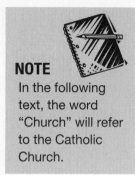

NOTE
In the following text, the word "Church" will refer to the Catholic Church.

positions. People also began to question whether or not clergymen should hold more than one church position. Neither of these practices, it was argued, seemed to benefit anyone other than the clergy. In addition, clerical positions tended to be quite lucrative in many cases, and people resented that. Not only were the clergy perceived as too wealthy, but the church itself also seemed to have entirely too much money at its disposal. Perhaps the laymen would not have minded so much if the money had been spent on the parishioners. Instead, though, the church spent exorbitant amounts of money on art, architecture, and the extravagant lifestyles of the popes.

Another major problem within the church was the uneducated priests. Many priests could hardly read or write in their native language, much less read or write in Latin, the language in which many theological works were written.

The tension had been building for some time when, in the fourteenth century, John Wycliffe (1329–1384) questioned some of the practices of the church. Among other things, Wycliffe argued against the wealth of the church and the selling of *indulgences*, or the practice of granting the buyer forgiveness for his sins. Wycliffe encouraged people to read the Bible themselves and interpret the Bible themselves, a practice that was unheard of in his day. To aid the people in doing so, Wycliffe translated the Bible into English. Wycliffe's teachings influenced a Bohemian named Jan Hus (1369–1415). Hus spoke out against the abuses of the church, too, and was later burned at the stake. The execution of Jan Hus did not have the desired effect on Hus's followers. Instead of squelching the voices that spoke out against the church, the execution incited a rebellion that took some time to put down. Wycliffe and Hus were both forerunners of the Reformation that was to follow in the next century.

MARTIN LUTHER

The issue that actually instigated the Reformation was that of indulgences. Individuals could purchase indulgences from the Catholic Church and in return receive remission of their sins. In 1517, Pope Leo X gave permission for Johann Tetzel (c.1465–1519), a Dominican friar, to sell indulgences. The revenue generated from the sale of the indulgences, by order of the pope, was to be used to repay a loan that was secured by the Catholic Church to build St. Peter's Church in Rome. A German Augustinian monk named Martin Luther (1483–1546) was outraged by the actions of the pope. According to tradition, Luther nailed his *95 Theses* to the door of the Castle Church at Wittenburg. Luther's *Theses* condemned the sale of indulgences and invited debate on the issue.

A few years and several publications later, Luther had successfully infuriated the pope by attacking the sacraments, transubstantiation (the belief that the bread and wine of Communion *actually* become the body and blood of Christ after they are consumed during Communion), and the means of a person's salvation. A papal bull, or an official statement by the pope, demanded that Luther recant. In an act of defiance, Luther burned the papal bull along with a volume of canon law. Outraged, the pope excommunicated Luther and called for him to appear before the Diet of Worms, an official meeting of electors, princes, and nobles. At the meeting, Holy Roman Emperor Charles V asked Luther to recant. Luther, in eloquent fashion, refused. Luther was banned from the Empire and was forced to seek refuge with Frederick the Elector of Saxony.

While in Saxony, Luther began to organize a new church based on ideas that he had been considering for several years. He also translated the Bible into German, an action that had a profound effect both on religion and on language in Germany. During the 1520s, Lutheranism spread throughout Germany, Denmark, Norway, Sweden, and Finland. Many people, especially in Germany, began to misinterpret Luther's message as a call for social equality and freedom. A large number of German peasants revolted and demanded freedom, using Luther's words as their battle cry. Luther published *On the Murderous, Thieving Hordes* in response to the peasant revolts. He condemned their actions and encouraged the princes to "exterminate the swine." The peasants, who had misinterpreted Luther's writings, felt betrayed by his condemnation of their actions.

> **NOTE**
> In all of Luther's writings, there are no accounts of nailing the *95 Theses* to the door. Whether or not he actually did does not change the fact that Luther openly challenged the papacy and church tradition, thus initiating the Reformation.

ULRICH ZWINGLI AND JOHN CALVIN

About the same time Luther's ideas were spreading, the teachings of Ulrich Zwingli (1484–1531) were taking hold in Zurich. Greatly influenced by humanism, specifically the work of Erasmus, Zwingli preached against all practices of the church that were not substantiated by Scripture. Zwingli went on to rule Zurich as a theocracy, or a government ruled by someone who claims to have divine authority. He did away with monasteries, religious icons, mass, and confession, and he preached that man did not need the pope or the church. In 1531, Zwingli, who was much more concerned with politics than was Luther, died in battle during a religious civil war.

A few years after Zwingli, a French humanist scholar and theologian named John Calvin (1509–1564) arrived in Geneva. After spending some time in Geneva assisting the reformation of the city, he was asked to leave. In 1541, Calvin was invited back to continue his reform of the church there. Although Calvin never became a citizen of Geneva, he drew up new ordinances for the city that governed both religious and secular aspects of life in the city. He imposed strict laws, and he saw that the laws were enforced. On occasion, Calvin was very harsh. For example, a man named Michael Servetus, who had managed to survive the Inquisition, wandered into Geneva. Calvin, along with others, burned Servetus at the stake for being a heretic. At any cost, Calvin was determined to hold Genevans to a high moral standard of living

During the 1540s and 1550s, Calvinism spread throughout Europe and found extraordinary success in Scotland under the leadership of John Knox (c.1513–1572), who founded the Presbyterian Church there. In England, the

Calvinists were known as the Puritans, and in France, Calvin's followers were known as the Huguenots.

THE ENGLISH REFORMATION

In sixteenth century England, nonreligious issues fueled the Reformation. Rather than a religious leader seeking religious reform, King Henry VIII (1491–1547, king 1509–1547) led the English Reformation for personal reasons. Henry, a supporter of the Catholic Church, married Catherine of Aragon (1485–1536) in 1509, but Catherine never produced a son for the king. In 1527, with no male heir, Henry announced his desire to divorce Catherine. Being Catholic, though, Henry was not able to get a divorce. Therefore, Henry sought an annulment on the grounds that the papal dispensation that allowed the marriage in the first place was invalid, thus making the marriage invalid. In the meantime, the king had fallen in love with Anne Boleyn (c.1507–1536), a young favorite from his court, and wanted to marry her.

When it became apparent that the pope would not grant an annulment, Henry began the *Reformation Parliament*. During the years of the Reformation Parliament, Henry initiated legislation that would no longer recognize the pope as the supreme authority in religious matters in England. This act was the Act in Restraint of Appeals. By 1533, Henry had managed to convince Anne Boleyn to share his bed, and she became pregnant. Henry and Anne were married in secret even though Henry and Catherine were still legally married. Conveniently, a tribunal led by Thomas Cranmer (who was appointed Archbishop of Canterbury by Henry!) declared Henry's marriage to Catherine null and void. Henry and Anne were married, and Anne's offspring were established as the heirs to the English throne. Unfortunately for Henry and for Anne, Anne's child was a girl, Elizabeth, who would grow up to be Elizabeth I (1533–1603, queen 1558–1603), the long-ruling Queen of England. In an attempt to secure a male heir, Henry married four more times.

In 1534, parliament passed the *Act of Supremacy*, which made Henry the official head of the Church of England. The Church of England, a Protestant church, was very similar to the Catholic Church in both theology and liturgy. Henry sought to keep the Church of England very Catholic in nature without being Catholic. However, Henry closed all the monasteries in England, which were Catholic, and he confiscated their lands so that their wealth became England's. After experiencing several doctrinal changes during the reigns of Henry's children, Edward VI (1537–1553, king 1547–1553) and Mary I (1516–1558, queen 1553–1558), the Church of England settled into a very moderate Protestant identity during the reign of Elizabeth I. Thus, the once-Catholic kingdom of England, through the political maneuverings of Henry VIII, broke away from the papacy and the Catholic Church and formed its own church.

CAUTION

Don't think that Henry VIII sought to reform the Catholic Church the way Luther originally did. Henry was only interested in resolving "the King's Great Matter" at any cost. Henry VIII's role in the Reformation was motivated by self-interest alone.

THE CATHOLIC REFORMATION

The Protestant Reformation brought many people into the Protestant fold and caused a noticeable decrease in the number of European Catholics. After several decades of Protestantism, the Catholic Church officially responded with its own reformation known as the *Catholic Reformation* or *Counter Reformation*. The Catholic Church, beginning with leadership of Pope Paul III, developed groups such as the Ursuline Order and the Jesuits to counter the actions of the Protestants and to bring souls back to the Catholic Church. The Church issued the Index of Prohibited Books that listed those books the Church deemed inappropriate and dangerous. This index included many writers such as Desiderius Erasmus. The Church revived the Inquisition and ruthlessly sought out and burned heretics. The most influential instrument of the Catholic Reformation, though, was the Council of Trent.

The Council of Trent (1545–1563) sought to answer the theological and philosophical questions raised by the Protestant Reformation. The Council affirmed that Church doctrine concerning the sacraments, the priesthood, and salvation were firmly rooted in both the Scriptures and in Church tradition. The Council determined that the sacraments and transubstantiation were valid, salvation was attained by both faith and by good works, and that monasticism and clerical celibacy were justified. The Council also addressed simony, indulgences, and issues relating to the clergy. Ultimately, the Council of Trent limited the sales of church positions and indulgences and decided that members of the clergy should receive a seminary education. The Council also called for more religious art to be produced. Modern historians have debated over the significance of the Council of Trent as it relates to the overall success of the Counter Reformation. However, most historians agree that the Council did increase the power and influence of the papacy.

RESULTS OF THE REFORMATION

First and foremost, the power and prestige of the Catholic Church in Europe suffered heavy blows by the Protestant movement. England, Scotland, Switzerland, Scandinavia, and parts of France and Germany all became Protestant. This resulted in a major split in Christendom. In effect, a new antagonistic element had been introduced into European politics and culture; this element was the Protestant-versus-Catholic mentality that, to this day, survives in many parts of Europe. Wars of religion erupted in Europe for nearly a century. Social and political interpretations of Protestantism led to nationalistic movements because of the idea that the state was superior to the church in all matters other than the spiritual.

NOTE
Mary I sought to reinstitute Catholicism in England during her reign. However, many Protestants remained and refused to convert to Catholicism. As a result, Mary burned these heretics at the stake and earned the nickname "Bloody Mary."

NOTE
The Jesuits, founded by Ignatius of Loyola (1491-1556), have left a legacy of outstanding education that dates back to the sixteenth century.

WARS OF RELIGION

As was mentioned previously, the Reformation resulted in an antagonistic, often hateful, relationship between Catholics and Protestants. In addition, the conflict between the two religious groups often strained and complicated international politics and diplomacy. In France, because of the Concordat of Bologna (an agreement between France and the pope that allowed the French crown to appoint church officials in France if the first year's income of the appointed officials went to the pope), the French government held close ties to Rome and the Catholic Church, and as a result, most Frenchmen were Catholic. Because of the influence of Calvin in France, though, growing numbers of Frenchmen became Calvinists, known as Huguenots. In the St. Bartholomew's Day Massacre in 1572, paranoid Parisian Catholics killed 20,000 Huguenots to prevent the possibility of a Protestant coup. This threw France into a bitter civil war between Catholics and Protestants. In 1589, Henry of Navarre, a Protestant, (1553–1610, king 1589–1610) became King Henry IV when the Catholic Henry III was assassinated. A Calvinist who was more interested in political than religious unity, Henry IV could not sway Paris away from Catholicism. Saying, "Paris is worth a mass," Henry became Catholic. However, he issued the *Edict of Nantes* that allowed the Huguenots to worship freely in France.

In England, Mary I, who was the daughter of the Catholic Catherine of Aragon, attempted to return England to Catholicism. She met with some resistance due to the large numbers of people who held on to the Protestant beliefs. Mary dealt with the resistance by executing many Protestants during her reign and consequently submitted England to the papacy.

This changed with Mary's successor, Elizabeth I. Elizabeth returned England to Protestantism, though only moderate Protestantism, and was not concerned when she was officially excommunicated. Elizabeth sought to compromise and reduce the tensions between Catholics and Protestants. However, in matters of international politics, Elizabeth openly supported Protestants. For example, Elizabeth supplied many troops to help support the efforts of the rebels in the Netherlands. As a result, England and Spain remained at odds for years.

The revolt in the Netherlands occurred for both political and religious reasons. Philip II of Spain wanted to exert more political control in the Netherlands. He also wanted to strengthen Catholicism in the Netherlands in response to the growing number of Calvinists there. Philip sent 20,000 troops to the Netherlands and ordered the Duke of Alva to establish the *Council of Troubles* to deal with the Calvinists there. Better known as the Council of Blood, the Council of Troubles executed thousands for heresy. The northern and southern provinces united in 1576 but ultimately separated into two sections. These two sections became modern-day Netherlands, which was Calvinist, in the north and modern-day Belgium, which was Catholic, in the south. In 1585, England sent troops and money to aid the

NOTE

King Philip II of Spain (1527–1598, king 1556–1598) sent the Spanish Armada to England in an attempt to make England Catholic. However, aided by poor weather conditions, a craftier English fleet crushed the Armada.

rebels there. At the end of the sixteenth century, the Spanish were driven from the northern Netherlands, and the war came to an end in 1609. In 1648, the northern Netherlands won their independence from Spain and became known as the United Provinces. As the Spanish Netherlands, the southern provinces remained under the control of Spain.

THE THIRTY YEARS' WAR

The final and most devastating war of religion was the *Thirty Years' War* (1618–1648). Although the war did not begin until 1618, the tensions that led to it date back to the Peace of Augsburg (1555), an agreement that allowed German princes to choose the religion of their territories. The only two religions that were recognized, though, were Catholicism and Lutheranism. In the early seventeenth century, Germany was divided into two main groups, the Protestant Union and the Catholic League of German States. The English, French, and Dutch supported the Protestant Union, while Spain and the Holy Roman Empire supported the Catholic League. The foundation was laid for the first continental war.

Generally, historians divide the Thirty Years' War into four phases. The first phase was the *Bohemian Phase* (1618–1625). The Bohemians, most of whom were Calvinists, distrusted their Catholic king, Matthias. After appeals to the king for intervention in the harsh acts of the Catholic Church in Bohemia went unanswered, the Protestants in Prague threw two of the king's officials out of a window. This act, known as the *Defenestration of Prague*, signaled the beginning of a national conflict. The following year, the Catholic king, died and Ferdinand, the Holy Roman Emperor's Catholic cousin, became King of Bohemia. The Protestants rejected Ferdinand and chose as their king Frederick Elector of the Palatinate, a Calvinist. In 1620, Bavarian forces fighting for Ferdinand crushed Frederick at the Battle of White Mountain. Spanish forces then conquered the Palatinate in 1622, thus ending Frederick's political career. Ferdinand confiscated the land of the Bohemian Protestant nobles and declared Catholicism the religion of Bohemia.

The second phase, or *Danish Phase* (1625–1629), began when the Lutheran King of Denmark, Christian IV (1577–1648, king 1588–1648), led an army into northern Germany in an attempt to aid the Protestants. Ferdinand responded by sending Albert of Wallenstein and his army of mercenaries to Germany. Wallenstein's army ravaged Germany and defeated Christian's army in 1626. In 1629, the emperor issued the *Edict of Restitution*, an act that outlawed Calvinism within the Holy Roman Empire and ordered Lutherans to turn over all property that they had gained since 1552.

In the third phase, or *Swedish Phase* (1629–1635), the French became disturbed by the resurgence of Habsburg power and offered monetary support to Gustavus Adolphus (1594–1632, king 1611–1632) for his help in

NOTE

Many historians believe that the conflict between the Bourbons (of France) and the Habsburgs (of Spain and the Holy Roman Empire) also contributed to the outbreak of war.

Germany. The Swedish king was a great military mind who commanded an outstanding army. He was also Protestant. Persuaded to involve himself and his troops in the war, Gustavus Adolphus moved into Germany and met with much success against the anti-Protestant forces until he was killed in 1632. The Swedes lost their effectiveness after his death and were eventually defeated, thus guaranteeing that southern Germany would remain Catholic. The Protestant states signed an agreement with the emperor that revoked the Edict of Resolution. The Swedes insisted on continuing the war effort, and France entered the war on the side of the Swedes.

The fourth and final phase of the war, the *French-Swedish Phase* (1635–1648), proved to be the most destructive. The French and Swedish forces fought against the Habsburgs and the Spanish. Both sides won several battles, but none were decisive. Finally, after the French defeated the Spanish at Rocroi, the war-weary participants wanted peace. Negotiations began at Westphalia, and after several years of peace talks, the countries signed the Peace of Westphalia (1648).

The Peace of Westphalia reinstated the Peace of Augsburg, except that Calvinists were given consideration, and the Edict of Restitution was revoked. Switzerland and Holland both gained independence. France and Sweden both received territories. Finally, German princes were granted sovereignty. As a result of the Peace, the Habsburgs and the Holy Roman Empire were severely weakened. Germany was devastated. Its agriculture took heavy losses, and its population was decimated. Entire towns were destroyed, and much of its culture was lost. In regards to the Reformation, Protestantism had established itself in Europe for good.

THEOLOGY OF THE REFORMATION

Although the Reformation often appeared to be political in nature, the heart of the movement was theological. To better understand the Reformation, it is important to understand the theological beliefs of those involved. One of the greatest theologians of the Reformation was Martin Luther. Although Luther never compiled a systematic theology, Luther explained his beliefs in his many writings. One area in which Luther differed from the Church was salvation. Whereas the Church argued that salvation required both faith and good works, Luther contended that salvation was possible through faith alone. In addition, Luther maintained that the weakness and utter helplessness of man required the grace of God for salvation. Luther also differed from the Church regarding the sacraments. The Church maintained seven sacraments were valid, while Luther reduced the sacraments to three—pennance, baptism, and the Eucharist, or the Lord's Supper. Luther also disagreed with the Church on the issue of transubstantiation, the idea that the bread and wine of the Eucharist are transformed into the body and blood of Christ. Luther's idea, later called consubstantiation, said that Christ was present in the bread and wine but the bread and wine did not change. He likened the process to putting an iron in a fire. The iron and fire are seemingly merged in the red-hot iron, but both the iron and the fire remain. Another point of contention between Luther and the Church was the role that Scripture and Church tradition played in the development of theology. Contrary to the theology of the Church, Luther claimed that the Scriptures alone were sufficient to determine theology and practice. Again contrary to the theology of the Church, Luther upheld the doctrine of the "priesthood of all believers." In other words, humanity no longer needed a mediator between themselves and God; man was sufficient to stand alone before Christ. This effectively reduced the need for a Church. Finally, Luther denounced the Church's policy of clerical celibacy. In fact, Luther married and had a seemingly happy marriage.

Another leading figure of the Reformation, Ulrich Zwingli, agreed with Luther on most issues. However, Zwingli disagreed with Luther on the issue of the "body and blood of Christ." Zwingli maintained that the Scripture should be taken figuratively and not literally when it spoke of the "body and blood of Christ" during the Last Supper. John Calvin, too, agreed with Luther on more points than most people realize.

Unlike Luther, Calvin developed a systematic theology that he outlined in his work, *Institutes of the Christian Religion* (translated 1561). Calvin, like Luther, believed in salvation by faith alone, but Calvin placed a great deal of emphasis on the sovereignty of God. Calvin's belief in the sovereignty of God led him to develop the concept of predestination. Calvin believed that God had predetermined who was to be saved (the elect) and who was to be damned (the reprobate). Also stemming from the sovereignty of God was the idea that believers could not be certain of their salvation; to be certain meant infringement upon God's sovereignty. Calvin reduced the sacraments to baptism and the Lord's Supper. Also, like Luther, Calvin argued that man had no free will.

Calvin's theology is generally outlined in the acrostic TULIP. *T* represents the total depravity of man. In other words, according to Calvin, man was totally corrupt. *U* represents unconditional predestination. This concept was explained in the preceding paragraph. *L* represents limited atonement, or the idea that Christ died only for the elect. *I* represents irresistible grace. Calvin believed that the elect were to be saved, and they had no choice in the matter. Finally, *P* represents perseverance of the saints. This concept is often summarized by the phrase "once saved, always saved." Calvin maintained that the elect always would be saved and never condemned.

Some of the more radical ideas that arose during the Reformation grew out of what is commonly called, believe it or not, the *Radical Reformation*. Among the leaders of the Radical Reformation were the *Anabaptists*.

NOTE
Zwingli denied being heavily influenced by Luther, and he claimed that he was preaching his beliefs long before anyone had heard of Luther. Many historians, however, believe that Zwingli took many of his ideas from the theology of Luther.

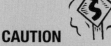

CAUTION
Do not make the mistake of referring to the Anabaptists as Baptists on the exam. The two groups are quite different. Your credibility would be damaged if you were to mention the "role of the Baptists during the Reformation.

Anabaptism appealed particularly to the peasants, workers, and lower classes, although there were some middle-class people devoted to Anabaptism. The Anabaptists believed that the true church was a voluntarily organized body of believers in which all believers were equal. The Anabaptists advocated adult baptism, or believer's baptism. Contrary to the teachings of the Church, they believed that the Lord's Supper was purely symbolic and was observed simply as a remembrance. What made the Anabaptists part of the Radical Reformation was their belief in the total separation of church and state. The Anabaptists were perceived as a threat to both religious and secular authority. Although most Anabaptists advocated peace, several Anabaptist groups turned to violence later in the Reformation.

THE MAJOR PLAYERS

Martin Luther (1483–1546)—Martin Luther was born to a successful miner who provided his son with a good education and wished for his son to become a lawyer. Martin Luther took advantage of his education and eventually enrolled to study law. However, during a terrible storm, Luther had a life-changing experience. In a desperate appeal to St. Anne, the patron saint of travelers in need of help, Luther promised to enter a monastery if he survived the storm. In 1505, he became an Augustinian monk, and after 1508, he spent time teaching in the University of Wittenburg. In 1510, he journeyed to Rome where he was appalled at the behavior of the clergy there. He returned to Germany and received his doctorate in theology in 1512. Luther preached and taught despite being troubled by questions of his own salvation. Through his studies, he came to believe that salvation was earned not through good works but by faith and by the grace of God.

After he posted his *95 Theses*, Luther became one of the leaders of the Protestant Reformation, especially in Germany. As has been discussed already in this chapter, Luther forever changed religion in Europe and, consequently, in the rest of the modern world. Luther's contributions to European history were more than just his theology, though. He published a number of works, including *On Christian Liberty* (1519), *The Babylonian Captivity of the Church* (1520), and the *Small Catechism* (1529). One of his most famous writings was *Against the Murderous, Thieving Hordes*, which denounced the peasants' revolt against the nobles in Germany. In 1532, he translated the Old Testament into German from the original Hebrew. Luther affected Europe not only through his religious teachings but also through his extensive writings. Because of the printing press, his writings were spread throughout Germany very quickly and had a profound effect on the German language.

Thomas Cranmer (1489–1556)—Both a lecturer and public examiner in divinity, Thomas Cranmer won the royal favor of Henry VIII in 1529. He suggested to the king that he not wait for an annulment order, but rather, refer the question of the legality of the marriage (to Catherine of Aragon) to legal scholars. Within three years, Cranmer had been appointed as the ambassador to the Holy Roman Empire. One year after that, in 1533, Henry VIII appointed

Cranmer as the Archbishop of Canterbury, the highest religious position in the land other than that of the king. Less than two months after being named Archbishop, Cranmer declared Henry's marriage to Catherine null and void, and Henry's marriage to Anne Boleyn legal.

During the Reformation, Cranmer played the role of perhaps the greatest reformer in England. Cranmer renounced his allegiance to the pope and removed the pope's name from the prayer book. He created the new liturgy for the new Church of England. When Henry VIII died, Cranmer became one of the regents of Edward VI, the new king. During the reign of Edward VI, Cranmer wrote two prayer books and the Thirty-Nine Articles (originally forty-two articles). When Edward died, Cranmer carried out the wishes of the dying king and helped Lady Jane Grey ascend to the throne where she sat for only nine days. When Mary Tudor overthrew Jane Grey, Cranmer was charged with treason, sentenced to death, spared, and then thrown in the Tower of London. Later, Cranmer was removed and taken to another prison. There he was forced to recant, only to be excommunicated and sentenced to death anyway. Upon the day of his execution, Cranmer recanted his recantations.

John Calvin (1509–1564)—Born in France in 1509, John Calvin was educated to become a priest. However, Calvin had some additional education because his father wanted him to pursue a career in law. Calvin became fascinated with the humanists and began studying Greek. In 1532, he published a commentary on *De Clementia*, a work by Seneca. In 1536, Calvin published the first of his *Institutes on the Christian Religion*, in which he began to lay out his systematic theology. Calvin also published a number of hymns and many commentaries on books of the Bible.

Aside from his theology, Calvin made a mark on European history because of the government he established in Geneva. Calvin helped adopt a new constitution for Geneva. He instituted a school system for the children of Geneva with a special academy for the best students. He sought good hospitals and care for the sick in Geneva. He encouraged new industries and hard work. The "Protestant work ethic" can be traced to Calvin and his ideals.

John Knox (c.1513–1572)—A Scottish religious reformer with a varied religious background, John Knox is remembered most for founding Presbyterianism in Scotland in the sixteenth century. Educated in Glasgow, Knox became a Catholic priest. However, after being exposed to Protestantism, Knox converted to Protestantism and began preaching the Protestant message. After serving with the Church of England under Edward VI, Knox found himself in danger when the Catholic "Bloody" Mary Tudor ascended to the English throne in 1553. He fled to Geneva where he was influenced by John Calvin. Knox later returned to Scotland where he helped the Protestants gain power. The Scottish Parliament eventually adopted Knox's ideology, which was similar to that of Calvin's, and it remained prominent in Scotland for nearly two hundred years. When the Catholic Mary, Queen of Scots, returned to Scotland in 1561, Knox spoke out against Mary and against Catholicism in general. Knox became even more influential in Scotland when he delivered sermons at the coronation of James VI of Scotland (who later became James I of England), a Protestant.

Ignatius of Loyola (1491–1556)—Ignatius of Loyola was born in Spain and grew up as a page to Ferdinand V of Castile. When he was old enough, Loyola entered the military. While recovering from being wounded in battle, he spent his time reading about the lives of saints. Deeply affected by the reading, Loyola decided to live the rest of his life as one of piety. He lived in a cave for several months and then journeyed to Jerusalem. After some study, Loyola founded the Society of Jesus, or the Jesuits. They were committed to pious living and education. The Jesuits played a major role in the Counter Reformation. Loyola wrote *Constitutions of the Order* concerning the Society of Jesus, and he wrote *Spiritual Exercises*, a manual on spiritual meditation. Loyola was canonized, or made a saint, in 1622.

CHRONOLOGY OF THE REFORMATION

1517—Johann Tetzel was authroized to sell indulgences to finance construction on St. Peter's Basilica in Rome.

1517—Martin Luther posted his *95 Theses* on the church door at Wittenburg castle in Germany.

1519—Luther debated John Eck and questioned the authority of the pope and church councils. In response, the papacy condemned Luther's propositions and ordered many of his books to be burned.

1519—Ulrich Zwingli began his teachings, thus spreading the Reformation to Switzerland.

1520—Thomas Munzer began the Anabaptist movement.

1520—Pope Leo X excommunicated Luther.

1521—Charles V and the Diet of Worms outlawed Martin Luther and forced him to seek refuge with Frederick the Wise.

1525—German peasants revolted in response to Luther's writings. Luther condemned the actions of the peasants but was later troubled by the behavior of the nobles.

1527—King Henry VIII first petitioned for a divorce from Catherine of Aragon.

1529—The term Protestant is coined at the Diet of Speyer, a meeting of the German princes.

1530—Archbishop of Canterbury Thomas Cranmer annulled the marriage of Henry VIII and Catherine of Aragon.

1531—Ulrich Zwingli was killed in battle.

1534—Henry VIII was recognized as the official head of the Church of England under the Act of Supremacy.

1536—John Calvin published the *Institutes of the Christian Religion* in Geneva.

1539—Parliament passed the Six Articles and affirmed many of the sacraments.

1540—The Jesuits were officially recognized and encouraged by Rome.

1541—John Knox began the Calvinist reform movement in Scotland.

1549—Thomas Cranmer published the *Book of Common Prayer*, which was used as a model for services in the Church of England.

1555—The Peace of Augsburg allowed German princes the right to choose the religion of their subjects.

1558—Elizabeth was crowned Queen of England and began a forty-five-year reign as a Protestant queen.

1568—Led by William of Orange, the Netherlands revolted against Spanish rule.

1588—The English fleet defeated the Spanish Armada.

1590s—William Shakespeare began some of his most famous works.

1603—Elizabeth I died, and James VI of Scotland ascended to the English throne as James I.

1618—Two of the king's men were thrown out of a window in the Defenestration of Prague. Amazingly, the men survived because they landed in a pile of manure. This marked the beginning of the Thirty Years' War.

1620—Holy Roman Emperor Ferdinand II defeated the Bohemians at the Battle of White Mountain.

1632—Swedish King Gustavus Adolphus was killed in battle while fighting on the side of the Protestants during the Thirty Years' War.

1648—The Peace of Westphalia marked the end of the Thirty Years' War.

CAUTION

These questions are for review purposes only, not to predict the questions that will be on the AP exam.

CAUTION

When writing essays about religion, be objective and write as a historian. Avoid making judgments of religions or religious leaders in your essays. The readers do not want to know whether or not you believe what these people believed; the readers want to know if you understand what these people believed.

SAMPLE ESSAY QUESTIONS

Now that you have reviewed the information about the Reformation, take a few moments to read through the following sample essay questions. The questions are intended to get you thinking about some of the ways the AP exam may test your knowledge of the Reformation. To completely answer the questions, you will need to draw upon the knowledge you gained during your own course of study in addition to your review with this book.

1. Compare and contrast the attitudes of the leaders of the Reformation toward political authority. Use specific examples to support your answer.

2. Analyze and discuss the social, economic, and political conditions that paved the way for the Reformation movement.

3. "The Counter Reformation had only moderate success in Europe in stopping the spread of Protestantism." Assess the validity of this statement using specific examples to support your argument.

4. Analyze and discuss the political, social, and geographic consequences of the Peace of Westphalia.

5. To what extent and in what ways did the Protestant Reformation change the society, politics, and economy of sixteenth century Europe as well as the centuries that followed?

6. To what extent and in what ways did the Thirty Years' War affect the society, politics, and culture of Europe?

7. Contrast the English Reformation and the Lutheran Reformation. Use specific examples to support your answer.

8. Discuss the political and religious conditions that led to the outbreak of the Thirty Years' War.

The Age of Expansion, Absolutism, and Constitutionalism

OVERVIEW

Europeans took the global lead in exploration and expansion primarily because of "God, gold, and glory". In the fifteenth century, a genuine desire to bring the "heathen" people of foreign lands into the fold of the Catholic Church existed. Religion, though, was not the only reason that Europeans began to sail abroad. During the fifteenth century, Europeans had access to non-European goods and cultures only through trade. Non-Europeans controlled this trade, and prices were very high. Many Europeans desired to bypass these traders and trade directly with the east, and individual explorers and adventurers often wanted fame, fortune, and the titles of nobility that might be lavished upon the leaders of successful expeditions.

The technology of exploration had been improving throughout the fourteenth and fifteenth centuries. The development of navigational devices, such as the compass and the astrolabe, made better navigation possible for Europeans. Improvements in the field of cartography also contributed to the ability of Europeans to venture farther away from home. Finally, new and improved shipmaking techniques provided the vessels that the Europeans needed to launch their expeditions.

During the Middle Ages and even during the Renaissance, kings ruled their subjects with the consent of the nobles. As that practice began to disappear, monarchs began to rule with more power and authority. Often, attempts were made to limit the power of the monarchs, but a few monarchs rose above these limitations. The greatest example of such a leader was Louis XIV of France. He epitomized the absolute ruler. Following in his footsteps in the eighteenth century were several eastern rulers who sought to be absolutists as well. While some nations developed strong monarchies, other nations, like England, developed a strong parliamentary government. Around the same time, Spain experienced its short-lived golden age.

EUROPEAN EXPANSION

TIP

The phrase "God, gold, and glory" is often used to sum up the motivations of the Europeans who went exploring during the fifteenth and sixteenth centuries. This is a good way to remember the reasons they went—just remember, their priorities were not always in that order!

Portugal led the way for overseas exploration during the fifteenth century by becoming the first European nation to explore the coast of Africa. Prince Henry the Navigator (1394–1460) explored Africa's coast in search of a Christian kingdom with which he could ally to fight against the Muslims who controlled many of the trade routes. He also searched for new trade opportunities for Portugal as well as opportunities to spread the Christian faith. Henry founded a school on the Portuguese coast where men could learn the skills of navigation and cartography. Within a few short years, Portuguese ships began sailing further and further down the African coast. The ships often returned with Africans who were sold as slaves. The Portuguese built forts along the African coast and established a thriving trade in gold, slaves, and ivory.

In 1487, Portuguese sailor Bartholomew Dias (c.1450–1500) became the first explorer to round the southern tip of Africa known as the Cape of Good Hope. In his lifetime, he explored many miles of Africa's coastline. Ten years later, Vasco da Gama (c.1469–1524) set sail from Portugal. He rounded the Cape of Good Hope and sailed into Calicut on the coast of India. After barely escaping from the Muslims who controlled the area, da Gama returned to Portugal as a hero. He was the first European to reach India by sea.

Gradually, Portugal sent more and more ships to India and established lucrative trade routes. At first, Portugal was intimidated by the Muslims and other traders that controlled the Indian trade. However, Portugal developed better and more heavily armed ships that allowed them to establish dominance. Perhaps the greatest improvement the Portuguese made was the mounting of cannons on their ships. This allowed the ships to battle from a distance instead of alongside enemy ships. Portugal's trade industry brought tremendous wealth, one that eventually rivaled that of the Italians.

Whereas Portugal's primary goal was the establishment of trade routes and trading ports, the Spanish had a much grander scheme. Spain's enormous wealth provided them with more resources to explore the world. One of the first men to tap these resources was a Genoese sailor named Christopher Columbus (1451–1506). Columbus persuaded the Spanish Queen Isabella to finance his expedition westward. Columbus convinced the queen, as he was convinced, that a sea route to the east could be found by sailing west across the Atlantic Ocean. In 1492, Columbus set sail westward and landed in the Caribbean. He was convinced that he had landed somewhere in the outer islands of Japan, or Chipangu, as he called it. In his three subsequent voyages, Columbus explored all the major islands of the Caribbean.

Vasco Nunez de Balboa (c.1475–1519) became the first European to view the Pacific Ocean in 1513. He landed in Panama and traveled through dense jungles across the isthmus until he reached the great sea, which he named the

South Sea. Several years later, Ferdinand Magellan (1480–1521) rounded the southern tip of South America, crossed the Pacific Ocean, and sailed to the Philippine Islands. Unfortunately, Magellan died in the Philippines at the hands of the natives. One of his original five ships continued the journey westward and sailed all the way back to Spain. Although Magellan did not make the entire journey, his name is associated with the first circumnavigation of the globe.

NOTE
Columbus did not really have to convince anyone that the world was round. Most people knew that the world was round, but they had no idea how great the earth's circumference actually was.

Sponsored by private, rather than state, funds, the Spanish *conquistadores*, or conquerors, set out to find wealth, fame, and power in the unexplored lands of the New World. In 1519, Hernan Cortes (1485–1547), accompanied by his troops, landed in Mexico. There he encountered the great Aztec civilization and the Aztec leader, Montezuma. The Spaniards, dressed in armor and riding atop horses, amazed the Aztecs. The Aztecs believed the Spaniards were sent by the god Quetzlcoatl, so they showered the Spaniards with gifts of gold and precious stones. Things went bad, and Cortes captured Montezuma, who died while in the custody of Cortes. Cortes' men destroyed many of the Aztec temples and buildings. Within three years, the conquistadores had wiped out the once-mighty Aztecs. The European weapons and diseases proved to be too much for the Aztecs. Those who didn't die of disease, brought over from Europe by the explorers, died at the hands of Cortes' men. Because of Cortes' expedition, Spain eventually controlled all of northern Mexico. Under the leadership of Francisco Pizarro (c.1476–1541), Spain established its dominance in western Latin America by destroying the Inca empire in 1532. In the years that followed, the Spaniards established colonies in the New World and searched for gold and silver. The pope granted Spain the ecclesiastical rights to the New World. As a result, Spain sent Catholic missionaries to the New World to Christianize the natives and to add souls to the Spanish empire.

The overseas expansion by Portugal and Spain had both positive and negative consequences. The trade developed by the two countries boosted their economies and introduced their subjects to many new goods and products. However, so much gold and silver flowed into Europe that Europe began to suffer from inflation. This inflation, coupled with the huge increase in population, contributed to what is generally referred to as the Price Revolution. However, the greatest negative consequence of the European expansion was the loss not only of the lives of the Indians but also of the civilizations.

THE RISE OF ABSOLUTISM IN FRANCE

With the death of Louis XIII in 1643, 5 year-old Louis XIV (1638–1715, king 1643–1715) ascended to the French throne. Louis' mother chose Cardinal Mazarin as his regent. Mazarin was not as shrewd as Cardinal Richelieu, who served as the most important adviser to Louis XIII. During Louis XIV's early years as king, he witnessed the Fronde, rebellions that

NOTE

It was quite common for absolutists to greatly increase taxes to pay for their increased spending and increased administrative expenses.

impressed upon Louis the need to tighten royal authority in France. After Mazarin's death, Louis was left to deal with the aristocracy, who were growing resentful of the growing power of the monarchy. To deal with the aristocracy, Louis adopted the concept of the *divine right of kings*. According to Bishop Bossuet, one of Louis' advisers, the king was chosen by God, and no one but God had the right to judge or question the king. This established the absolute sovereignty of Louis and his monarchy. The famous line *L'etat, c'est moi* is often attributed to Louis. Translated "I am the state," this line represents the mindset of Louis XIV.

Louis chose Jean-Baptiste Colbert (1619–1683) to administer the government of France. Colbert played a pivotal role in centralizing the monarchy of France. One of the ways Colbert did so was through the implementation of a mercantilistic economic policy. Colbert reshaped the French economy through government control of industry and trade. He organized factories and systems of production, trading companies and colonies, and intricate systems of canals and roadways. By the 1680s, France had trading colonies as far away as Canada and the Caribbean. All of his new policies helped put gold into the state coffers.

Louis decided to strengthen his grip on France in addition to controlling their economy. Louis believed that a unified France had room for only one religion. Louis also believed that more than one religion could not coexist in France. Therefore, Louis revoked the Edict of Nantes, which had allowed Calvinists to worship freely. Louis closed Huguenot institutions and stripped the Huguenots of their rights. Many Huguenots were exiled from France altogether.

Louis XIV took control of the military actions of the state, too. He had a strong desire to increase the size of his kingdom, and he used military might to do so. Louis used the money in his coffers to establish a vast, professional army, and France had great success early in his military campaigns. Parts of Germany and the surrounding area were added to French holdings. However, by the end of the seventeenth century and the beginning of the eighteenth century, the powers of Europe joined together to contain Louis' aggression.

By establishing absolute control over every aspect of the government, Louis epitomized the absolute monarch. As king, he controlled the economics, religion foreign and domestic policies, and military exploits of France. Louis ran the state and acted as if the state were there to serve him. He used the money in his royal coffers to finance not only his military expeditions, but also his extravagant lifestyle. He built a magnificent palace at Versailles that was home to thousands. He surrounded himself with fantastic art and beautiful landscaping. He used the wealth of the nation to flaunt his power for all to see. Louis also used his extraordinary wealth to intimidate foreigners who visited France.

NOTE

One of the characteristics of an absolute government was a professional standing army like the one employed by Louis XIV.

THE RISE OF ABSOLUTISM IN THE EAST

When Alexis I of Russia died, his daughter Sophia ruled as regent for Alexis' two sons, Peter and Ivan. At the age of 17, Peter took control from his sister and became Peter the Great (1672–1725, czar 1689–1725). Peter admired Western Europe and was determined to westernize Russia. His first priority was the strengthening of the army and the creation of a navy. He reorganized the government of Russia and divided Russia into provinces. He required members of the nobility to serve in the military or in some civil service position. After studying the policies of Western European nations, Peter attempted to install a mercantilistic economy in Russia by increasing exports and introducing new industries. However, when those efforts did not produce enough money, he simply raised taxes.

Peter really began to take on the look of a Western absolutist when he tried to gain control of the Russian Orthodox Church. Peter turned his attention to architecture. Using the grand Versailles as a model, Peter spent vast sums of money on architecture and art that testified to the greatness of Russia, just as Versailles did for France. Also, like a Western absolutist, Peter used his military to attack other territories and make them his own, as was the case in the Baltic region owned by Sweden.

THE RISE OF CONSTITUTIONALISM IN ENGLAND

England's history ran a much different course than that of France. England had experienced relative success with monarchy rather early in its history. The monarchy was solidified with the establishment of the Tudor dynasty in 1485. Henry VIII strengthened the position of the monarchy in England, and his daughter, Elizabeth I, went on to become the most successful of all the Tudor monarchs. However, the Tudor dynasty ended when Elizabeth died in 1603 and her cousin ascended to the throne of England. James VI of Scotland (1566–1625, King of Scotland 1567–1625, King of England 1603–1625), who became known as James I of England, began his reign on the wrong foot with Parliament. In his first meeting with Parliament, James, in an arrogant manner, informed them that he did not want to be challenged. Although James had the power to call and dismiss Parliament, Parliament had control over the revenues of the land. This antagonistic relationship between king and Parliament would later play a major role in the historical development of England.

James' son, Charles I (1600–1649), also ran into problems with Parliament. Parliament refused to grant Charles a lifetime of customs duties and opted, instead, to grant him only one year's worth. Charles found money elsewhere and wasted it on a failed military expedition to Spain. To pay for his mistake, Charles required the wealthy to cover his expenses. Several members of Parliament refused to pay, and they were jailed. In 1628,

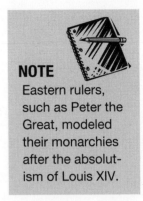

NOTE
Eastern rulers, such as Peter the Great, modeled their monarchies after the absolutism of Louis XIV.

NOTE

James I was strongly influenced by writings from France that used the divine right of kings concept to justify the strong monarchy there.

Parliament forced Charles to sign the *Petition of Rights*, which said that the king couldn't force a loan without Parliament's approval. The following year, Charles I dissolved Parliament. Charles began an eleven-year period during which he ruled without Parliament. To raise revenue, Charles collected ship money—money collected from coastal towns for their defense. Charles also collected ship money from landlocked towns.

A few years later, Charles found himself in a dangerous situation with Scotland. Charles tried to impose religious changes on the Scots, and riots ensued. The Scots vowed not to change their church. For the first time in more than ten years, Charles called Parliament in an attempt to raise funds to punish the Scots. The Parliament, called the Short Parliament, refused to give Charles the money he wanted. After a failed military campaign, Charles needed more money to pay the Scots to leave northern England. Charles contacted Parliament, called the long Parliament because it was in session for twenty years, in order to get more money. Parliament dismissed two of Charles' ministers and abolished many of the king's rights. They presented the king with a list of 204 grievances, known as the *Grand Remonstrance*. After a failed attempt to arrest some of the leaders of Parliament, Charles fled London to gather his troops. This began the English Civil War (1642–1649).

Oliver Cromwell (1599–1658) and his New Model Army, composed mostly of well-trained, well-disciplined Puritans, supported Parliament and captured Charles in 1646. A dispute arose among the troops, and Charles fled. Once again, Oliver Cromwell and his army captured Charles I. All of the Presbyterians were removed from Parliament, leaving what was known as the *Rump Parliament*. The Rump Parliament condemned the king to death, and Charles lost his head in 1649. The Civil War was over, and the monarchy had been toppled. Cromwell replaced the monarchy with a republic, called the Commonwealth. Designated Lord Protector, Cromwell ruled the Commonwealth as a military dictator until his death.

Charles II (1630–1685, king 1660–1685) returned from exile to take the throne in England. During his reign, Parliament restored the Church of England as the official church. Charles signed a secret treaty in which he had agreed to make England Catholic. Parliament became suspicious of Charles and passed the Test Act in 1673, which said only Anglicans could hold public office. Later, Parliament tried to pass legislation that would keep Charles' brother, James II, from ascending to the throne because he was Catholic. However, Charles dismissed Parliament. Charles died a few years later, and James II (1633–1701, king 1685–88) took the throne. When James and his wife had a son in 1688, England faced the possibility of a Catholic dynasty being established. William of Orange (1650–1702, king 1689–1702) and his wife Mary invaded England, and James fled with his family. With virtually no bloodshed, the old monarch was overthrown and a new monarchy was established. This was called the *Glorious Revolution*.

Parliament offered the throne to William and Mary under the condition that they would accept the Declaration of Rights, which later became the Bill of Rights. The Bill of Rights laid the foundation for the constitutional monarchy in England. Also, with the ascension of William and Mary to the throne, the idea of the divine right of kings had been destroyed in England.

THE GOLDEN AGE AND DECLINE OF SPAIN

The grandson of King Ferdinand and Queen Isabella of Spain, Charles, a Habsburg, became the first king of a united Spain. Three years later, in 1519, Charles became Charles V, Holy Roman Emperor. During the reign of Charles, Spain flourished because of the wealth that flowed from the New World. In 1556, Charles abdicated the Spanish throne to his son Philip (1527–1598, king 1556–1598). Because France was involved in its own religious turmoil, Spain went unchallenged. This marked the beginning of the Golden Age of Spain's art and culture. A devout Catholic and absolutist, Philip persecuted the Protestants in the Netherlands, an action that drained the Spanish coffers and led to war with England's Elizabeth I. It was Philip who lost the Spanish Armada to the English in 1588. Philip's successor, Philip III (1578–1621, king 1598–1621) ceased action against the Dutch and reduced Spanish spending.

Philip IV (1605–1665, king 1621–1665) ushered Spain into the height of its Golden Age. Because Philip IV did not concern himself much with politics, he gave governmental control of Spain to Gaspar de Guzman, conde de Olivares. Olivares renewed action against the Dutch and involved Spain in the Thirty Years' War, which then led Spain to war with France. After Olivares was removed, Spain began to decline. Ultimately, the grandson of Louis XIV, Philip V (1683–1746, king 1700–1746) ascended to the throne and sparked international controversy. The other European powers dreaded the idea of Louis' influence extending into Spain. Because of the controversy, Europe erupted into the War of the Spanish Succession. The Grand Alliance challenged Spain and France. At the end of the war, Philip kept his Spanish throne, to which he brought absolutism that he learned from the best, his grandfather, Louis XIV.

THE MAJOR PLAYERS

Christopher Columbus (1451–1506)—Known in Spanish as *Cristobal Colon* and in Italian as *Cristoforo Colombo*, Christopher Columbus was born into the family of a weaver in Genoa, Italy. Columbus took his first voyage in the 1470s and continued sailing after that. He married in 1479 and had his first child in 1480.

Columbus calculated that the earth was actually about 25 percent smaller than scholars had previously believed. (Columbus did not try to convince people that the world was round.) Based on these calculations, Columbus tried in vain to persuade the king of Portugal to finance a westward voyage

NOTE
The Petition of Rights also prohibited the imprisonment of individuals without a cause, and it prevented the quartering of troops in people's homes.

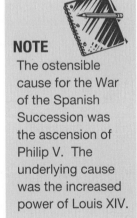

NOTE
The ostensible cause for the War of the Spanish Succession was the ascension of Philip V. The underlying cause was the increased power of Louis XIV.

to prove his theory. After failing in Portugal, Columbus went to Spain where he tried to find sponsors for a voyage. By this time, his wife had died, and he had a second child with his mistress, whom he later married. After several attempts, Columbus managed to convince King Ferdinand and Queen Isabella to sponsor a westward voyage of discovery. Columbus completed four voyages for Spain and opened the door for the Spanish occupation of the New World.

Most children learn about Columbus at an early age. However, the traditional stories about the heroic Columbus now seem to be inaccurate. Recent scholarship has shown that Columbus' motives were less than pure and that his treatment of the natives was harsh at best. Accounts from Columbus' own journal support the relatively new belief that Columbus had much less integrity than originally believed. Columbus' character aside, the fact remains that Columbus was a great pioneer in the area of overseas exploration.

Jean-Baptiste Colbert (1619–1683)—Colbert is often regarded as the greatest statesman in French history. Colbert began his civil service career at the age of 19 when he first went to work for the office of the minister of war in France. In 1651, Cardinal Mazarin hired Colbert to manage his finances. In 1665, Colbert was made the comptroller of finance for France. In his new role, Colbert completely reworked the nation's finances and employed the doctrine of mercantilism. He worked to control the French economy and direct all profits to the French coffers. Colbert controlled French industry, trade, navigation laws, trading companies, and colonization efforts for the economic prosperity of France. In addition, he built factories, roads, and canals, all of which boosted the French economy. He fortified coastal towns and strengthened the French navy. Colbert patronized the arts and sciences and established several institutes of higher learning. Unfortunately, as hard as Colbert worked, his efforts were no match for the unprecedented spending power of his king, Louis XIV. At the time of Colbert's death, he was unjustly blamed for France's financial problems.

James VI of Scotland, James I of England (1566–1625, King of Scotland 1567–1625, King of England 1603–1625)—Born in Edinburgh Castle in Scotland, James was the only son of Mary, Queen of Scots. Mary abdicated the throne in 1567, and James became king, although regents ruled for him until 1576. He was kidnapped in 1582, but he escaped the following year. In 1586, James signed the Treaty of Berwick and formed an alliance with Queen Elizabeth I of England, his cousin. In 1587, Mary, Queen of Scots, was executed, and James reduced the power of the Catholic nobility. Later, James suppressed the Protestants, too. He claimed the divine right of kings and established a strong central monarchy.

In 1603, James became the first Stuart king of England when Elizabeth I died without children. The following year, he ended England's war with Spain but began his long struggle with Parliament. James is famous for authorizing an English translation of the Bible. During his reign, he treated the Catholics very harshly. In 1605, as a result of his harsh treatment of Catholics, a group of Catholics entered into the Gunpowder Plot. These conspirators, along with Guy Fawkes, placed thirty-six barrels of gunpowder beneath Parliament in an attempt to kill Parliament and the king. Guy Fawkes was arrested and tortured until he admitted his guilt and revealed the names of the conspirators. The conspirators who were not killed while being arrested were hanged later with Fawkes. James considered himself a peacemaker, and in an attempt to promote religious peace in Europe, James gave his daughter in marriage to Frederick V, the Protestant German Leader. James also attempted to marry his son Charles to the daughter of the king of Spain, a Catholic. His subjects interpreted this move as pro-Catholic and anti-Anglican. These actions, along with his hesitation to support Protestant troops in the Thirty Years War, led many to question his loyalty to the Anglican Church.

NOTE
The Gunpowder Plot is celebrated annually in Great Britain on November 5 by burning in effigy a resemblance of Guy Fawkes.

Oliver Cromwell (1599–1658)—Originally from Wales, Oliver Cromwell was educated by a Puritan who wished to purify the Church of England of its remaining Catholic elements. As a member of Parliament in 1628 and 1629, Cromwell criticized the toleration of Catholic practices in the Church of England. Cromwell returned to Parliament in the crucial year 1640. After the outbreak of civil war, Cromwell used religious zeal to motivate troops to fight on the side of Parliament. After demonstrating his outstanding abilities in battle, Cromwell earned the nickname Ironsides. He opposed the king at every opportunity. Cromwell approved the removal of Presbyterians from Parliament and approved the execution of Charles I. He dismissed the Rump Parliament and became Lord Protector of the new Commonwealth; he later refused to be king. By acting as a military dictator in England, Cromwell managed to provide peace, stability, and religious toleration in England. Many people throughout history have vilified Cromwell, but his military and administrative skill is generally recognized as the best of his time.

Miguel de Cervantes Saavedra (1547–1616)—Cervantes overcame great odds to become one of Western Civilization's greatest writers. During a battle against the Turks, while he was in military service in Naples, Cervantes lost the use of his left hand. On his way back to Spain, he was captured by Barbary pirates and held for ransom. He tried unsuccessfully to escape several times. Fortunately, his family ransomed him, and he returned to Spain. He tried in vain to find employment with the nobility. He tried writing, but he couldn't support himself. With no other options available to him, Cervantes took government jobs. He found himself in prison, though, for a problem he encountered on one of his government jobs. It was during his prison term that he conceived the idea for *Don Quixote*, the story of a knight who traveled about looking for adventures. In addition to *Don Quixote*, Cervantes wrote *Exemplary Novels* and *Persiles y Sigismunda*. Cervantes is considered the greatest of all Spanish authors.

CHRONOLOGY OF THE AGE OF EXPANSION, ABSOLUTISM, AND CONSTITUTIONALISM

1418—Prince Henry the Navigator established his navigation school in Portugal.

1455—The War of the Roses began in England between the House of Lancaster and the House of York.

1488—Bartholomew Dias reached the Cape of Good Hope.

1492—Christopher Columbus set sail for India.

1493—Pope Alexander VI established the Line of Demarcation. Everything east of the line belonged to Portugal, and everything west of the line belonged to Spain.

1494—The Treaty of Tordesillas moved the Line of Demarcation west and gave Brazil to Portugal.

1497—Vasco da Gama reached the coast of India.

1497—John Cabot landed on and explored the coast of Newfoundland and New England.

1513—Vasco Nunez de Balboa became the first European to view the Pacific Ocean.

1519—Hernan Cortes conquered the Aztec empire in Mexico.

1519–1522—Ferdinand Magellan became the first ever to circumnavigate the globe.

1531—Francisco Pizarro began his conquest of the Inca empire.

1534—Jacques Cartier began exploration of Canada.

1553—Mary Tudor, also known as Bloody Mary, became Queen of England.

1558—Elizabeth I was crowned Queen of England.

1576—The Northern Provinces signed the Pacification of Ghent and drove out the Spaniards.

1584—William of Orange was assassinated.

1588—The English fleet defeated the great Spanish Armada.

1588—Henry III was assassinated, and Henry of Navarre became King of France.

1603—James VI of Scotland became James I of England, the first Stuart king.

1611—The authorized English version of the Bible, or the King James Bible, was published in England.

1618—Bohemians threw two of the king's officials out a window in the Defenestration of Prague, thus signaling the start of the Thirty Years' War.

1630—Swedish King Gustavus Adolphus entered the Thirty Years' War in defense of the Protestants.

1632—Swedish King Gustavus Adolphus was killed and the Swedish troops lost heart in their war efforts.

1637—Charles I forced a new prayer book on the Presbyterians of Scotland.

1640—Civil war broke out in England.

1643—Louis XIV became King of France, although a regent ruled for him.

1648—The Thirty Years' War ended with the signing of the Treaty of Westphalia.

1661—Louis XIV assumed control of the French throne.

1685—The Edict of Nantes was revoked by Louis XIV.

1688—The Glorious Revolution in England replaced James II with William and Mary with virtually no violence or bloodshed.

1689—Peter the Great became czar of Russia.

1701—The War of the Spanish Succession began.

1713—The War of the Spanish Succession ended with Philip V, grandson of Louis XIV, on the Spanish throne.

CAUTION
These questions are for review purposes only, not to predict the questions that will be on the AP exam.

SAMPLE ESSAY QUESTIONS

Now that you have reviewed the information about the Age of Expansion, Absolutism, and Constitutionalism, take a few moments to read through the sample essay questions that follow. The questions are intended to get you to think about some of the ways the AP exam may test your knowledge of the Age of Expansion, Absolutism, and Constitutionalism. To completely answer the questions, you will need to draw upon the knowledge you gained during your own course of study in addition to your review with this book.

1. Analyze and discuss the economic and social effects of the interaction between Spain and Portugal and the Americas.

2. Analyze and discuss the effects of mercantilism on France between 1600 and 1715.

3. Compare and contrast the reigns of Louis XIV and Peter the Great.

4. "God, gold, and glory were the primary motivations of the explorers and conquistadors who traveled to the New World during the Age of Expansion." Assess the validity of this statement.

5. Discuss the background, major events, and consequences of the Thirty Years' War.

6. Analyze and discuss the economic, social, and political consequences of Louis XIV's absolutism in France.

7. Analyze and discuss the extent to which the English Civil War and the Glorious Revolution contributed to the rise of constitutionalism in England.

8. Analyze and discuss the concept of divine right of kings. Use specific examples to support your answer.

9. Contrast absolutism and constitutionalism as they appeared in England and in France.

10. Analyze and discuss the extent to which religion played a role in the peace, or lack thereof, in Europe between 1600 and 1700. Use specific examples to support your answer.

The Scientific Revolution and the Enlightenment

OVERVIEW

During the sixteenth and seventeenth centuries, the knowledge of the world changed. The Scientific Revolution shook the foundations of the intellectual and theological traditions that had been formed during the Middle Ages. It would be a misrepresentation to classify the Scientific Revolution as either scientific or as a revolution. The science of the world didn't change, but rather the methodology of science, or the way man thought, underwent a transformation. In addition, the change took an extended period of time and was not revolutionary in the sense of the old being replaced immediately by the new; it was a gradual process of new ideas replacing old. Nevertheless, the Scientific Revolution permanently altered modern thought and the modern conception of the world around us.

The science of the Middle Ages, known then as natural philosophy, consisted of a mixture of Aristotelian, Ptolemaic, and Christian ideas about the world and universe. This natural philosophy, which supported the idea that God created a finite universe, became deeply rooted in and vigorously defended by Church orthodoxy. It was inconceivable to medieval scientists that the natural world could be examined outside the realm of religion and theology. After all, the universe was God's creation; he designed the universe and everything in it, so the truth about the nature of the universe must be compatible with the Christian religion and traditions. However, many of the ideas of sixteenth- and seventeenth-century thinkers were not only incompatible with but also contrary to the traditional Church dogma and, therefore, were strongly opposed by the Church.

For centuries, the intellectuals and theologians of Europe embraced the Ptolemaic concept of a geocentric universe, a universe with earth at the center. The ever-changing earth was thought to be composed of four basic elements: earth, water, fire, and air. Surrounding the imperfect earth were ten perfect crystal spheres that orbited the earth in circular orbits. Beyond the tenth sphere was heaven. For many, this was a logical, if not comfortable, arrangement. The entire finite universe revolved around the earth. The

NOTE

Ptolemy was an ancient astronomer who placed the earth at the center of the universe. His full name was Claudius Ptolemaeus. The name Claudius indicates a Roman heritage, and the name Ptolemaeus indicates an Egyptian heritage—but he wrote in Greek!

universe had limits, and man knew what and where those limits were. Beyond the limits of the universe was heaven, where God kept order in the universe. Is it any wonder that when these concepts were challenged, the Church reacted as if its very foundation was being attacked?

The Scientific Revolution instilled in European thinkers a new sense of self-confidence and self-reliance. This era of confidence in the human mind and faith in reason was known as the *Enlightenment*. Inspired by such intellectuals as Newton and Locke, Enlightenment thinkers used rational thinking and focused on such issues as moral improvement, economic growth, and political reform. This new breed of intellectuals believed that if reason could be applied to the laws of nature, then reason could also be applied to the laws of society. Enlightenment thinkers were optimistic about the possibility of changing the human condition.

The most famous and influential figures of the Enlightenment were the *philosophes*. These writers and thinkers sought the reform of government and society, and they made their thoughts known through the use of print. The *philosophes* thrived in the print culture of Europe, and they produced numerous books, pamphlets, and periodicals. During the era of the *philosophes*, the number of secular books increased tremendously, reflecting the idea of the Enlightenment that man did not need religion to find truth. Prose and poetry began to be considered of equal value, and the novel came into its own as a genre. The most famous of the philosophes were Voltaire, Montesquieu, Diderot, Rousseau, Hume, Smith, and Kant.

THE SCIENTIFIC REVOLUTION

At the dawn of the Scientific Revolution, the accepted ideas about the universe were still based upon those of Aristotle and Ptolemy. These medieval ideas were accepted because they easily supported what could be seen with the naked eye and because they were compatible with Christian doctrine. However, medieval universities and Renaissance thought helped create a group of intellectuals who were not afraid to think for themselves, even if that thought diverged from traditional thinkers. Furthermore, Europeans were beginning to explore lands further and further away from home, and they needed more advanced navigational methods and instruments. This, combined with a new way of thinking, spurred the movement of the Scientific Revolution.

One of the first truly revolutionary minds of the Scientific Revolution was Nicolaus Copernicus (1473–1543). Copernicus spent much of his early life studying church law and astronomy. It was during his study of astronomy that he became fascinated by the heliocentric universe, an ancient Greek idea that placed the sun at the center of the universe. This idea, of course, contradicted contemporary scientific thought and challenged hundreds of years of traditional thought. Although he came to believe in a heliocentric rather than geocentric universe, Copernicus did not publish his work for fear of ostracism and ridicule. Rather, his work was published posthumously. The implications of the theories of Copernicus were immense. His theory implied that the universe was actually unimaginable in size, contrary to the traditional idea of a finite universe and that the earth was no longer the center of the universe. This greatly reduced the importance of earth in the grand scheme of the universe. Religious leaders across Europe, including both Calvin and Luther, criticized Copernicus for his ideas, which, according to them, directly contradicted the teachings of the Bible. The Catholic Church reacted a little slower but finally declared his work false in 1616.

Copernicus paved the way for other thinkers such as Tycho Brahe (1546–1630). This Danish scientist spent twenty long years observing the stars and collecting data. His lack of mathematical genius prevented him from using the data to develop theories and laws. Brahe's assistant, however, possessed the mathematical ability necessary to formulate scientific laws based upon the mountains of Brahe's research data. Johannes Kepler (1571–1630) used Brahe's work and findings to develop three very important natural laws. First, he said the orbits of the planets were elliptical and not circular. Second, Kepler said the planets move at different speeds in their orbits. Third, he said the time it takes for a planet to complete its orbit of the sun is relative to its distance from the sun. These three laws smashed the Aristotelian and Ptolemaic concepts of the universe to which Europe had clung for centuries, and he proved these laws mathematically.

Galileo Galilei (1564–1642) continued the break with tradition in his findings as well. A genius who became a math professor at age 25, Galileo used observation instead of speculation as he developed his theories. Among other things, Galileo worked with laws of motion and discovered Jupiter's moons. He destroyed the idea that the planets were mere crystal spheres and proved that the heavenly bodies were not always as they appeared to the naked eye. After the publication of his *Dialogue on the Two Chief Systems of the World* (1632), Galileo was arrested, tried for heresy, and imprisoned. This episode occurred only a few years after the pope had instructed Galileo that he could continue to write about the possible systems of the world that might exist, as long as he did not say in his writings which of those actually did exist. Galileo's trial has come to represent the conflict between science and religion both during and after the Scientific Revolution.

The greatest achievement of the Scientific Revolution was the synthesis of Copernicus, Kepler, and Galileo into a single system of thought. Sir Isaac Newton (1642–1727) developed a system of mathematical laws known as *universal gravitation*. Based on mathematics, Newton determined that every body in the universe is attracted to every other body in the universe in a mathematical relationship. He also asserted that the attraction of these bodies is based upon the amount of matter of the bodies and the distance between them.

NOTE
Descartes believed humans have innate knowledge and ideas. Bacon disagreed and argued that knowledge is based on experience.

MAKING OF THE MODERN SCIENTIFIC METHOD

The Scientific Revolution changed not only the knowledge of the times but also the methodology of obtaining knowledge. The two men most responsible for the development of the methodology were Francis Bacon (1561–1626) and René Descartes (1596–1650). Although Bacon and Descartes contrasted each other concerning methods of acquiring knowledge, the combination of their ideas results in the modern scientific method. Bacon, an English writer, championed a new experimental method of acquiring knowledge. He rejected the Aristotelian idea of speculative reasoning and advocated the inductive method. He believed that it was important to observe something in order to determine its nature and to learn more about it. Bacon's method is often referred to as *empiricism*. Descartes, a French mathematician who developed analytic geometry, advocated deductive reasoning. Descartes had great faith in the ability of the human mind. Therefore, Descartes method was to doubt everything, then use logic and reason to deduce the nature of things and the scientific laws that govern those things. Descartes reduced all substances to matter and mind, or the physical and the spiritual, which is a concept known as *Cartesian dualism*. The modern scientific method is a combination of the thinking of Bacon and Descartes. The scientific method employs both observation and logical thinking in the development of scientific theories and laws.

THE ENLIGHTENMENT

The Scientific Revolution changed the way Europeans thought, and this new trend in intellectual activity was known as the *Enlightenment*. The contemporaries of the age believed they were experiencing a new, enlightened period of reason and science. Although the Enlightenment occurred largely in the eighteenth century, its roots lay in the time period between Sir Isaac Newton and Louis XIV of France. The writers of the Enlightenment were greatly influenced by the unanswered questions of religious and scientific certainty and uncertainty that were brought to light during the Scientific Revolution. Because of the impact of the Scientific Revolution on the power of the human mind, the Enlightenment became a profoundly secular movement that demonstrated man's independence from religion. In general, the Enlightenment affected the middle class and aristocracy of Europe and played almost no part at all in the lives of the lower classes.

The thinkers of the Enlightenment were heavily influenced by such thinkers as Newton and John Locke (1632–1704), both Englishmen, but, for a few reasons, the Enlightenment reached its pinnacle in France. First, the international language of the educated elite in Europe was French. Second, although French thinkers and writers were sometimes jailed or forced to flee the country, they were never executed for their statements. Consequently, the French thinkers never faced insurmountable odds like some thinkers and writers in Central and Eastern Europe.

The Age of Enlightenment brought with it three main ideas that were manifest in the writings of the times. First, Enlightenment thinkers believed that the methods of natural science, which were developed during the Scientific Revolution, were applicable to all aspects of life. Second, they believed the scientific method was capable of discovering the laws of human society. Third, and perhaps most importantly, the Enlightenment thinkers believed in the possibility of both societal and individual progress and improvement for humans. In other words, the thinkers of the Enlightenment believed in the power of reason and in the power of the human mind to discover the laws that govern man and society. They also believed that the application of these laws to society could improve both man and society. Overall, the Enlightenment was a time of optimism.

NOTE
Enlightenment thinkers were reformers and not revolutionaries. They advocated change from the top down and not from the bottom up.

Although some of the important intellectuals of the Enlightenment were the skeptics, such as Pierre Bayle (1647–1706), the most important and most influential of all Enlightenment thinkers were the *philosophes*. The *philosophes* claimed that they were bringing knowledge to Europe. They believed that they were shedding light on the dark, uneducated continent. The *philosophes* sought to educate the public, or educated middle class. They saw no need to educate the people, or the commoners of Europe, who the *philosophes* regarded as ignorant and deeply affected by superstition.

Because governments usually did not allow individuals to speak out directly against the government or against the established Church, many *philosophes* found clever ways to spread their ideas. Some of the *philosophes* produced their work in the form of books, encyclopedias, or pamphlets that were full of satire. By writing in this cryptic manner, the writers prevented their writings from being burned or banned. One such writer was the Baron de Montesquieu (1689–1755), who wrote *The Persian Letters* (1721), a satirical look at the customs and practices of Europe. Another *philosophe* who employed such methods was Voltaire (1694–1778). Voltaire criticized the established Church and other things in his satirical work *Candide* (1759). The volumes of work produced by the *philosophes* increased both the demand for and sales of books in Europe. In addition, Europe saw a slight increase in literacy during this period, probably as a result of the increased interest in reading. The illegal book trade also prospered during this period.

Another step that was taken to prevent government interference in intellectual issues was the use of *salons*. Elite women began to organize and host salons in their homes. Salons were meetings of *philosophes* and other educated elites who gathered to discuss philosophy, politics, and current events. The salons allowed the free discussion of ideas and the uninhibited expression of public opinion. The women who hosted these salons began to rise in prominence, especially in France. The elite women hosting salons influenced not only intellectual trends but artistic trends as well. Through their political work, they began to influence a new artistic style known as *rococo*. The popular rococo style was characterized by delicacy and ornamentation and was reflected in the style of the drawing rooms where the *salons* were held.

NOTE
The illegal book trade in Europe centered around scandalous and often pornographic accounts of the lives of prominent Europeans.

CAUTION

Do not think that all of the thinkers of the later Enlightenment were atheists like d'Holbach. Many of them simply had strong beliefs, like d'Holbach, and insisted on the validity of their beliefs.

The later Enlightenment saw the exaggeration of original Enlightenment ideas. These exaggerations were manifest in the inflexible and often dogmatic systems of thought, which often went far beyond traditional Enlightenment thought. Baron Paul d'Holbach (1723–1789) exemplified the later Enlightenment thinkers through his aggressive atheistic beliefs. This inflexibility and rigidity caused many Enlightenment thinkers to turn their backs on these new stubborn intellectuals. Ultimately, this disagreement in ideology caused a division between the traditional Enlightenment thinkers and those of the later Enlightenment.

EFFECTS OF THE ENLIGHTENMENT

The Enlightenment thinkers believed that an educated monarch would be ideal, supposing that he would make better laws and decisions concerning his or her subjects. Several central and eastern European rulers such as Catherine the Great of Russia, Frederick the Great of Prussia, and Joseph II of Austria, were inspired by the Enlightenment thinkers and made conscious efforts to rule as enlightened monarchs.

Catherine the Great (1729–1796, empress 1762–1796) studied the writings of Voltaire, Bayle, and others. She worked to bring Western culture to Russia. She tried to make better laws. In other words, she wanted to introduce enlightened, more tolerant legislation, legislation of which the *philosophes* would approve. Therefore, she introduced reforms such as the abolishment of torture; she even allowed limited religious toleration. Catherine never questioned whether or not she should rule absolutely—she just did—but she tried diligently to rule as an enlightened absolutist. Frederick the Great of Prussia (1712–1786, king 1740–1786) sought to institute humane policies for his kingdom. He allowed religious freedom and philosophical freedom. He advocated education by improving the schools in his kingdom. He simplified his laws and put in place hardworking, honest members of the judiciary. Frederick once expressed to Voltaire his desire to enlighten his people. Joseph II of Austria (1741–1790, emperor 1780–1790) acted as an enlightened absolutist by extending toleration to Protestants and Jews and by abolishing serfdom.

THE MAJOR PLAYERS

Thomas Hobbes (1588–1679)—Hobbes, an English philosopher, met with Galileo and Descartes and was affected by their philosophies. The English Revolution deeply disturbed Hobbes and played a major role in the development of his idea that man was totally depraved. He believed that, because of man's depravity, an absolute, sovereign ruler was necessary to keep man under control. His absolutist views, however, were not based on the concept of the divine right of kings. He outlined his views on sovereignty in his classic work *Leviathan* (1651).

Blaise Pascal (1623–1662)—Pascal was a brilliant French scientist and mathematician who invented a mechanical calculator. Pascal's objective was to unite Christianity and science by proving that Christianity was not contrary to reason. Pascal said, "This is what constitutes faith: God experienced by the heart, not by the reason." Pascal's greatest work, published posthumously, is known as *Thoughts on Religion and Other Subjects*, or *Pensees*.

Baruch Spinoza (1632–1677)—Educated in the Jewish tradition, the Dutchman Baruch Spinoza was later alienated from Judaism because of his study of Descartes and Hobbes. Spinoza advocated pantheism, the idea that everything that exists is God and God is the substance of things. He followed Descartes' ideas about knowledge and the separation of mind and matter. He rejected the ideas of both providence and free will. Spinoza's greatest work was *Ethics Demonstrated in the Geometrical Manner*.

John Locke (1632–1704)—Locke, an English philosopher, played a major role in the development of modern western thought and government. Locke emphasized the role of empiricism rather than the Cartesian concept of innate ideas. In his famous work *Essay on Human Understanding* (1690), Locke argued that the human mind was a *tabula rasa*, or blank slate, at birth. According to Locke, experiences formed and shaped man's knowledge. Locke also argued that man was born good, not depraved, and equal. In his *Two Treatises of Government* (1690), Locke attacked the divine right of kings, thereby contradicting the ideas of Hobbes. Locke said that the sovereignty of the state lay within the people and that the people possessed unalienable rights, called natural rights. Locke went even further by saying that the people have a right, if not an obligation, to rebel or revolt if the government were to infringe upon those rights. In addition, Locke advocated freedom of religion and separation of church and state. Locke had a profound influence on the development of the United States Constitution and the government of the United States. The thinkers of the Enlightenment regarded Locke, along with Newton, as one of the greatest European minds of all time.

Pierre Bayle (1647–1706)—Pierre Bayle, a French philosopher and skeptic, led the way for skepticism. Born a Protestant, Bayle converted to Catholicism and then back to Protestantism. His works, the most famous of which was *Historical and Critical Dictionary*, attacked superstition, religious dogma, and religious tradition. He also attacked traditional religious heroes like David of the Bible. Bayle believed that Christianity and morality did not necessarily go hand in hand. Bayle also argued against religious intolerance, probably in reaction to Louis XIV.

CAUTION
Be very cautious when making superlative statements like "Galileo was the greatest..." or "Descartes was the most intelligent..." because you may, by mistake, attribute a superlative quality to a person who is not generally accepted as the "greatest" or "most important." An erroneous statement like that may damage your credibility.

NOTE

Voltaire's *Candide* is a book that you need to read if you haven't already done so. It provides a fantastic glimpse into the world of Voltaire, and it is quite entertaining. In addition, college representatives who do interviews love to hear students discuss their high school readings lists when they include books like *Candide*.

Bernard de Fontenelle (1657–1757)—Fontenelle was a French scholar who knew a great deal about science. For several years, he served as secretary for the French Royal Academy of Science. Fontenelle is best remembered for his book *Plurality of Worlds*. Written as a conversation between a man and woman sitting under the night sky, *Plurality* made the world of science accessible to non-scientists by integrating science with literature. Fontenelle downplayed the importance of religion and the Church, thus contributing to the skepticism of the seventeenth and eighteenth centuries.

Montesquieu (1689–1755)—Montesquieu's full name was Charles Louis de Secondat, Baron de la Brede et de Montesquieu. This French writer produced some of the most important works of the Enlightenment. His early work *Persian Letters* (1721) satirized and criticized French politics and social practices. It was written as a collection of letters between two aristocratic Persians who had traveled to Europe and discussed what they had seen. Montesquieu chose this manner of writing to avoid persecution for his statements. Montesquieu also dealt with the philosophy of history in his *Thoughts on the Causes of the Greatness and Downfall of the Romans* (1734). In 1748, he produced his most famous writings, *The Spirit of Laws*. In this book, Montesquieu examined the republic, monarchy, and despotism. He contended that a country's geography and general conditions helped determine what type of government evolved there. He advocated a balance of power within the government to protect and preserve individual freedoms. He also spoke out against slavery because it was a violation of a person's individual freedom and of natural law.

Voltaire (1694–1778)—Francois Marie Arouet assumed the name Voltaire for his writings. Voltaire may have been the greatest of all the *philosophes*. Much of Voltaire's life and career were shaped by a journey he made to England. After that journey, Voltaire forever preferred England to his native France. Voltaire admired England's religious toleration and respect for Sir Isaac Newton. Although Voltaire received a Jesuit education, he despised the Catholic Church. In fact, he disapproved of all organized religion. Voltaire was a deist who saw organized religion as oppressive. He voiced this opinion in the wake of the Lisbon earthquake in 1755 by publishing his greatest work, *Candide*, in 1759. In *Candide*, Voltaire tried to show the evils of the Church and of organized religion. Through this work, he contended that individuals should seek peace within themselves instead of in a set of beliefs or doctrines. In 1763, Voltaire published his *Treatise on Toleration,* in which he eloquently pleaded for religious toleration. He believed in freedom of thought and respect for all, and he used his writings to champion these ideals.

David Hume (1711–1776)—David Hume was a Scottish historian and philosopher who advocated skepticism and empiricism. He said that careful observation of human experiences would lead to the knowledge of human nature. He also argued that since man's ideas are based on his experiences, reason cannot answer questions that can't be answered by empiricism. Hume also argued against the existence of miracles. One of his most famous works was *Philosophical Essays Concerning Human Understanding* (1748).

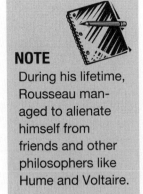

NOTE
During his lifetime, Rousseau managed to alienate himself from friends and other philosophers like Hume and Voltaire.

Jean-Jacques Rousseau (1712–1778)—The French philosopher Jean-Jacques Rousseau began his scholarly career working alongside Diderot on the *Encyclopedie*. Rousseau developed the idea that man in the state of nature, or as primitive man, was morally superior to modern civilized man. Rousseau argued that modern man had become corrupt by art, science, and modern institutions and innovations. With this idea, he alienated himself from some of the *philosophes*. In 1762, Rousseau published *The Social Contract* in which he said that man agreed to be ruled by creating a sort of social contract between the government and the governed. Rousseau said that in this relationship, the individual should submit to the general will, or the will of the community, in order to be free. Rousseau downplayed individualism and said that the individual was part of the greater community.

In 1762 Rousseau also published *Emile*, another book that created a stir among his contemporaries. In *Emile*, Rousseau told the story of the education of a young boy named Emile. Rousseau advocated the development of children's emotions instead of the development of children's reason and logical thinking. Rousseau also suggested that children be treated like children and not like adults. Because of his view of emotions over reason, Rousseau found himself at odds with Voltaire.

Denis Diderot (1713–1784)—Diderot was a French writer of novels, essays, plays, and criticisms. His most famous work, though, was the *Encyclopedie*. He was asked to work on a French translation of the English *Cyclopaedia*. He, along with Jean Le Rond d'Alembert, overhauled the work and produced a thirty-five volume *Encyclopedie*. Diderot enlisted the help of some the greatest contemporary writers like Voltaire and Montesquieu. The *Encyclopedie* was an attempt to organize information in a rational and scientific fashion. Diderot hoped these volumes of information would change the way people thought. The *Encyclopedie* drew attention from far and wide. Several of his volumes were banned across Europe and included in the *Index of Prohibited Books*. Catherine the Great of Russia, on the other hand, financed some of the work by Diderot. Even Thomas Jefferson and Ben Franklin had copies of the *Encyclopedie*.

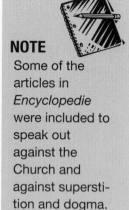

NOTE
Some of the articles in *Encyclopedie* were included to speak out against the Church and against superstition and dogma.

Adam Smith (1723–1790)—Adam Smith, once a professor in Glasgow, emerged as the most important and influential economists of the Enlightenment. The Scottish Smith met with a group of economists called *physiocrats* on the Continent and was heavily influenced by their ideas. He adopted much of their ideology that maintains that economics is based on natural law, wealth, and order. In 1776, Smith produced *Inquiry into the Nature and Causes of the Wealth of Nations* (usually referred to as *Wealth of Nations*). In this book, he advocated the abolition of mercantilism and all government interference in economics. Smith preferred a *laissez-faire* economic policy, one in which the government takes a hands-off economic approach. Smith believed that individuals who were left alone to invest and spend on their own would act as if an invisible hand is leading them. This invisible hand would lead them, according to Smith, to act in the best interest of everyone. In *Wealth of Nations*, Smith created a classic economic text that is still used and studied by Economics students today.

Immanuel Kant (1724–1804)—The German philosopher Kant has been called the most influential modern philosopher. His tow great works were *The Critique of Pure Reason* (1781) and *The Critique of Practical Reason* (1788). He examined in these books the nature and basis of knowledge. One of Kant's most well-known concepts is that of the categorical imperative. This concept is that humans possess an innate morality, which compels a man to act in any given situation the way one would want others to act in that same situation. Kant used this imperative to support the existence of God. He realized this could not be proved, but he still accepted it. He also accepted rationalism and reason. Kant's work later influenced Hegel and Marx.

NOTE
Kant said that thinkers should be allowed to express themselves through writing and that enlightenment would follow when that came to pass.

Edward Gibbon (1737–1794)—Gibbon was the greatest English historian of the Enlightenment. In 1776, Gibbon began his voluminous work *The History of the Decline and Fall of the Roman Empire*. Although we have data that refutes some of his work, Gibbon's masterpiece remains a classic. The work illustrates Gibbon's skepticism of religion through his treatment of early Christianity as a natural phenomenon instead of as a religion of miracles and providence.

CHRONOLOGY OF THE SCIENTIFIC REVOLUTION AND THE ENLIGHTENMENT

1543—Copernicus' *On the Revolution of the Heavenly Spheres* was published posthumously.

1577–1640—Flemish painter Peter Paul Rubens epitomized the baroque style of painting. He painted many religious scenes and portrayed even saints and angels as sensual nude figures.

1590—Zacharias Jansen invented the microscope.

1605—Francis Bacon's *The Advancement of Learning* was published.

c.1608—The telescope was invented.

1609—Johannes Kepler's *On the Motion of Mars* was published.

1628—William Harvey developed his theory of the circulation of blood.

1632—Galileo's *Dialogues on the Two Chief Systems of the World* was published.

1633—Galileo was tried and imprisoned for heresy.

1637—René Descartes' *Discourse on Method* was published.

1642–1649—Civil war raged in England.

1651—Thomas Hobbes' *Leviathan* was published.

1685–1750—Johann Sebastian Bach became the greatest of the baroque musicians. His brilliant music was characterized by its ornate fashion.

1687—Sir Isaac Newton's *Principia Mathematica* was published.

1690—John Locke's *Essay Concerning Human Understanding* was published.

1717—Jean-Antoine Watteau painted *The Embarkation for the Island of Cythera*, one of the best examples of the French rococo artistic style.

1751—Diderot's first volume of *Encyclopedie* was published.

1751—Carolus Linnaeus was the first to use binomial nomenclature to classify genus and species of living organisms in the field of taxonomy.

1755—The Lisbon earthquake killed thousands and sparked a Continental debate on theology, natural science, and other great issues.

1756—Wolfgang Amadeus Mozart was born in Austria.

1759—Voltaire published *Candide*.

TIP
Use this chronology to begin to frame the big picture. Chronologies are helpful when you are trying to see how a story unfolds; in this case, the story is that of the Scientific Revolution and the Enlightenment.

1762—Catherine the Great began her rule in Russia.

1765—Jean-Honore Fragonard began painting in the rococo style.

1776—Adam Smith's *Wealth of Nations* was published.

1781—Joseph II of Austria began policy of religious toleration.

SAMPLE ESSAY QUESTIONS

Now that you have reviewed the information about the Scientific Revolution and Enlightenment, take a few moments to read through the sample essay questions that follow. The questions are intended to get you thinking about some of the ways the AP exam may test your knowledge of the Scientific Revolution and Enlightenment. To completely answer the questions, you will need to draw upon the knowledge you gained during your own course of study in addition to your review with this book.

1. Analyze and discuss the ways in which the scientific method differed from the medieval approach to scientific knowledge.

2. Contrast the philosophies of Bacon and Descartes.

3. Analyze and discuss the extent to which humanism had an effect on thinkers of the Scientific Revolution and of the Enlightenment.

4. "The Enlightenment presented an optimistic outlook of the future of Europe." Assess the validity of this statement using specific examples to support your answer.

5. Analyze and discuss the extent to which Central and Eastern European rulers were affected by the intellectuals of the Enlightenment.

6. Discuss the reasons why the Catholic Church felt threatened by the Scientific Revolution and by the Enlightenment.

7. Contrast the political philosophy of Thomas Hobbes and John Locke, including a treatment of the implications of their philosophies.

8. Discuss which of the Enlightenment thinkers played the greatest role in the shaping of modern government.

9. Discuss which of the thinkers of the Scientific Revolution played the greatest role in the shaping of modern science.

10. "The Scientific Revolution was not a revolution in science but rather was a revolution in the thought." Assess the validity of this statement using specific examples to support your answer.

11. "The Enlightenment thinkers accomplished their goal of bringing knowledge to many Europeans." Assess the validity of this statement using specific examples to support your answer.

The French Revolution and the Napoleonic Era (1789–1815)

OVERVIEW

Despite the influence of the Enlightenment and the abundance of resources France possessed, the French government of the eighteenth century had become corrupt and ineffective. Much of the French social structure was a holdover from the Middle Ages, and the French social classes resented one another for a number of reasons. Most importantly, though, the French government found itself buried beneath a mountain of debt with no way to dig itself out. Fueled by the fire of class resentments, a moderate reform movement spiraled out of control and resulted in a bloody revolution that destroyed the old regime. The French Revolution sent shockwaves through the rest of Europe by threatening the traditional social and political orders of other nations. In 1799, Napoleon Bonaparte began his meteoric rise to greatness by seizing control of France. After establishing himself in France, Napoleon moved on to the rest of Europe where he established one of the greatest modern empires, one in which he instituted a number of landmark reforms. After losing many of his troops, Napoleon lost the Battle of Nations in 1813. The following year, Napoleon abdicated the throne. The European powers came together and established a policy of balance of power to prevent international domination by one nation, as was the case with France under Napoleon.

BACKGROUND OF THE REVOLUTION IN FRANCE

One of the biggest problems facing France in the eighteenth century was its social structure. The entire population of France fell into one of three legal divisions or categories called *estates*. The First Estate included the clergy of the Catholic Church. This group accounted for a tiny fraction of the total population, yet they owned between one tenth and one fifth of the land in France. In addition, they paid virtually no taxes aside from a voluntary tax

NOTE
The *taille* was an annual tax on land or property that did not need to be approved by the Estates-General.

once every five years. The First Estate was somewhat divided, with the higher clergy often having different interests than the parish priests. The nobility made up the Second Estate. The Second Estate owned between one fourth and one third of the land in France, yet they also numbered but a fraction of the population. Although there were some divisions between the upper nobility and the lower nobility, none of the nobles paid taxes. With the First Estate and Second Estate both exempt from taxes, particularly the *taille*, the tax burden fell upon the Third Estate. The Third Estate included everyone in France who was neither nobility nor clergy. Although legally considered commoners, the Third Estate, which owned the majority of the land and property in France, included people of many economic, occupational, and educational backgrounds. Peasants, artisans, the urban poor, middle class merchants, bankers, and professionals, such as doctors and lawyers, all found themselves together as members of the Third Estate. If the interests of the people in the First and Second Estates were varied, the interests of and differences between the people of the Third Estate were almost irreconcilable. The wealthiest members of the Third Estate seemed to have more in common with the Second Estate than with the poor members of their own social group. Therefore, class resentments and struggles were not as clearly defined as you might have imagined.

Perhaps the greatest challenge facing the French government during the eighteenth century was the national economy. The economic dire straits in which France found itself dated back to the uncontrolled spending of Louis XIV and the mismanagement of the government by Louis XV (1710–1774, king 1715–1774). The expense of the French and Indian War, combined with the expense of supporting the American colonies against Great Britain, placed an almost unbearable economic burden on France. By the time of the Revolution, France devoted approximately 50 percent of its national budget to the debt and the interest on that debt. In an effort to keep up with the debt, the king sold political offices and government positions. France's three primary taxes, the *taille*, the *gabelle,* and the *aide,* simply did not produce the revenue that France needed. The nobility repeatedly rejected the crown's attempt to tax them, so the tax burden fell on those least able to support it, the peasants. Louis XVI (1754–1793, king 1774–1792) appointed a number of economic advisers throughout the 1770s and 1780s, but all were forced to resign because of their attacks on the rights of the privileged. In 1788, Louis XVI gave in to the Paris Parlement, or one of the courts, and agreed to bring back the Estates-General. The Estates-General, a legislative body that included representatives from each of the three estates, had not met since 1614. Louis ordered an election and declared that the Estates-General would meet at Versailles in May of the following year.

NOTE
The *gabelle* was a tax on salt, and the *aide* was a tax on food and drink.

THE ESTATES-GENERAL

Although the chance for the Third Estate to participate in government brought great excitement, it also brought great concern. The Estates-General traditionally seated 300 people from each estate, and each estate voted equally. The Third Estate realized that the nobility controlled the First and Second Estates and would, therefore, vote in a manner that would benefit the nobles and not the commoners. The Third Estate demanded that the number of their representatives be raised to 600, and in 1788, Louis doubled the number of representatives in the Third Estate. Because each estate was to have an equal vote, though, the members of the Third Estate were not satisfied. They understood that they outnumbered the First and Second Estates combined, but they were to receive the same vote as the other two estates. For the Third Estate, this unequal representation was completely unfair. This raised the issue of whether the Estates-General should vote according to tradition with each order, or estate, voting equally, or whether the Estates General should vote by head, that is with each member of the Estates General receiving one vote. The traditional voting method favored the First and Second Estates, while the voting-by-head method favored the Third Estate. This issue was left unresolved. The members of each estate drew up a list of grievances, known as the *cahiers*, and sent them to Versailles. The cahiers from each estate had concerns about the need for reform of the French government, in particular the state bureaucracy. The cahiers indicated that people of every walk of life in France had concerns about the current state of affairs, and those concerns were relatively similar, despite the economic and social differences of the estates.

On May 5, 1789, the Estates-General convened for the first time in more than 150 years. The occasion began with great pomp and circumstance but deteriorated quickly. After initial tensions arose over issues of the Third Estate's clothing and their desire to wear hats before the king, the members of the First and Second Estates became deadlocked with the Third Estate over the method of voting. The Third Estate demanded that the vote be by head, thus making their collective voice equal to or greater than those of the First and Second Estate. The privileged members of the Estates-General, of course, demanded that the vote be by order, thus giving the nobility the distinct advantage. The impasse lasted for weeks and rendered the Estates-General powerless to act.

Influenced by Abbe Sieyes (1748–1836) and Honore Gabriel Victor de Mirabeau, the Third Estate changed its name to the National Assembly and began its own meetings. After being locked out of their meeting hall by the king's guards, supposedly because of repairs, the new National Assembly met on an indoor tennis court and vowed not to disassemble until they had written a new constitution. This famous event is known as the *Tennis Court Oath*. The Tennis Court Oath essentially marked the beginning of the French Revolution. Only days later, Louis granted some concessions and agreed to recognize the National Assembly. However, the king's efforts were too little too late.

NOTE
One of the most famous paintings of the French Revolution is the *Tennis Court Oath* by Jacques-Louis David. The painting depicts the event and features Sieyes and Robespierre, among others.

THE FIRST, OR MODERATE, STAGE OF THE REVOLUTION

In the meantime, the people of Paris grew increasingly unhappy with their condition. The poor faced food shortages, high prices, and backbreaking taxes, and their frustrations were compounded by the virtual stalemate at Versailles. As if the people of Paris didn't have enough to worry about, rumors began to spread that the king was amassing troops for an offensive measure that would disband the National Assembly and reassert royal power. To defend themselves, the people of Paris stormed the Bastille, a royal armory, and ordered the garrison to leave their posts and surrender the arms inside; the crowd numbered about 80,000 strong. The crowd cut off the head of the commander of the forces and paraded about Paris with the decapitated head on a pike. This served as a brutal foreshadowing of events to follow. The rebellion spread from Paris into the countryside, where the *Great Fear* dominated the summer of 1789. During the Great Fear, peasants attacked nobles and the nobles' estates and burned all the documents on which were recorded the peasants' financial obligations. The nobles reacted by renouncing all their feudal rights and ended feudalism in France.

The bourgeoisie of Paris feared further action by the commoners, so they established a militia known as the National Guard. They chose the Marquis de Lafayette (1757–1834) to head the new National Guard. Lafayette had been a hero during the War for American Independence, and the people rallied behind him. Under his leadership, the flag bearing the Bourbon *fleur de lis* was replaced by the tricolor flag still used in France today. Lafayette also played a role in the development of one of Europe's most important documents since the Magna Carta. With the help of Thomas Jefferson, Lafayette and others wrote the *Declaration of the Rights of Man and the Citizen*. They based this document on the American Declaration of Independence and on such Enlightenment ideas as the right to life, liberty, and property. This powerful document made all men equal under the law and restricted the monarchy. It also guaranteed freedom of speech, religion, and due process of law.

NOTE
The *Declaration of the Rights of Man and the Citizen* raised the issue of women's rights. Olympe de Gouges responded to the document with her own *Declaration of the Rights of Woman and the Female Citizen*. Her demands, however, were largely ignored.

On October 5 of the same year, a mob of Parisian women marched from Paris to Versailles, which was 12 miles away. They wanted to express their discontent to the king and the National Assembly. Armed with pitchforks, broomsticks, and guns, the women marched on Versailles and received their audience with the king. The mob then demanded that the king and his family return to Paris with them. Louis was in no position to argue. Carrying the heads of the king's guards on sticks, the mob of women "escorted" the royal family back to the *Tuileries*, the king's residence in Paris, where they remained virtually as prisoners until they were executed. The National Assembly also returned to Paris

In 1790, the Revolution opened the door for dissent with the Civil Constitution of the Clergy. This legislation, reluctantly approved by Louis, basically made the Church a state institution and made members of the clergy, by virtue of an oath of allegiance, employees of the state. In essence, those who took the oath supported the Revolution, and those who did not take the oath were considered counter-revolutionaries. Pope Pious VI denounced this legislation and the principles of the Revolution. The National Assembly confiscated much of the Church land and used it to pay off some of the national debt—an act that infuriated Catholics. The friction between Church and state served as a catalyst for counter-revolutionary activity.

The National Assembly, also called the Constituent Assembly for its work on a new constitution, completed its work on the constitution in 1791. The new constitution limited the power of the "king of the French" by creating a Legislative Assembly, the members of which were to be chosen by electors. The National Assembly also divided France into eighty-three departments, thus eliminating the old provincial system. The Assembly extended rights to Protestants and Jews, perhaps due in no small part to the influence of some Enlightenment thinkers. In addition, the National Assembly abolished slavery in France.

In 1791, the brother of Louis XVI encouraged the king to flee France with his family. The king got as far as Varennes before he was recognized and taken back to Paris. The National Assembly, still working for a constitutional monarchy, told the public that the king had been kidnapped; the Assembly did not want the public to know that their king had attempted to leave the country. Also in 1791, the King of Prussia and the Emperor of Austria, partially persuaded by the *emigres*, issued the Declaration of Pillnitz. In this document, the foreign monarchs threatened to intervene in French affairs and restore the old regime of France. As a result, the Legislative Assembly declared war on Austria the following year.

NOTE
Because of the economic qualifications to become an elector, only about 50,000 French men qualified as electors in 1791.

NOTE
The *emigres* were French nobles who fled to the countryside of France and fought to restore the ancient regime.

THE SECOND, OR RADICAL, STAGE OF THE REVOLUTION

The war with Austria went poorly, and the French suffered miserable defeats. After the defeats, everyone in France was looking for someone else to blame. Combined with the agony of defeat, the economic hardships that faced the French people sparked a radical group of Parisian citizens to storm the Legislative Assembly in August of 1792. The mob forced the Assembly to call for a National Convention that was to be elected by universal male suffrage. The mob was composed of the *sans-culottes*, which literally means "without breeches." The *sans-culottes* were the working people who did not wear the fine breeches of the elite. These radicals ushered in the next stage of the Revolution. The *sans-culottes*, under the leadership of Georges Danton (1759–1794), carried out the September massacres. The mob executed thousands of people, including many already in prison, that they believed to be traitors and counter-revolutionaries.

NOTE

The Jacobin clubs were political clubs that originally occupied a Jacobin convent in Paris. They served as a discussion group and later as an activist group for those who were interested in the politics of France.

In September of 1792, the National Convention met for the first time with the task of abolishing the monarchy and developing a new constitution, one that would create a republic. The task would be a nearly impossible challenge, since the Convention was split into two major factions. One group was the *Mountain*, named for the raised platform on which they sat in the Convention. The Mountain generally represented the radical Parisians and advocated the execution of the king. The second group was the *Girondists*. The Girondists represented the countryside and sought to preserve the king's life. Both groups were members of the Jacobin club. The Mountain won the first great battle in the Convention and condemned the king to death. On January 21, 1793, Louis XVI lost his head on the brand-new guillotine. The execution of the king outraged many people in France and in other countries.

In 1793, the radical Paris Commune dominated the political scene in Paris. Early in the summer of 1793, the members of the Paris Commune broke into the Convention and arrested the leaders of the Girondists. The Mountain now controlled the Convention. Under the Mountain's control, the National Convention faced a daunting task. Several European nations had joined together to confront France. Led again by Danton, the radical French welcomed the challenge. They formed the Committee of Public Safety that helped put down counter-revolutionary activity. The Committee also sought to raise a national army to defend France from foreign invaders. Maximilien Robespierre (1758–1794) rose to a prominent leadership position on the Committee of Public Safety. Between August 1793 and September 1794, France raised a staggering 1.1 million–man army, the largest Europe had ever seen. The formation of the national army and the defeat of the European forces greatly contributed to the formation of the modern notion of nationalism.

NOTE

The new republican calendar featured months like *Floreal*, which meant seeding, and *Vendemiaire*, which meant harvest.

France more or less rid itself of external dangers, but the country still faced internal problems. These internal problems centered around those Frenchmen who were thought to be counter-revolutionaries and conspirators with other countries. To deal with these problems, the Committee of Public Safety instituted the infamous *Reign of Terror*. The Committee formed courts that tried people suspected of treachery against the Republic. Between 1793 and 1794, the Reign of Terror claimed more than 40,000 lives. Many of the executed lost their lives to the guillotine, some to gunfire and cannon fire, and still others were drowned. In addition to executing enemies of the state, the Committee enforced economic policies, including price controls and food rationing. Later in 1793, the Committee declared France a Republic of Virtue. They attempted to de-Christianize the Republic by pillaging churches and creating a new, non-Christian calendar.

THE THIRD, OR REACTIONARY, STAGE OF THE REVOLUTION

In 1794, the Committee of Public Safety began to lose its appeal, and public opinion swayed against the Committee. Contrary to public opinion, Robespierre continued his authoritarian rule, and he even executed Danton for speaking out against the Reign of Terror. A group of leaders of the National Convention became convinced that if they did not get rid of Robespierre, Robespierre would get rid of them. The convention decided to move, and Robespierre was arrested and then guillotined the next day, July 28, 1794; this day was the Tenth day of Thermidor, one of the months of the new non-Christian calendar. The death of Robespierre began the Thermidorian Reaction, in which the moderates regained control of France. In 1795, a new two-house legislature was established. The new National Convention consisted of a lower house, the Council of 500, and an upper house, the Council of Elders. In order to begin the healing process in France, the Convention reduced the power of the Committee of Public Safety, closed the Jacobin clubs, and granted amnesty to many people formerly persecuted during the Reign of Terror. In addition, the National Convention relaxed old economic controls, made divorce more honorable for women, and allowed Catholic services to be held again.

In 1795, the National Convention vested governmental authority in a five-man body known as the *Directory*. The period during which France operated under the Directory was filled with controversy and corruption. The economic situation in France did not improve. People from the political left and the political right disagreed with and disapproved of the Directory and its methods. Power began to slip away, and the Directory turned to the military as a tool by which it would maintain control. On October 5, 1795, a royalist rebellion broke out in Paris against the Directory, and General Napoleon Bonaparte was ordered to crush the rebellion. Napoleon did as instructed and saved the Directory from the rebels.

THE NAPOLEONIC ERA

In November 1799, Napoleon Bonaparte (1769–1821) overthrew the Directory in a *coup d'etat* and created the *Consulate*. Under the Consulate, France received male suffrage, but the power actually remained in the hands of the Consuls. Napoleon was one Consul, and the other two Consuls were Roger-Ducos and Abbe Sieyes. Under the constitution in late 1799, Napoleon was First Consul. In 1802, the constitution made him Consul for life, and in 1804, the constitution made him Emperor. For each of these constitutions, Napoleon held a national vote (called a *plebiscite*), and the people of France approved the new constitution.

Napoleon instituted numerous domestic policies that helped France get back on its feet after the exhausting Revolution. One of Napoleon's first

NOTE
One of the ways Napoleon financed his military exploits was through the sale of the Louisiana Territory to the United States.

moves was reconciliation with the Church. In 1801, Napoleon signed a concordat with Pope Pius VII. The concordat recognized Catholicism as the religion of the majority of Frenchmen, but it did not make Catholicism the sole religion France, as the Pope had wished. In fact, Napoleon maintained the upper hand throughout the negotiations. Because of Napoleon's negotiating skills, France kept the Church land it had confiscated during the Revolution, and France retained the right to nominate bishops in France. After the concordat, the state had virtual control over the Church in France.

Napoleon's next move was the reform and overhaul of the laws of France. He systematically arranged laws into a single organized code, called the *Civil Code* (often referred to as the Napoleonic Code or Code Napoleon), by which everyone was treated equally under the law. The new laws abolished serfdom and granted religious toleration to Protestants and Jews. Unfortunately for women, though, Napoleon's new laws negated much of the progress women had achieved during the Enlightenment and Revolution by making men superior to women.

The great reformer reworked the French bureaucracy and made it more efficient. Although he kept the departments in France, he appointed new prefects for each department. He chose experienced officials to occupy the positions in his new government. Napoleon promoted people based on a merit system instead of title or social status. He practiced nepotism, or showing favoritism toward relatives, as often as he could. For example, Napoleon's stepson, three of his brothers, and his brother-in-law were all made rulers of conquered territories. He eliminated tax exemptions and created a new, more efficient tax collection system. Napoleon's domestic reforms strengthened and stabilized the government of France.

As busy as Napoleon was in France introducing reforms, he was even busier abroad engaging in one of his favorite pastimes—war. When Napoleon assumed power in 1799, France was at war with the *Second Coalition*, which consisted of Russia, Austria, and Great Britain. In 1802, Napoleon bought himself some time by signing a temporary peace agreement at Amiens. The peace lasted until 1803 when France resumed war with the *Third Coalition*, which included Austria, Russia, Prussia, and Great Britain. After many major battles between 1805 and 1807, Napoleon's Grand Army, the largest Europe had seen to date, defeated the armies of the Coalition. In the wake of his grand victory, Napoleon formed the Grand Empire. The new Grand Empire included the French Empire, Holland, Spain, the German states (excluding Austria and Prussia), Warsaw, the Swiss Republic, and Italy. Napoleon forced Austria, Russia, and Prussia to help him against Great Britain, although they were not included in the Grand Empire. In each place that Napoleon added to the Grand Empire, he instituted reform. He sought equality under the law and religious toleration and relaxed economic policies for his new subjects. He stripped the nobility and the aristocracy of their privileges in an attempt to stamp out the old regime across Europe. Like in France, Napoleon enacted the Civil Code in his new lands.

Napoleon wanted very much to invade England, the final thorn in his side. However, the British fleet, under the direction of Admiral Nelson, crushed the French Navy at the battle of Trafalgar. Since a military defeat of the British seemed unlikely, Napoleon decided to break the economic back of Great Britain. Napoleon began his *Continental System*, his plan to cut off Britain from the countries on the European continent, with the intent to prevent British goods from being distributed throughout Europe. Unfortunately for Napoleon, many European nations did not abide by his commands, and the French Empire suffered worse economically than did Great Britain. This economic turn of events began the downward spiral of the Grand Empire and Napoleon's dream of total European domination.

Historians generally agree that nationalism played a major role in the defeat of Napoleon. First, Napoleon tried to place his brother, Joseph, on the Spanish throne. In reaction to Napoleon's actions, a Spanish nationalist rebellion erupted and sidetracked hundreds of thousands of Napoleon's men for a number of years. Nationalism spread through other French holdings in Europe as well, especially Germany. Also contributing to Napoleon's downfall was his invasion of Russia. In 1812, Napoleon led well over a half million men into Russia. The Russians refused to engage the Grand Army and instead retreated deeper into Russia. As they retreated, they burned farms and villages, so the French troops were left with no means of gathering food or finding shelter. When the French reached Moscow, they found it in ashes. At this point, Napoleon began the Grand Retreat, in which the Grand Army turned and headed for Poland. Only 40,000 of the original Grand Army soldiers made it out of Russia.

After Napoleon's disastrous expedition in Russia, the countries of Great Britain, Russia, Prussia, and Austria fought together to liberate Europe from Napoleon's rule. In 1814, after a defeat, Napoleon abdicated his throne. He was then exiled to Elba, a small island off the Italian coast, where he could be emperor of the tiny island and nothing else.

In France, Louis XVIII (1755–1824, king 1814–1815, 1815–1824), a Bourbon, ascended to the throne. In Vienna, the major European powers gathered for a landmark conference known as the *Congress of Vienna*. Under the heavy influence of Prince Clemens von Metternich, the participants, Austria, Russia, Prussia, and Great Britain, wanted to make sure that nationalism and liberalism were put to rest in Europe. In addition, the Congress wanted to prevent France, or any other nation, from dominating Europe as Napoleon had done. They were more than fair in granting concessions and demanding reparations from France, mostly to discourage France from becoming angry and retaliating. They allowed France to keep all the territory it acquired prior to 1792. Then, the Congress established a geographic barrier around France to prevent its expansion.

NOTE
The Russians knew that Napoleon did not use a supply line to provide food for his troops but that he encouraged his men to live off what they could gather or confiscate during their journey. Therefore, they intentionally left the French with nothing to gather or confiscate in Russia.

Although Napoleon had been exiled, Europe had not seen the last of him. In 1815, Napoleon escaped his island prison and returned to France. Upon his return, Napoleon discovered a large group of his supporters who were still loyal to him. Napoleon even convinced a group of guards, originally sent to arrest him, to join his cause. When the king heard of Napoleon's return, he fled for his life. Napoleon once again became Emperor. He knew, though, that the other European nations would not sit idly by and allow him to rule. Therefore, Napoleon raised an army for the inevitable confrontation. On June 18, 1815, a British commander named Wellington defeated Napoleon at the famous Battle of Waterloo. Thus ended the Hundred Days, Napoleon's second stint as Emperor. Louis XVIII returned, and Napoleon was exiled to the remote of island of St. Helena, where he died in 1821.

THE MAJOR PLAYERS

Louis XVI (1754–1793, king 1774–1792)—Born in 1754 at Versailles, Louis became the Dauphin in 1765 when his father, Louis XV's only son, died. He married Marie Antoinette, the daughter of Maria Theresa, in 1770. Louis was generally regarded as a weak and unintelligent ruler who devoted as much time to hobbies like hunting as he did to governing the country. He frequently allowed himself to be persuaded and even controlled by his wife.

When he became king, Louis inherited a nation with a great debt and millions of subjects living in poverty. He tried to institute economic reforms but often was challenged by the aristocracy and the courts. Later, he contributed to the economic problems by sending large sums of money to support the American colonies against the British. In addition, he borrowed until he could borrow no more, and he spent a great deal on his lavish lifestyle. Finally, the notables, or the clergy and the nobility, forced Louis to call a meeting of the Estates-General for the first time since 1614. The notables had hoped the Estates-General would prevent Louis from instituting economic reform that limited their rights and privileges.

When the situation deteriorated during the French Revolution, Louis and his family tried unsuccessfully to flee the country. In 1792, the king was tried as a traitor and sentenced to death. On January 21, 1793, Louis XVI was executed on the guillotine.

Marie Antoinette (1755–1793, queen 1774–1792)—Marie Antoinette was born in Vienna in 1755 to Holy Roman Emperor Francis I and Maria Theresa of Austria. She was married to Louis in 1770 in an attempt to form an alliance between France and the Austrian Habsburgs. After Louis became king in 1774, she bore him a daughter and two sons. The French people never accepted Marie because she was a foreigner and because she devoted much time and interest to the affairs of Austria. She earned a bad reputation with the French as an extravagant spender and is notorious for her statement, "Let them eat cake." She was tried for and convicted of treason in

1793 and was guillotined on October 16, 1793, nearly nine months after her husband.

Abbe Emmanuel Joseph Sieyes (1748–1836)—As a young man, Emmanuel Joseph Sieyes studied to become a member of the clergy, and he became a priest in 1773. In 1789, he wrote a famous pamphlet called *What is the Third Estate?* He served as a member of the Estates-General, the National Convention, the Council of Five Hundred, and the Directory. He worked with Napoleon and helped him achieve greatness. In 1799, he became a member of the Consulate along with Pierre Roger Ducos and Napoleon Bonaparte. He drafted a constitution for Napoleon, but Napoleon reworked most of Sieyes' original draft. Sieyes was exiled from France in 1815, but he returned to France in 1830.

Marquis de Lafayette (1757–1834)—Lafayette was born to a noble family of France in 1757. He joined the French army and served from 1771–1776. After the Americans declared their independence from Britain, he went to the United States Congress to offer his assistance. Congress made him a major general in the Continental Army and a member of George Washington's staff. In 1778, he returned to France and helped convince the French to offer further support to the Americans and their cause. He went back to America once more in 1780 and served in Virginia.

Years later, in 1789, Lafayette became a member of the National Assembly where he supported a constitution modeled after the United States Constitution. He later became commander of the newly formed French National Guard. Lafayette commanded the French army against Austria. After being declared a traitor by the Jacobins, he fled the country, was arrested by the Austrians, and was thrown in prison. He returned to France in 1799 and remained inactive in politics until after the fall of Napoleon. Lafayette played a key role in the French Revolution and always supported equality, tolerance, and other popular rights, such as those granted by the United States Constitution.

Georges Danton (1759–1794)—Georges Danton was born in France in 1759. He studied law and became a wealthy lawyer. He became involved in politics in 1789 with the outbreak of the Revolution. Danton's prominence came in 1792 after he was elected to the National Convention. He became a fierce opponent of the Girondists. Danton went on to serve on the Committee of Public Safety after the fall of the Girondists. However, Danton became overshadowed by Robespierre. Eventually, Robespierre attacked Danton and had Danton sent to the guillotine in 1794.

Maximilien Robespierre (1758–1794)—Maximilien Robespierre was born in France in 1758 and received a good education as a young man. During his studies, he was greatly influenced by the work of Jean-Jacques Rousseau. He became a member of the Estates-General in 1789 and then was a member of the National Constituent Assembly. He was elected president of the Jacobins in 1790. He opposed the monarchy and the Girondists. In 1792, after the fall of the monarchy, he was elected to the National Convention where he argued for the execution of Louis XVI. In 1793, Robespierre succeeded in ridding the National Convention of the Girondists. Shortly thereafter, he joined the Committee of Public Safety and initiated the Reign of Terror. During the Reign of Terror, he ordered the elimination of many "enemies of the Revolution." He persuaded the National Convention to institute the Cult of the Supreme Being, a theology based on Rousseau's deism. Robespierre went on to become the president of the National Convention. However, in 1794, many members of the National Convention began to fear for their own safety, and they arrested Robespierre. He and 100 of his followers were guillotined in 1794.

Jean Paul Marat (1743–1793)—Jean Paul Marat left his home at the age of 16 and eventually earned a medical degree. He spent several years in Britain and then returned to France where he tried to become a successful writer. Marat wrote on politics and science but found little success. When the Revolution broke out, he began a radical French newspaper called *The Friend of the People* in which he called for violence against moderates. His writings greatly influenced the violence of the Revolution in France. He was elected to the National Convention where he fought against the Girondists. Marat was assassinated in his bathtub in 1793 by Charlotte Corday. His death is the subject of a famous painting by Jacques-Louis David.

Charlotte Corday (1768–1793)—Marie Anne Charlotte Corday d'Armont was born in Normandy in 1768 and spent her younger years in a convent. She supported the Girondists and hated Marat for his role in the Reign of Terror. In 1793, she said she had information for Marat about the Girondists, and she was allowed inside Marat's home. She found Marat in his bathtub and killed him. Marat's friends caught her before she could escape and guillotined her in 1793.

Jacques-Louis David (1748–1825)—Jacques-Louis David was born in Paris in 1748. He studied art under the direction of a rococo painter. However, he was influenced more by the classical art of Rome that he saw on a trip there. Because of this influence, David developed the neoclassical style and introduced it with *Oath of the Horatii* in 1784. After 1789, he painted in a realistic style in which he painted Revolutionary scenes such as the *Tennis Court Oath* and

NOTE

Jean Paul Marat had a terrible skin condition, so he spent much of his time soaking in the bathtub. He was soaking his skin when Charlotte Corday found him and killed him.

Death of Marat. David became Napoleon's official painter and created for the Emperor such works as *Coronation of Emperor and Josephine.*

Napoleon Bonaparte (1769–1821)—Napoleon Bonaparte was born in Corsica in 1769. After his father entered the French aristocracy, Napoleon received a French military education. Napoleon joined the artillery and became a second lieutenant at the age of 16. In 1791, he became a colonel in the Corsican National Guard but then fled to France when Corsica declared its independence. In France, he became a captain and won a great victory over the British at Toulon. Because of that victory, Napoleon was promoted to brigadier general at the age of 24.

In 1795, he crushed a revolt in Paris and saved the government. The following year, he became commander of the French forces in Italy and defeated four superior Austrian generals and their armies. In 1798, Napoleon conquered Egypt in order to cut off British trade with the East. In a battle with the British navy, Napoleon lost his fleet to the fleet of Admiral Nelson. In 1799, Napoleon led a *coup d'etat* in Paris, seized the government, and formed the Consulate. He eventually became Emperor of France where he codified the laws and initiated major reforms.

As Emperor, Napoleon fought against the coalition of Austrian, Russian, and Prussian forces and won major victories at Austerlitz, Jena, Auerstadt, and Friedland. He seized Naples, Westphalia, and Warsaw and created Holland and the Confederation of the Rhine. In 1807, he seized Portugal and made his brother king of Spain. In all of his lands, he abolished feudalism, established a civil code and constitution, and granted religious toleration.

In 1812, however, Napoleon began his downward slide when he led a fateful military campaign into Russia where he lost a majority of his Grand Army. In 1814, he abdicated the throne and left France in exile for the island of Elba. He escaped Elba in 1815 and returned to France where he ruled for the Hundred Days. He was arrested and exiled to St. Helena, where he died in 1821.

Arthur Wellesley, Duke of Wellington (1769–1852)—Arthur Wellesley was born in Dublin and educated in the French military academy as a young man. He entered the British army in 1787 and fought against France in the First Coalition. He went on to participate in battles against the French in Hanover, Denmark, and Spain. As the Duke of Wellington, he participated in the Congress of Vienna and then took command of the allied armies when Napoleon escaped from Elba. In his most famous battle, Wellington defeated Napoleon at the Battle of Waterloo. He stayed in France for the following three years as commander of the allied forces occupying France.

NOTE

Many people have heard of the Battle of Waterloo, and the term *Waterloo* has come to mean a person's undoing or defeat. However, most people do not know that the Battle of Waterloo took place in what is now Belgium.

TIP
Use this chronology to begin to frame the big picture. Chronologies are helpful when you are trying to see how a story unfolds; in this case, the story is that of the French Revolution and the Napoleonic Era.

CHRONOLOGY OF THE FRENCH REVOLUTION AND THE NAPOLEONIC ERA

1784–1785—Jacques-Louis David completed his neoclassical masterpiece *Oath of the Horatii.*

1787—Louis XVI ordered a meeting of an Assembly of Notables in the hope that they would approve his new system of taxation.

May 5, 1789—The Estates-General met for the first time since 1614.

June 17, 1789—The Estates-General declared that they would only meet before the king as a National Assembly.

June 20, 1789—The members of the Third Estate met on an indoor tennis court at Versailles and vowed that they would not disband until they had created a new constitution. This event is known as the *Tennis Court Oath.*

June 27, 1789—Louis XVI agreed to recognize the National Assembly.

July 14, 1789—A mob of angry Parisians stormed the Bastille in search of arms with which to defend themselves.

Summer 1789—The *Great Fear* plagued the countryside of France as peasants attacked noble estates and burned all documents showing their debts and obligations.

August 4, 1789—Nobles in the National Assembly renounced their feudal rights and effectively ended feudalism in France.

August 26, 1789—The Declaration of the Rights of Man and the Citizen was adopted as the forerunner to the French Constitution.

October 5–6, 1789—Thousands of angry Parisian women marched 12 miles from Paris to Versailles to seek audience with the king. The mob forced the royal family to return to Paris with them in a most bizarre parade.

July 12, 1790—The French government adopted the Civil Constitution of the Clergy and effectively made the Catholic Church a state institution.

June 20–21, 1791—Louis XVI attempted to flee France but was caught and arrested before he could get to the French border.

August 27, 1791—Other European monarchs issued the Declaration of Pillnitz and threatened to intervene in the French affairs and restore the old regime to power.

1791–1792—The Legislative Assembly convened and eliminated the traditional provincial system, abolished slavery, and granted religious tolerance to the Protestants and Jews.

April 20, 1792—France declared war on Austria.

August 10, 1792—The *sans-culottes* stormed the Assembly and demanded a National Convention elected by universal male suffrage.

1792–1795—The National Convention governed France.

September 21, 1792—The National Convention met with the goal of abolishing the monarchy and creating a new constitution.

January 21, 1793—King Louis XVI of France was guillotined for treason.

July 28, 1794—Out of concern for their own safety, members of the National Convention arrested Maximilien Robespierre and executed him along with about 100 of his followers on July 28 and 29, 1794.

1795–1799—The Directory ruled France ineffectively and inefficiently.

August 22, 1795—Constitution of 1795 was adopted in France.

November 9, 1799—Napoleon led a coup d'etat in which he overthrew the Directory and seized control of the government.

July 15, 1801—Napoleon signed a concordat with Pope Pius VII that gave the French government virtual control over the Church in France.

March 25, 1802—Napoleon signed the Treaty of Amiens with Britain.

December 2, 1802—Napoleon crowned himself Emperor of France.

October 1805—Nelson defeated Napoleon in the Battle for Trafalgar.

1805–1807—Jacques-Louis David completed his *Coronation of Napoleon and Josephine*.

March 1810—Napoleon married Marie Louise of Austria.

1812—Napoleon led his troops into Russia and then began the Grand Retreat in the winter, consequently losing the majority of his troops.

October 1813—The Grand Alliance defeated Napoleon at the Battle of the Nations.

1814—Napoleon was exiled to Elba, and Louis XVIII was crowned King of France.

February 1815—Napoleon escaped Elba and began his rule of the Hundred Days.

June 18, 1815—Wellington defeated Napoleon in the famous Battle of Waterloo.

CAUTION
These questions are for review purposes only, not to predict the questions that will be on the AP exam.

SAMPLE ESSAY QUESTIONS

Now that you have reviewed the information about the French Revolution and Napoleonic Era, take a few moments to read through the sample essay questions that follow. The questions are intended to get you thinking about some of the ways the AP exam may test your knowledge of the French Revolution and Napoleonic Era. To completely answer the questions, you will need to draw upon the knowledge you gained during your own course of study in addition to your review with this book.

1. Describe the economic conditions of Paris and the French countryside on the eve of the French Revolution and both the causes and effects of those conditions.

2. Identify and discuss the different social groups in France and their concerns and goals on the eve of the French Revolution. Also discuss their successes and failures during the course of the Revolution.

3. Analyze and discuss the extent to which Louis XVI's actions as King of France contributed to the outbreak of the French Revolution.

4. "Napoleon was an Enlightened ruler." Assess the validity of this statement using specific examples to support your argument.

5. "Nationalism is the element that ultimately led to the downfall of Napoleon." Assess the validity of this statement using specific examples to support your argument.

6. Discuss the consequences of the French Revolution for both Spain and the rest of Europe.

7. Using specific examples, contrast the leaders of moderates and of the radicals during the French Revolution. Include a treatment of their goals, successes, and failures.

8. Analyze and discuss the reforms made by Napoleon and their short-term and long-term consequences on Europe.

The Agricultural and Industrial Revolutions

OVERVIEW

For some time, historians have hotly debated whether or not the Agricultural Revolution was truly a revolution. Although the speed at which new machines and agricultural techniques were developed was less than revolutionary, these developments revolutionized the way Europe farmed. New crops, new techniques, and new ways of organizing and managing the farmland allowed Europeans to grow more crops and livestock than they ever had before. The increase in food, combined with other factors, led to a population explosion in Europe, particularly in Britain. The Industrial Revolution, which occurred first in Britain, was revolutionary in the same way that the Agricultural Revolution was. Although the developments were at first somewhat slow, the consequences were quite dramatic. Society changed from agrarian to industrial in less than a century, and the population, which was booming, moved from the country into the cities. The combination of new agriculture and new industry carried first Britain and then the rest of Europe into the modern era.

THE AGRICULTURAL REVOLUTION

In the sixteenth century, more than three fourths of all Europeans made their living by way of agriculture. Farming was a difficult way to survive, as farmers had to deal with the often-uncooperative climate and inconsistently arable land. One of the biggest challenges facing European farmers was the low yield their land produced. (*Yield* refers to the amount of produce relative to the amount of seed planted.) The farmers needed new and innovative ways to increase the yield of their land with relatively little risk. Experimental techniques often had a high failure rate, so naturally, farmers were reluctant to try new, unproven methods of farming. Unfortunately for the earlier farmers, these low-risk innovations would not be available until the late sixteenth and seventeenth centuries. Because of the low yields, the reserves of grain ran low, and grain prices rose. In many parts of Europe during the sixteenth century, the grain reserves were completely exhausted. With grain reserves low or exhausted and the land yielding small amounts

NOTE

The three-field system, used throughout Europe during the Middle Ages, required the planting of crops in two fields while one field remained fallow. The following season, the fallow field was planted and one of the other two fields was left fallow, and so on each season thereafter.

NOTE

To employ methods of crop rotation, everyone in the village or community had to agree on the crops and the rotation schedule. As you know, people are often slow to accept change, and many people initially resisted the new farming techniques. This initial reluctance led some people to argue for enclosure.

of produce, much of Europe faced famine conditions. The poor turned to famine foods such as nuts, roots, berries, and even bark as an alternative to grains. In these lean years, many people died, and many more got sick from weakness due to malnutrition. Europe desperately needed a change in its agriculture.

The most important change Europeans made in their farming techniques involved the management of their land. The traditional method of farming, which dated back to the Middle Ages, was the open field system. In the open field system, a village often owned a section of land, and that section was divided into strips. The individual farmers in the village cultivated particular strips. Even the large estates owned by the aristocratic landowners were divided in this manner. Occasionally, the land produced a very nice yield, but usually, the yield was quite meager. One of the main reasons the land produced modest crops was the depletion of the minerals in the soil by the constant presence of food crops. To remedy this, strips of land were left fallow, or unplanted. Across Europe, so much land was left fallow that the production of the land would have increased as much as 50 percent if the fallow land had been planted. The Dutch developed a method for rejuvenating soil and still maintaining high levels of yield. They planted crops in the fallow fields that actually replenished the soil's nutrients. At first, peas and beans were used, and then new crops, such as turnips, potatoes, and clover, were introduced. These crops were rotated every year or every few years to prevent soil exhaustion.

The impact of this new method can hardly be overemphasized. By eliminating fallow land, farmers increased the total amount of land that could be cultivated and improved the quality of the land on which they were planting crops. The better-quality soil meant a higher yield, and this, in turn, meant a larger amount of food was available for the farmer and his family. In some cases, rather than food, a fodder crop was planted in the field that was once left fallow. The fodder could support increased numbers of livestock, and more livestock meant more manure. More manure meant more fertilizer for farmland, and this cycle greatly increased the production of both crops and livestock.

In addition to pioneering new farming techniques during the sixteenth and seventeenth centuries, farmers in the Low Countries, or what is now Belgium and the Netherlands, began the development and employment of new and improved ways of building dikes and irrigation canals. The Dutch also invented methods of creating farmland by draining swamps, marshes, and wasteland. The Dutch engineers became so famous that English landowners employed them to drain English wastelands. One of the most famous of these Dutchmen was Cornelius Vermuyden who drained nearly 40,000 acres of English land in the seventeenth century. In 1701, Jethro Tull (1674–1741) invented a new drill that planted seeds in a row. No longer did farmers have to sow their seeds by casting them by hand and risking the loss of seed to birds. Tull believed it was very important for air and moisture to reach the roots of plants, and he developed a hoe to help with that task. Tull's methods reduced the need to leave fields fallow because his new method permitted cultivation between the rows, thus increasing the amount of food that could be produced by a given plot of land. Tull also advocated the use of horses instead of oxen to pull plows.

Charles "Turnip" Townsend (1674–1738) also contributed to the agricultural revolution in England. He advocated the use of the turnip as a new crop in England and was said to have talked incessantly of the turnip, hence his nickname. Townsend experimented with turnips in crop rotation along with wheat, barley, and clover. These crops actually helped replenish the soil's nutrients, thus reducing the need to leave fields fallow. The introduction of the potato and maize, or corn, combined with the English agricultural developments greatly increased the amount of produce that was available for consumption.

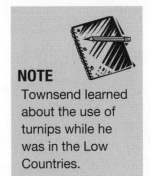

NOTE
Townsend learned about the use of turnips while he was in the Low Countries.

Robert Bakewell (1725–1795), also an Englishman, developed new breeding techniques that led to greater milk and meat production. Advancements in animal husbandry led to an increased amount of meat that was available for consumption by the lower classes. This new, improved diet led to longer lifespans and better health for the people of Europe.

The next step taken by Europeans was the enclosure, or actual fencing off, of land. This practice was generally advocated by the large landowners, especially in Britain. Because Parliament primarily consisted of the landed nobility, Parliament passed a series of enclosure acts that fenced off much of Britain. The enclosure of the land was expensive because of the surveying and fencing that was involved. Although the large landowners absorbed much of the cost, many peasants were required to shoulder the financial burden as well. Many of the peasants could not afford their share. Some of the landless peasants were removed altogether from the land worked. These landless peasants became wage laborers on the new, larger, enclosed tracts of land. Therefore, contrary to what some historians once believed, enclosure did not always force people off the land completely. The enclosure of the land allowed large landowners to employ new and innovative farming techniques on a large scale. This, in turn, produced high yields on a large scale and made many landowners wealthier than they ever had been before.

THE POPULATION EXPLOSION

The population of Europe grew tremendously in the eighteenth century, and the population growth continued at a high rate until the twentieth century. The primary reason for the rapid increase in population was the decrease in the death rate. The decrease in the death rate occurred not only for adults but also for children. In addition, the newborn and infant mortality rate decreased during this time. Determining the cause or causes of the decreasing mortality rate has not been easy for historians to do, but they have narrowed the reasons to a few possibilities. First, the bubonic plague, or *Black Death*, virtually disappeared during the seventeenth and eighteenth centuries. Also, Europeans developed an inoculation against smallpox. No longer were Europeans at the mercy of these diseases that had ravaged the continent in the previous centuries. Across Europe, countries made dramatic improvements to their sewage and water systems. By cleaning up cities and creating more sanitary conditions, governments helped control the spread of such diseases as cholera. The importance of the increased food production, which was the result of the agricultural revolution, should not be overlooked. The addition of new and better foods to the European diet helped to improve the general health of the people. Vitamins and minerals from new vegetables and from meat bolstered their immune systems and helped them fight diseases. The large quantities of food helped protect against famine by providing reserves that could be stored. Finally, the nature of the warfare of the late seventeenth and eighteenth centuries changed. A more "gentlemanly" and "civilized" style of warfare reduced the number of casualties of war. While historians disagree about the extent to which each of these factors contributed to the population explosion, all of these factors were important.

PROTOINDUSTRIALIZATION

As the population of Europe increased during the eighteenth century, the population pressure also increased in Europe. This population pressure strained the economic resources and the economic opportunities that were available. One of the consequences of the increased population was a growing number of landless people who needed a means of survival. Many people also found themselves with the need to supplement their income. The agrarian economy could not support the increased population, and people looked for other means of economic stability. Many found the stability they sought in the cottage industry.

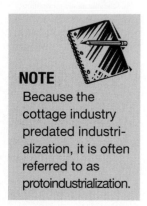

NOTE
Because the cottage industry predated industrialization, it is often referred to as protoindustrialization.

The cottage industry centered on the relationship between capitalist merchants, or merchants with raw materials, and rural workers. In the cottage industry, or "putting out system," the merchant, who was usually from the city, provided the rural workers with raw materials. The workers labored in their homes and worked the raw materials into a finished product. All the members of the family participated in the manufacture of goods. At the end of each week, the merchant picked up the finished product, dropped off the next week's raw materials, and paid the workers. The workers often produced textiles, housewares, or goods that might have been used on a daily basis. This system worked because the capitalists needed finished products but wanted cheap labor. In addition, by hiring rural workers, the capitalists avoided conflicts with the guilds in the cities. The workers needed the income and were willing to accept lower wages because they didn't have to travel into the cities to find work.

This system first appeared in Britain, but it eventually spread across Europe. Across the board, the textile industry employed the most workers of all the cottage industries. The "putting out system" worked well for many years. However, in the long run, the system proved in many cases to be inefficient, and the workers were sometimes unreliable. As the efficiency decreased, the merchant capitalists sought new and better ways to produce their goods. The cottage industry began to shift towards full-blown industrialization.

THE INDUSTRIAL REVOLUTION

Just as the cottage industry had done, the Industrial Revolution occurred first in Britain. Britain had abundant natural resources, including coal and iron, and a large body of eager workers. The ever-expanding colonial empire provided a growing market for new goods. In addition, an increasingly healthy economy allowed Britain to provide a strong domestic market for manufactured goods. The British government also allowed the economy to operate on its own and free from the rigid controls that other nations employed as a part of their economic policy. Due partly to an increase in food and a decrease in food prices, British people had more money to spend on goods that they had never before been able to afford. Therefore, the market for goods increased. The Industrial Revolution grew out of the pressure to produce more goods for an expanding market.

One of the greatest and fastest-growing markets was that of textiles. The people of Britain and those on the continent purchased wool and cotton fabrics at an unprecedented rate in the eighteenth century. To meet the growing demand for textiles, merchants searched for more efficient methods of production. What developed were new and better spinning wheels. In 1765, James Hargreaves invented a cotton spinning jenny, and about the same time, Richard Arkwright invented the water frame, a mill powered by water. With these innovations, the textile industry took off. Textiles became cheaper, and the demand for textiles increased.

After the introduction of the jenny and the mill, textile production moved into factories. At first, people were hesitant about working in these factories, and labor shortages were prevalent. In response, factory owners turned to child labor. The children that worked in factories were there because their parents took them or because they lived in foundling institutions that exploited those in its care.

The earliest factories were placed along streams and rivers because they were powered by water. In order to move the factories to locations away from the rivers, owners needed a new way to power their operations. The answer to their problem was steam. James Watt (1736–1819) developed a number of devices that allowed steam to be used to power equipment. Watt's inventions increased the power of steam engines because they prevented great losses of steam from the engines' cylinders, thus harnessing

NOTE
 The issue of child labor became a topic of great debate in England during the nineteenth century. Eventually, Parliament passed laws restricting the use of child labor and the length of the workday.

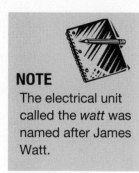

NOTE

The electrical unit called the *watt* was named after James Watt.

the power of greater quantities of steam. In addition, other Watt inventions enabled the steam engines to turn wheels.

Traditionally, English refineries used charcoal to smelt iron, but by the eighteenth century, England had depleted many of its forests, the primary sources of charcoal. Therefore, England needed to find an alternative to charcoal for use in smelting iron. Englishman Abraham Darby (1677–1717) developed a method of smelting iron using coal instead of charcoal. This development allowed the mass production of iron that, in turn, greatly increased the speed of industrialization. Darby built the great Ironbridge in northwest England, the first successfully erected cast-iron bridge that demonstrated the potential of this new metal. His bridge paved the way for such architectural feats as the Crystal Palace, the structure made entirely of glass and steel that was erected for the Great Exposition in London in 1851. Henry Cort then created the puddling furnace that allowed refineries to remove large amounts of impurities from the iron, thereby creating cleaner, stronger iron. Cort also worked with large mills that produced iron in all shapes and sizes. In the seventy years after the development of steam and iron technology, Britain's iron production increased at a phenomenal rate.

The development of steam engines led to steam-powered cars and wagons. At first, these vehicles traveled on flat surfaces or along roads constructed of wooden planks. The friction created by the heavy cars on the roads reduced the efficiency of the steam power, so in 1816, the steam-powered engines began running on rails. By reducing friction, rails had been used to allow horses and people to pull cars with relative ease. The new combination of rails and steam power seemed to hold unlimited potential. In 1825, George Stephenson rocketed from Liverpool to Manchester at a blistering 16 miles per hour on his new locomotive. The rail road, now called a railroad, unleashed the industrial beast within Britain. During the next fifty years, Britain and the rest of Europe lay railroad lines at a furious pace. These railroad lines connected all of the major cities and industrial sites and increased the speed and efficiency at which goods and passengers could be transported. The rails also reduced the cost of transporting goods, thereby boosting the economy of all who employed the new system.

CONSEQUENCES OF THE INDUSTRIAL REVOLUTION

The Industrial Revolution resulted first and foremost in the increased production and increased availability of goods. Manufactured goods were cheaper than the goods of pre-Industrial Europe, and, therefore, more people were able to afford them. A large market and able, willing consumers meant increased wealth for the entrepreneurs who produced these articles. The increased consumption also led to an increase in the number of available jobs. Because cities tended to grow up around the industrial area, the jobs were in the cities. Eager to work, entire families flocked to the cities by the thousands. The workers, especially the women and children, endured deplorable conditions in the factories, including extended hours with little or no breaks and dangerous machinery. As if that weren't bad enough, conditions where the workers lived were even worse. The houses and apartments were crowded, and the conditions were incredibly unsanitary. Human waste often leaked into basements and into the streets because of poor sewage and water systems. The streets were crowded with people who unwittingly carried and spread germs everywhere they went. These conditions led to cholera outbreaks as well as other diseases that were related to unsanitary conditions.

Some people embraced the new technology despite the poor living and working conditions that accompanied industrialization. Others, however, despised the new technology and the new problems it caused. Many people lost their jobs and were simply replaced by machines. One group, known as the *Luddites*, firmly believed that the new machines would take their jobs from them and often tried to destroy the machines in the factories. Another group of opponents of the new factories protested in an entirely different way. The *Romantics*, including such poets as William Blake (1757–1827) and William Wordsworth (1770–1850), wrote of the destruction of the countryside and the terrible conditions of the workers.

When laborers decided they could not deal with the new problems on their own, they began to join together as societies. These societies were the forerunners of unions. In the mid–nineteenth century, workers organized unions that lobbied for better wages and better working conditions. In 1834, after an earlier attempt at forming a union failed, Robert Owen (1771–1858) helped organize the Grand National Consolidated Trades. Eventually, laborers from many different fields were forming labor unions all over Europe. Many Europeans embraced the new unions, while others believed unions did not go far enough to help the workers. For those who sought a better solution than unions, socialism appeared to be the answer. *Socialism* was a political and economic system that encouraged the nationalization of resources, capital, and industry. The most influential of the socialists was Karl Marx (1818–1883). Marx believed that the history of society was a history full of class struggles. He believed that the capitalists were exploiting the workers of the world, the *proletariat*. Marx, along with Friedrich Engels (1820–1895), published *The Communist Manifesto*, a document in which their socialist ideas were explained. Marx argued that the workers would rise up and overthrow the capitalists in a violent struggle. Eventually, society would develop into one of communism, a classless society with no private property. Marx wanted to unite the workers of the world by creating socialist parties. In the late nineteenth century, the First International and the Second International were created as parties to unite socialists everywhere. Socialism grew into a powerful force across Europe, and its effects are still evident around the world today.

NOTE

Many people have used Malthus' principles as arguments against helping the poor escape their undesirable living conditions.

THE MAJOR PLAYERS

Thomas Malthus (1766–1834)—Thomas Malthus was born in England in 1766 where he attended Cambridge as a young man. He was one of the leading British economists of his time, although his outlook was not as optimistic as the outlooks of most other economists. In 1798, Malthus published *An Essay on the Principle of Population*. Malthus believed that the population increases faster than the food supply needed to sustain the population. Whenever there is a large gain in food production, he argued, the population soon increases and offsets the gain. According to the same principles, if the population grows too quickly, famine and disease keep the population in check. This pessimistic view of society contradicted the rather optimistic outlook of most nineteenth-century British economists. Malthus' ideas greatly influenced David Ricardo.

Robert Owen (1771–1858)—Robert Owen was born in Wales in 1771. Owen successfully experimented with improving worker productivity by improving their working conditions. Based on the results of this experiment, Owen concluded that mankind could be improved if the living conditions were improved. He believed that the quality of an individual's character was directly related to the quality of that individual's surroundings. In another grand experiment, Owen purchased land in Illinois and Indiana where he established a commune called New Harmony. Unfortunately for Owen, the commune failed and cost him most of his life savings. A Utopian socialist, Owen helped found the first British union in 1833. Although the union ultimately failed, Owen is considered the father of the international cooperative movement.

David Ricardo (1772–1823)—British economist David Ricardo left home at the age of 14 and made his fortune before he turned 30. In 1809, he wrote *The High Price of Bullion, a Proof of the Depreciation of Bank Notes* in which he advocated a currency backed by a precious metal. In 1817, Ricardo published *Principles of Economy and Taxation* in which he advocated freedom of competition. Influenced by Malthus, Ricardo believed that a growing population would lead to a shortage of productive land. He said that wages are determined by food prices, which are determined by the cost of production, which is determined by the amount of labor required to produce the food. In other words, labor determines value. This principle played a major role in the development of Marxism. During the final years of his life, David Ricardo served as a member of Parliament.

Karl Marx (1818–1883)—Karl Marx was born in Germany in 1818. He attended several colleges in Germany before he became editor of the German newspaper *Rheinische Zeitung* in Cologne. In 1843, he resigned as editor because his criticism of the current political situation was too radical and controversial. He left Germany and went to Paris. Once again, he was too radical and controversial, and he was instructed to leave Paris in 1845. Marx left Paris and settled in Belgium. Marx began the Communist Correspondence Committees in several European cities and later formed the Communist League. Marx, along with Friedrich Engels, worked on a statement of principles and beliefs for the Communist League and as a result produced the *Communist Manifesto*. They based the *Manifesto* on a materialist view of history, a view also known as *historical materialism*. The *Manifesto* said that the dominant economic system of each historical era, or epoch, determines the social and political history of that era. The *Manifesto* also said that the history of society is the history of class struggles between the exploiting class and the exploited class. The *Manifesto* went on to say that the current (1848) exploiting class, the capitalists, would be overthrown in a violent revolution by the exploited class, the workers. Eventually, according to the *Manifesto*, a classless society would emerge.

In 1848, the year of the many revolutions in Europe, Belgium expelled Marx for fear of his revolutionary influence, and Marx returned to Germany. After being arrested and later acquitted for inciting insurrection, Marx went to London, where he spent the rest of his life. In London, Marx wrote the great work *Das Kapital*, a multivolume history of the economy of capitalist society, some of which was published posthumously. It was in *Das Kapital* that Marx explained how capitalists exploited the working class. Eventually, the Communist League dissolved, and Marx helped form the First International in 1864. In 1871, he wrote *The Civil War in France*, an examination of the 1871 Paris Commune. For Marx, the Paris Commune served as a validation of his theories. Marx and his ideas proved to be far more influential after his death than during his lifetime. His systematic socialism is now known as *Marxism,* or *scientific socialism.* Marx's ideas were adopted by Lenin and were at the heart of Bolshevism.

Friedrich Engels (1820–1895)—Friedrich Engels was born to a Protestant family in Germany in 1820. He was strongly influenced by the writings of German poet Heinrich Heine, German philosopher G. W. F. Hegel, and German socialist Moses Hess. Engels believed that history could be explained as an economic history and that the current social situation in Europe was a result of private property. Furthermore, a class struggle could eliminate private property and would lead to a classless society. Engels met Marx in 1842, and the two realized that they shared the same views. Together, they produced the *Communist Manifesto* in 1848. He and Marx collaborated on projects, and he provided Marx with financial support while they were in England. He was a member of the First International but did not participate in the Second International. In addition to his work on the *Manifesto*, Engels wrote *Socialism: Utopian and Scientific* (1892), *Origin of the Family, Private Property and the State* (1884), and *Dialectics of Nature*, which was published posthumously in 1925.

TIP
Use this chronology to begin to frame the big picture. Chronologies are helpful when you are trying to see how a story unfolds; in this case, the story is that of the Agricultural and Industrial Revolutions.

NOTE
Thomas Savery actually created the first steam engine, but it was *very* primitive. Watt improved upon it to the extent that some people erroneously credit Watt with the invention of the steam engine.

CHRONOLOGY OF THE AGRICULTURAL AND INDUSTRIAL REVOLUTIONS

1698—Thomas Savery created the first steam engine.

1701—Jethro Tull invented a drill that improved the planting of seeds.

1705—Thomas Newcomen adjusted the steam engine and used it to pump water.

1733—John Kay invented the flying shuttle.

1740—Henry Cort invented the puddling furnace.

1765—James Hargreaves invented the cotton spinning jenny.

1768—Richard Arkwright invented the water frame.

1785—Edmund Cartwright invented the power loom, one of the most significant inventions to the development of the Industrial Revolution.

1792—American Eli Whitney invented the cotton gin.

1798—Thomas Malthus published *Essays on the Principle of Population*.

1799—Parliament passed the Combination Acts and banned labor unions.

1812—Factories were attacked by the Luddites because they thought the machines would take away their jobs.

1824—Parliament repealed the Combination Acts.

1825—George Stephenson developed the locomotive.

1833—Parliament passed the Factory Act and restricted the employment of children in factories.

1834—The Poor Law was passed in an attempt to relieve the poverty in industrial towns in England.

1846—The Corn Laws were repealed by Parliament.

1848—Karl Marx and Friedrich Engels published the *Communist Manifesto*.

1866—The transatlantic telegraph wire connected Europe to the United States.

SAMPLE ESSAY QUESTIONS

Now that you have reviewed the information about the Agricultural and Industrial Revolutions, take a few moments to read through the sample essay questions that follow. The questions are intended to get you thinking about some of the ways the AP exam may test your knowledge of the Agricultural and Industrial Revolutions. To answer the questions completely, you will need to draw upon the knowledge you gained during your own course of study in addition to your review with this book.

1. Analyze and discuss the economic, cultural, and social changes that led to the population explosion in Europe prior to 1800.

2. Contrast the economic views of Adam Smith with those of Thomas Malthus and David Ricardo.

3. Discuss the positive and negative social and economic consequences of the Industrial Revolution on Europe.

4. "The Industrial Revolution began in England purely by chance." Assess the validity of this statement using specific examples to support your argument.

5. Explain the extent to which Marx's theories are valid in light of the Industrial Revolution.

6. Discuss the major developments in technology prior to and during the Industrial Revolution, and analyze their effects on Europe.

7. Choose one of the following economists, and discuss the Agricultural and Industrial Revolutions according to his economic philosophy.

    a.   Adam Smith

    b.   Thomas Malthus

    c.   Karl Marx

Europe from 1815–1900

OVERVIEW

Perhaps no other century in European history has seen the ebb and flow of national powers, ideologies, and warfare as did the nineteenth century. Beginning with the Age of Metternich, a few dynamic personalities dominated the politics and diplomacy of nineteenth-century Europe. Regimes fell and nations grew up in their place as nationalism swept the continent. Violent and bloody revolutions scarred many nations. In the last quarter of the century, Europeans carried their "superiority" across oceans and imposed their culture on the "primitive" peoples of "uncivilized" lands. Industrialization launched some nations into modernity, while other nations lagged behind. The growing pains of industrialization forced governments to turn their attentions toward the growing number of working poor and the revolutionaries who sought to end poverty by eliminating social classes and property.

NEW IDEOLOGIES

Thinkers of the nineteenth century introduced new ideas to Europe. The most important ideological trends were liberalism, nationalism, romanticism, conservatism, and socialism (discussed in Chapter 8 with Marx and Engels). These ideologies often overlapped chronologically, so they will be discussed together.

LIBERALISM

The liberal thinkers concerned themselves primarily with the rights of the individual and advocated the limitation of the powers of state. Liberals often advocated freedom of religion, freedom of the press, equal treatment under the law, and a free-market economy. In general, liberals were influenced by the theories of Adam Smith concerning little or no governmental interference in the economy.

One of the greatest liberals was Jeremy Bentham (1748–1832), author of *Introduction of the Principles of Morals and Legislation* (1789). Bentham founded the philosophy of utilitarianism, the idea that decisions should be made based on what's best for the greatest number of people. He said the government should not interfere in people's lives except to bring order and harmony. John Stuart Mill (1806–1873) went even farther than Bentham and said that it was the role of the government to provide happiness for the people. Mill worked for the rights of the poor and of women. Later in his life, Mill argued for an equitable distribution of property among the people. Mill's most influential writings were *Utilitarianism* (1836), *On Liberty* (1859), *Principles of the Political Economy* (1848), and *On the Subjection of Women* (1869).

NATIONALISM

In its purest and most simple form, nationalism was people's feeling of unity against an absolutist or against oppression from outsiders. Nationalism was very often fueled by religion, geography, culture, or history that people had in common with each other. Nationalism made people feel like a national citizen, a member of a nation. The spirit of nationalism was a driving force and often inspired people to join the army and fight and to rise up against their oppressors. Nationalism, arguably, first emerged during the Hundred Years' War, then again during the French Revolution, and then spread across Europe during the Napoleonic Era. With its seeds firmly planted in the early nineteenth century, nationalism shaped the course of European history during the next hundred years.

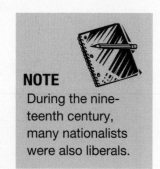

NOTE
During the nineteenth century, many nationalists were also liberals.

CONSERVATISM

Contrary to the more radical ideologies of the nineteenth century, conservatism advocated a slower, more gradual process of change. Conservatives believed change should come only through a gradual process and not by way of the destruction of the tradition or the old order. Conservatism emphasized the importance of tradition. Frenchman Joseph de Maistre demonstrated his extreme conservatism by defending the monarchy and opposing any and all political reform. One of the most influential writings of conservatism was Edmund Burke's *Reflections on the Revolution in France* (1790).

ROMANTICISM

Unlike some of the other nineteenth-century ideologies, Romanticism tended to be more of an artistic and literary movement. Romanticism involved a new outlook on life and a new way of looking at the world. Inspired by Rousseau, the emotion of the Romantic Movement appeared in stark contrast to the cold, rational Enlightenment. Generally, the Romantic Movement celebrated Europe's medieval past, whereas the Enlightenment looked down upon the Middle Ages. This fascination with the Middle Ages was nowhere more apparent than in Sir Walter Scott's *Ivanhoe* (1820) and Victor Hugo's *Hunchback of Notre Dame* (1831). The Romantics developed a deep appreciation for nature, unlike the thinkers of the Scientific

and Enlightenment, who merely studied it. Romantic writers
radition and encouraged free thinking, emotions, and imagina-
am Wordsworth (1770–1850) and Samuel Taylor Coleridge
) were the first Romantic poets. When they published *Lyrical*
798, they introduced the world to emotional poetry about nature.
fgang von Goethe (1749–1832) wrote in a style called *Sturm und*
m and Stress) that was both romantic and tragic. Germaine de
–1817), a French Romantic, followed Rousseau's example and
a child's proper education that should be centered on the
eeds and development of the child. Romanticism affected all
including music and painting. Frederic Chopin (1810–1849)
and Franz Liszt (1811–1886) were the musical geniuses of the Romantic
period. J. M. W. Turner (1861–1932) painted emotional landscapes in rich,
vibrant colors. Eugene Delacroix (1798–1863) showed an experimental use
of color and expression of spirit in such paintings as *Liberty Leading the
People* (1830). The Romanticism of the nineteenth century is perhaps best
characterized by its intense passion and emotion in art, music, and literature.

THE AGE OF METTERNICH (1815–1848)

ENGLAND IN THE AGE OF METTERNICH

After 1815, Parliament represented only the wealthy. Tory, or conservative,
reform in the 1820s reinstated labor unions, reworked the justice system, and
granted religious toleration to Catholics. In the revolutions of 1830 on the
continent, suffrage was a major issue. In Britain, the main concern was
representation in Parliament. Largely because of urban industrialization,
people left the country to go find work in the cities. The urban populations
increased, but the representation for the urban areas did not always increase
at the same rate. Therefore, the underrepresented urban areas were upset
about the gross overrepresentation of the rural areas. In many rural areas,
which happened to have the same representation in Parliament as large
urban areas, there lived more sheep than people. These overrepresented
rural districts were called *rotten boroughs*. The Great Reform Bill of 1832
increased the electorate by almost 50 percent and redrew the voting district
lines, thereby abolishing the rotten boroughs. Later, a group of people
introduced the People's Charter, a document that demanded universal male
suffrage. Supporters of this document were called *Chartists*. The Chartists
also demanded the secret ballot, annual elections, salaries for Parliament,
and equal voting districts. The Chartist movement lasted about ten years
before it dissolved. One of the greatest issues facing Britain was that of the
Corn Laws, or tariffs on imported grains to benefit domestic grains sales.
These Corn Laws were repealed in 1846 in a controversial legislative move.
Those who supported the repeal hoped it would mean lower wages for
factory workers, while those who opposed the repeal feared a decline in the
domestic grain industry.

NOTE

Louis Philippe ruled as the citizen king because he was content to rule without many royal privileges in order to satisfy the republicans.

FRANCE IN THE AGE OF METTERNICH

After the fall of Napoleon, Louis XVIII returned to the French throne. Louis granted a constitution, but the constitution was weak, giving power to only a few in France. His successor, Charles X (1757–1836, king 1824–1830), ruled as an ultraroyalist and angered many liberals during his short reign. In 1830, Charles sparked the July Revolution by trying to undo the results of an election that was won by the liberals. After the Revolution, Louis Philippe (1773–1850, king 1830–1848) became king. He honored the constitution and replaced the Bourbon flag with the tricolor of the French Revolution, but he ignored the demands of the workers. Under his rule, troops repeatedly were required to put down workers' revolts. Louis Philippe ruled until 1848.

THE GERMAN STATES IN THE AGE OF METTERNICH

After the Congress of Vienna in 1815, Germany was organized into a Germanic Confederation composed of thirty-nine independent German states. Many people in the German states sought unification under a liberal government, such as those of England and France. The leaders of Prussia and Austria (especially Austria) strongly opposed such a plan. At the time, Austria was under the leadership of Prince Clemens von Metternich (1773–1859). In 1819, Metternich pushed through the Carlsbad Decrees that censored and controlled nationalistic student organizations called *Burschenschaften*. The secret police also persecuted everyone who advocated political changes. When the July Revolution erupted in France, many liberal Germans spoke out against the repressive government. In response, the ultraconservative Metternich prohibited public assemblies and petitions. Metternich continued his rule until 1848.

RUSSIA IN THE AGE OF METTERNICH

In 1815, the Congress of Vienna granted the Duchy of Warsaw to Russia, which was led by Czar Alexander I (1777–1825, czar 1801–1825). After 1815, many Russians became increasingly liberal, especially the students and the younger nobility. These young liberals formed secret political societies; the members longed for a new government that was not corrupt and that was actually concerned about the people. When Alexander died in 1825, Nicholas I (1796–1855, czar 1825–1855), his younger brother, ascended to the throne.

At the time of his succession, a group of young army officers staged a revolt known as the *Decembrist Revolt*. The Decembrists wanted a more liberal, even constitutional, government. After the revolt was crushed and some of the Decembrists were executed, Nicholas became increasingly reactionary and repressive. He created the Third Section, the secret police, which was designed to squelch further revolutionary activity. During the violence as a means of venting their frustration and anger.

In France, Louis Philippe's repressive administration prohibited any political meetings when the politics might be unfavorable to the regime. In February of 1848, Louis' chief minister, Francoise Guizot (1787–1874), banned a political meeting that was to be held in honor of George Washington. In response, angry Parisians took to the streets. Louis forced Guizot to resign, but Louis later abdicated, too. Later in 1848, the socialist Louis Blanc (1811–1882) convinced the provisional government to establish national workshops to provide employment opportunities to those without work. In June of 1848, the government did away with the national workshops, and again angry Parisians stormed the streets. During the June Days, approximately 10,000 people, defeated by the republican army, died in a violent class struggle. In November, France created the Second Republic and elected Louis Napoleon as their president. Through political maneuvering, he won a re-election and then declared himself Emperor Napoleon III in 1852. The revolution in France proved to be a failure.

As news of the revolution in France spread throughout Europe, liberals demanded governmental reforms. In the Austrian Empire, Hungarians demanded autonomy and additional liberal concessions. The workers and students in Vienna took to the streets in revolt when the government balked at the demands. As a result, Emperor Ferdinand I (1793–1875, emperor 1835–1848) promised reform, abolished serfdom, and then capitulated. Fearing that the new wave of anti-conservative violence might threaten his life, Metternich fled the country and went to London. However, imperial forces overthrew the revolutionary government. Francis Joseph (1830–1916, emperor 1848–1916) became Emperor of Austria in December of 1848. Six months later, with the aid of the Russians, the revolution in Hungary was crushed. The revolution in the Austrian Empire had also failed.

Prior to 1848, German liberals desired a unified German state. When revolution broke out in France, Prussian liberals stated their demands. After a revolt in Berlin, Frederick William IV (1795–1861, king 1840–1861) promised a new German state and a constitution. Although the desires of the aristocracy and the middle class differed, Frederick allowed the election of

and liberal ideas and were remembered as martyrs by Russian revolutionaries who followed.

NOTE
The First Republic was created by the French Revolution in 1792.

TIP

Just in case you see the term on the AP exam, remember that a *constituent assembly* is one whose purpose is the creation of a constitution.

a *constituent assembly* that was to draw up a constitution for Prussia. Meanwhile, in Frankfurt, the National Assembly, called the Frankfurt Assembly, met to create a unified German state. In 1849, the National Assembly completed its constitution and elected Frederick William IV emperor of the new German state. However, Frederick refused to accept a "crown from the gutter," so he granted a conservative constitution and reasserted his authority. Attempts to unify the German states had failed.

The revolutions of 1848 failed mostly because the revolutionaries were united only by their desire to reform or replace the current governments. The revolutionaries in each example were divided by social and economic differences. Each time, after the revolutionaries gained control or made progress, they fought amongst themselves and afforded the old regimes opportunities to regain power.

THE CRIMEAN WAR (1854–1856)

The Crimean War began as a dispute between Russia and France over who should protect certain holy Christian sites in the Ottoman Empire. The British and French worried about the increasing Russian influence in the Balkans because of the weakness of the Ottoman Empire. In 1853, France and Britain declared war on Russia. Most of the fighting took place on the Crimean Peninsula, and most of the casualties were from disease and poor conditions. Russia ended their fighting when Austria threatened to join the side of the French and British. Unfortunately for Europe, this undid what the Congress of Vienna had tried to accomplish in the Concert of Europe. After the war, Britain isolated itself to avoid being dragged into further conflicts on the continent. Humiliated, Russia resented Austria along with Britain and France. However, the Crimean War served as a wake-up call for Russia. Russia realized just how far it had lagged behind the rest of Europe technologically, economically, and culturally.

THE UNIFICATION OF ITALY

In 1848, liberals attempted and failed to create a unified state of Italy. For years afterward, however, people still wanted a unified Italy. Prior to unification, Italy consisted of the Kingdom of Sardinia (also known as Piedmont-Sardinia), Lombardy-Venetia, the Papal States, and the Kingdom of Naples (also known as the Two Sicilies). The only independent state was Sardinia. In Sardinia, Victor Emmanuel II (1820–1878, king of Sardinia 1849–1861, king of Italy 1861–1878) ruled as a constitutional monarch. In 1854, Camillo de Cavour (1810–1861) became prime minister. Cavour was a nationalist who broke away from the romantic nationalism of such thinkers as Giuseppe Mazzini (1805–1872). Cavour was a reformer who strengthened Sardinia by encouraging industrial development and freeing the peasants. He sought a unified Italy, but he knew that goal would be reached

NOTE

Tennyson's *Charge of the Light Brigade* is about a famous battle of the Crimean War.

only by force and only by ridding Italy of Austria. Not letting the idea go, Cavour developed a plan to get rid of Austria. He convinced Napoleon III to come to the aid of Sardinia in the event of a Sardinian war with Austria. Napoleon agreed because Sardinia had entered the Crimean War on the side of France, and Sardinia had promised France some territory in return for help. In 1859, Austria declared war on Sardinia and, as promised, Napoleon III came to Sardinia's aid. Before the war was over, though, Napoleon withdrew his forces because of Prussian threats. Angered and humiliated, Cavour resigned (only to resume his duties the following year).

Inspired by the war, many people throughout the Italian states cried out for unification. Several of the regions held plebiscites and voted to join Sardinia. Cavour persuaded Giuseppe Garibaldi (1807–1882), a throwback to romantic nationalism, to invade Sicily. Garibaldi led his Red Shirts, only a thousand strong, into Sicily and Naples and defeated the much larger Bourbon forces. Soon after the stunning victory, Victor Emmanuel II became king of a unified Italy. Within ten years, the Papal States and Venetia were part of the Kingdom of Italy, too. Although Italy was unified, the north and the south often resented each other, and a rivalry developed between the two regions. In addition, the relations between the Church and the state remained icy for years.

THE UNIFICATION OF GERMANY

After the Napoleonic Era, Austria and Prussia dominated the German states. Prussia, in particular, enjoyed superiority due in part to the *Zollverein*, the trade and customs union, and in part to its industrialization. In 1860, William I of Prussia (1797–1888, king 1861–1888) appointed Otto von Bismarck (1815–1898) as chancellor. Bismarck was a spirited Junker, or a member of the landed nobility, and a statesman. He told the Prussian parliament that Germany would be united by blood and iron and that Germany needed Prussia's power to lead the struggle for unification. Despite his speech, Parliament refused to grant the military budget that William and Bismarck wanted. Therefore, Bismarck collected the taxes himself, enlarged the army, and instituted his own reforms. No one stood in his way.

In 1864, Prussia and Austria led the German states into war with Denmark over the territories of Schleswig and Holstein, a war in which Denmark was easily defeated. Bismarck then schemed to create a dispute between Austria and Prussia over the government of the new territories. Bismarck entered into an agreement with France that France would remain uninvolved. Bismarck then enlisted the aid of Italy against Austria. With all the plans in order, Prussia declared war on Austria, thus beginning the Austro-Prussian War. The Prussian army smashed the Austrians in just seven weeks. Bismarck intentionally made the peace terms lenient at the end of the war so as not to alienate Austria. After the war with Austria, Bismarck created the North German Confederation. The Prussian king and a bicameral legislature ruled the union of twenty-one states. The *Reichstag*, or lower house, represented the people, and the *Bundesrat*, or upper house, represented the German princes.

In 1870, Bismarck began a dispute with France over the Spanish throne. William I agreed to settle the dispute, but Bismarck would not settle for it. He took an account of William's meeting with the French and reworded it to make France feel as though William insulted them. Bismarck then made the *Ems Dispatch* public, thus inciting Napoleon III to declare war on Prussia. Prussia defeated France in the Franco-Prussian War and took Alsace-Lorraine.

In 1871, four German states in the south joined the northern states. Then William I became the emperor, or *kaiser*, of the new German Empire. Both France and Britain resented and feared the new German Empire. The German Empire was not entirely stable, though. To increase its stability, Bismarck launched his *Kulturkampf,* which comes from the German words for culture and struggle. Bismarck's *Kulturkampf* was an attack on the Catholic Church in an attempt to bring the Church under strict control. He attempted to repress socialists as well. In both cases, though, the repression backfired by making the two more popular. When William II (1859–1941, emperor 1888–1918) became emperor, Bismarck was dismissed. William II ruled as an arrogant, oppressive ruler until 1918.

ENGLAND FROM 1848–1900

England began the second half of the nineteenth century in style with the Great Exhibition of 1851 and the unveiling of the *Crystal Palace*, the great English building constructed entirely of steel and glass. The Crystal Palace symbolized the seemingly unlimited potential of industrialization. In the 1860s, William Gladstone (1809–1898), the Whig, or liberal, prime minister, attempted unsuccessfully to expand the franchise, or vote . A year later, Benjamin Disraeli (1804–1881), a Tory, pushed through the Second Reform Bill, legislation that doubled the size of the electorate. Disraeli lost the next election to Gladstone, who instituted many reforms, including the secret ballot and free public education. This era of British history saw the rise of the two-party system and the decline of the power of the monarchy under Queen Victoria (1819–1901, queen 1837–1901).

FRANCE FROM 1848–1900

The Second Republic of Napoleon III was soon replaced by the Second Empire (the first being that of Napoleon I). Napoleon III led France to prosperity. He constructed numerous canals and roads that led to further economic expansion. He rebuilt Paris with the help and direction of George

Haussmann (1809–1891). He ruled initially in an authoritarian manner but became increasingly liberal, even creating a Liberal Empire in 1859. Shortly thereafter, he involved France in the Franco-Prussian War in which he was captured. He was soon exiled.

The Second Empire was replaced by the Third Republic. Immediately, the Third Republic was challenged by the Paris Commune. The Paris Commune was destroyed, and 20,000 Parisians lost their lives. The Third Republic stabilized and finished the nineteenth century as the best of hitherto French Republics. However, near the end of the century, France became divided over the Dreyfus Affair. In 1893, a Jewish artillery captain named Alfred Dreyfus stood accused of treason for drawing up secret French documents that allegedly were to be delivered to the Germans. Dreyfus was found guilty and exiled to Devil's Island where he was to remain for the rest of his life. A few years later, another French officer discovered that someone other than Dreyfus wrote the documents. That officer was silenced and then removed from the military. About the same time, though, Dreyfus' friends and family also discovered evidence that Major Marie Charles Esterhazy had written the document. The army court-martialed Esterhazy, but he was later acquitted. Another French officer, Lieutenant Colonel Hubert Joseph Henry, was arrested in 1898 for forging documents that implicated Dreyfus; Henry later committed suicide. The following year, Dreyfus stood before a new trial where he once again was found guilty. Fortunately for Dreyfus, a new government nullified the verdict within a few weeks. The Dreyfus Affair divided France politically, socially, and religiously as accusations of anti-Semitism and government conspiracy became widespread. The famous French writer Emile Zola wrote a letter accusing the government of lying and covering up conspiracies. For this letter, Zola was sent to prison. Zola eventually escaped from prison, though, and moved to England. The prestige and credibility of the military and civil authorities in France declined significantly after the Dreyfus Affair.

NOTE

In modern French history, there have been five republics. The First French Republic was declared by the National Convention in 1792, the Second Republic began in 1848, the Third Republic in 1875, the Fourth Republic in 1945, and the Fifth Republic in 1958.

RUSSIA FROM 1848–1900

After the Crimean War, Russia realized how far behind the rest of Europe it actually was. In 1861, Alexander II (1818–1881, emperor 1855–1881) freed the serfs. He created the *zemstvos*, or local governments, that were empowered to deal with local issues. Alexander II went on to reform the legal system as well. Alexander II was assassinated in 1881 and was replaced by Alexander III (1845–1894, emperor 1881–1894). In addition to political strides, Russia made great progress with industrialization. Through the construction of railroads and factories, Russia established itself as a legitimate industrial power by the turn of the twentieth century.

IMPERIALISM

Imperialism was nothing new to Europeans. Under the old imperialism of the sixteenth, seventeenth, and eighteenth centuries, countries sent explorers and colonists to all parts of the globe. But the new imperialism of the nineteenth century often involved military domination of a weaker country or geographic area. The industrialized nations of Europe were constantly seeking raw materials and new markets for their manufactured goods. Although much of the commerce of the nineteenth century was done with other European nations, non-European markets seemed promising. The Europeans heavily invested in foreign lands that produced raw materials. Then, they established colonies to protect those investments. In addition, the European nations established military bases and naval ports around the world in order to protect their colonies and, if need be, to launch offensives. The military played a large role in imperialism when other nations began to compete for land and when subjugated lands began to revolt.

Imperialism also grew out of the desire to spread European thought, culture, and religion to the underdeveloped and "inferior" people of the world. *Social Darwinism* proposed that some people were more fit than others to rule, and, of course, the Europeans were the most fit of all. Prodded by the "white man's burden" to take their culture abroad and "civilize" the uncivilized, the Europeans of the nineteenth century believed it was their duty to "improve" the "inferior" people of the world.

European powers scrambled for Africa. Britain, France, Italy, Germany, and Belgium all wanted pieces of Africa. To prevent any major conflicts, Bismarck called the Berlin Conference of 1885. There, the ground rules were laid that a country must occupy land in order to have a legitimate claim to it. After that, the Europeans continued to grab up pieces of Africa. European conquest of Africa was not without incident. Europeans clashed with natives such as the Zulu. They also clashed with the Afrikaners, descendants of the early Dutch settlers, in the Boer War (1899–1902).

In Asia, the British controlled India, the "crown jewel of the British Empire." There, they instituted social reforms, advocated education, and introduced technology. The Dutch held the Dutch East Indies (Indonesia), and the French took Indochina. Even the Russians got involved by establishing control over Persia. China remained independent but was forced to open its doors to Western trade. In 1900, the Chinese revolted in the unsuccessful *Boxer Rebellion*. Japan, although initially resistant to westernization, changed its government and its economy because of the European influence.

NINETEENTH-CENTURY CULTURE

As Europe became more industrialized, European cities grew at alarming rates. As the cities grew, conditions in the cities worsened, due mostly to

TIP

If you have not already done so, find a copy of Rudyard Kipling's *White Man's Burden* and read it. Kipling's work provides great insight into the era of imperialism.

overcrowding. People flocked to the cities to find work or to find a mate, because life in the city seemed much more promising than life in the country. As a result, the cities exceeded their population limits. People lived in subhuman conditions amongst rats, fleas, and human waste. The housing was cramped, and the streets were overcrowded. The terrible conditions forced the governments to turn their attentions to the cities. Through major building and renovation projects, European governments made major improvements in water and sewage systems and public transportation systems. Slums were torn down and replaced by parks, wider streets, and new buildings.

One of the major changes brought about by industrialization was an increase in the average person's standard of living, especially in the second half of the nineteenth century. Although the living conditions didn't always improve, salaries increased tremendously. During this time, the gap between the rich and poor didn't necessarily shrink. However, the middle class expanded significantly. Professionals such as engineers, accountants, and even teachers moved into the middle class. Across the board, families began having fewer children, and parents gave their children more attention, affection, and opportunities than at any other point in European history.

Many women left the country to find employment in the cities. Outside the home, though, employment often came in the form of maid service or prostitution. In most middle class scenarios, women were expected to stay at home and manage the household. Toward the end of the century, women mobilized and sought economic and social reform and equality under the law for themselves. Many women even demanded suffrage.

Near the end of the nineteenth century, art and literature moved away from Romanticism and into Realism. The realists focused on the everyday struggles and triumphs of life. Realists also focused on inequality and championed a more progressive world view.

NOTE
Although families had fewer children, the birthrate didn't necessarily decrease. In fact, the nineteenth century experienced an illegitimacy explosion.

THE MAJOR PLAYERS

Prince Klemens Wenzel Nepomuk Lothar von Metternich (1773–1859)—Metternich was born into an aristocratic German family and then married into an aristocratic Austrian family. Under the employment of the Habsburgs, he served as ambassador to Saxony, Prussia, and France. Metternich played a major role at the Congress of Vienna in 1815 by stopping Russia from taking all of Poland and by stopping Prussia from taking Saxony. Metternich established himself as the leading statesman in Europe until 1848. He repeatedly attacked liberalism and nationalism. A consummate conservative, Metternich defended the power of the aristocracy. He truly believed that the privileged class deserved to rule, a characteristic that has made him appear vain and arrogant to many of his contemporaries and to many historians.

Sir Robert Peel (1788–1850)—Robert Peel was born in England and educated at Oxford. As a young man, Peel went into politics. Early in his conservative career, Peel denied religious freedom to the Catholics in Ireland. Later, though, he introduced and pushed through legislation that granted equality to the Irish Catholics. One of Peel's accomplishments was the reorganization of the police force. English policemen are known as *bobbies* now because of Robert Peel. Also early in his political career, Peel opposed the idea of free trade in Britain. Later, though, Peel changed and repealed the Corn Laws. He resigned from politics after the repeal because of all the controversy surrounding the legislation.

Benjamin Disraeli (1804–1881)—Born to a Jewish family in England, Benjamin Disraeli later converted to Christianity. Disraeli wrote novels as a young man to pay bills. He moved from novels to pamphlets and articles that outlined his conservative views. He supported governmental reform and aid for the middle class. He also sought to preserve the power of the monarchy. In 1837, Disraeli became a member of Parliament. He continued writing novels in the 1840s, novels that showed his support for government reform. He earned the respect of his colleagues and eventually became Prime Minister. As Prime Minister, Disraeli improved housing and working conditions for many in England. He persuaded the government to invest in the Suez Canal. He even created the title of Empress of India for Queen Victoria. Later, he became concerned about Russia's power and influence. At the Congress of Berlin, Disraeli limited the power of Russia after Russia defeated Turkey in the Russo-Turkish War. Disraeli is remembered as a great politician who was conservative regarding the empire but liberal regarding government reform.

Napoleon III (1808–1873, emperor 1852–1870)—Charles Louis Napoleon Bonaparte was the nephew of Napoleon I. As a young man, he led unsuccessful attempts to overthrow King Louis Philippe. One of the failed attempts landed him in prison, but he later escaped. In 1848, he was elected president of the new French republic, mostly because of the popularity of his name. The new president was limited to a four-year term, so he led a coup, seized power, and granted himself a ten-year term as president. The following year, Napoleon changed the Second Republic to the Second Empire. He, of course, became emperor. Napoleon censored writers and newspapers and ruled authoritatively. However, he grew more liberal as opposition rose against his rule. Even though he didn't tolerate anyone who challenged him or questioned him, he was very popular.

Napoleon III built roads, railroads, and canals that helped France grow prosperous. Napoleon also rebuilt Paris and made it one of the grandest of all European cities. His construction and political reform greatly improved France. However, Napoleon spent too much money on wars like the Crimean War. He foolishly involved France in the Franco-Prussian War. During this war, he was captured. Afterward, his regime came undone, and Napoleon III left in exile.

CAUTION

When dealing with Darwinism, or any other controversial subject, on the AP exam, avoid making value judgments like "Evolution is wrong" or "Darwin is an idiot." The importance of people like Darwin is not whether or not his ideas are right or wrong. Rather, he is important because of the enormous impact he made on the history of the world.

Charles Robert Darwin (1809–1882)—The English scientist and writer Charles Darwin proved to be one of the most influential and important of all nineteenth-century thinkers. After college, Darwin traveled around the world on the HMS *Beagle* and served on the voyage as a naturalist. After the voyage and after reading the work of Thomas Malthus, Darwin applied Malthus' ideas to plants and animals. He developed his theories of evolution and natural selection. Darwin published his ideas about natural selection in *Origin of the Species* (1859), often called the book that shook the world. Some called Darwin a genius, while others claimed he could not prove his theories. The religious reaction to Darwin tended to be the most vocal and antagonistic. Many religious leaders said that Darwin's ideas completely contradicted the Bible and the teachings of the Church. Another one of Darwin's famous and influential works is *The Descent of Man* (1871).

William Ewart Gladstone (1809–1898)—A very religious and moral man, William Gladstone was first elected to the British Parliament in 1832 as a Tory, or conservative. Early in his life, he was conservative, but he grew more liberal with age. He sought moral and religious reforms and advocated the admission of Jews to Parliament. Gladstone was concerned about Ireland, and he disestablished the Anglican Church there. He wanted Home Rule for Ireland, and he wanted to pacify the Irish. Gladstone opposed the Boer War and imperialism in general. Throughout his political career, morality and religious beliefs guided Gladstone. He served as Prime Minister four times and was always Disraeli's rival.

NOTE
The issue of Home Rule for Ireland centered around Ireland's independence from Britain. The Catholics in Ireland wanted Home Rule, while the Protestants did not want to leave the Protestant influence of England.

Prince Otto Edward Leopold von Bismarck (1815–1898)—Bismarck was born a Junker. He studied law and then worked briefly for the government before entering politics in 1847. He soon became Prussia's representative to the German Confederation, then ambassador to Russia, and then ambassador to France. Because of his hard work and abilities, Bismarck was appointed as minister-president of Prussia. He immediately ignored Parliament and collected taxes on his own to increase the size of the military. He fought for German unification and said that the issue would not be settled by speeches but by blood and iron. A skilled diplomat and politician, Bismarck provoked war with Denmark, France, and Austria. He then used the foreign enemies to unite the people by focusing German attentions on the foreign aggressors. He established numerous alliances and dealt strongly with anyone who challenged his ideas or his authority. In a brilliant political move, Bismarck introduced social security and unemployment insurance to the German people, the first programs of their kind. His greatest achievement, though, was the unification of Germany.

TIP

Use this chronology to begin to frame the big picture. Chronologies are helpful when you are trying to see how a story unfolds; in this case, the story is that of Europe from 1815–1900.

CHRONOLOGY OF EUROPE FROM 1815–1900

1798—William Wordsworth and Samuel Taylor Coleridge published the Romantic work *Lyrical Ballads*.

1815—The Congress of Vienna was held to reestablish political boundaries after the Napoleonic Era.

1818—Prussia created the *Zollverein*, the international trade union.

1818–1819—Theodore Gericault painted his Romantic masterpiece *Raft of the Medusa*.

1819—Metternich imposed the Carlsbad Decrees upon the Germans.

1824—Charles X became king of France.

1824—England repealed the Combination Acts and allowed labor unions.

1829—Frederic Chopin presented his first piano concerts in Vienna.

1830—Revolution broke out in France. Eugene Delacroix painted his Romantic masterpiece *Liberty Leading the People*.

1832—The Great Reform Bill increased the electorate and reduced the requirements for holding public office in England.

1833—The Factory Act in England restricted child labor.

1838—The Chartists presented their People's Charter.

1845–1846—The Great Potato Famine in Ireland killed thousands and drove thousands of Irish to other parts of the world in search of food and better economic opportunities.

1846—The Corn Laws were repealed by Parliament.

1847—The Ten Hours Act limited the number of hours that women and children could work daily in factories.

1848—Revolutions erupted in Paris, Hungary, and Vienna. All the revolutions proved unsuccessful in their nationalistic efforts.

1851—Louis Napoleon became Emperor Napoleon III.

1851–1877—Franz Liszt composed some of his greatest sonatas, concertos, and etudes.

1852—Camillo de Cavour became Prime Minister in Sardinia.

1858—The British Empire added India to its vast holdings that were ruled directly.

1860—Giuseppe Garibaldi and his 1,000 Red Shirts invaded Sicily.

1861—Italy became unified under Victor Emmanuel II.

1862—Prince Otto von Bismarck became minister-president of Prussia.

1866—Bismarck provoked Austria into fighting the Austro-Prussian War.

1871—The German Empire was created under the direction of Bismarck.

1878—The Congress of Berlin set ground rules for European imperialism.

1894—The Dreyfus Affair drove a wedge into France.

1898—The Chinese revolted against westerners in the Boxer Rebellion.

1899–1902—The British and the Afrikaners battled in the Boer War.

SAMPLE ESSAY QUESTIONS

Now that you have reviewed the information about Europe from 1815–1900, take a few moments to read through the sample essay questions that follow. The questions are intended to get you to think about some of the ways the AP exam may test your knowledge of Europe from 1815–1900. To completely answer the questions, you will need to draw upon the knowledge you gained during your own course of study in addition to your review with this book.

CAUTION
These questions are for review purposes only, not to predict the questions that will be on the AP exam.

1. Analyze and discuss the most important economic developments in Europe during the nineteenth century.

2. Analyze the extent to which industrialization affected the culture of nineteenth-century Europe, and discuss its impact on European culture.

3. Discuss the extent to which Romanticism might be perceived as a reaction to the Enlightenment.

4. Compare and contrast the personalities and politics of Napoleon I and Metternich.

5. "By the end of the nineteenth century, England and France were very similar politically although each took a different path to democracy." Assess the validity of this statement. Be sure to include examples to support your answer.

6. Analyze and discuss the political situation in Europe prior to 1848 that led to the revolutions of 1848.

7. Analyze and discuss the motives of Europeans during the imperialism of the late nineteenth century.

8. Using specific examples, contrast the ideologies of liberalism, conservatism, and nationalism during the nineteenth century.

9. Analyze and discuss the extent to which European rulers attempted to suppress nationalism and liberalism between 1815 and 1848.

10. Compare and contrast the unification of both Italy and Germany. Be sure to include a treatment of the motives and methods of the driving forces behind each of the unifications.

Europe in the Twentieth Century and Beyond

THE RUSSIAN REVOLUTION OF 1905

Russia's industrialization in the late nineteenth century left laborers upset with their working conditions, much the same way other European workers felt in the early nineteenth century. The Russian factory workers organized an illegal labor movement and sought the reforms other European nations had granted earlier in the century. The governmental reforms of the nineteenth century, which failed to provide a constitution and a representative assembly, left them completely unsatisfied. To make matters worse, Japan defeated Russia in the Russo-Japanese War in 1905 and prevented Russia from expanding too far into the east. These events and conditions contributed to a climate of political unrest in Russia.

In 1905, workers in St. Petersburg peacefully assembled in front of the Winter Palace to appeal to the czar, Nicholas II (1868–1918, czar 1894–1917), for relief from the poor conditions. Little did the workers know that the czar had already left St. Petersburg. On that cold Sunday in January, the czar's troops opened fire on the demonstrators. A thousand men, women, and children were killed on what became known as *Bloody Sunday*. That summer, fueled by resentment for the czar, workers and peasants alike held strikes, mutinies, and small revolts. Finally, in October 1905, the czar gave in and issued the October Manifesto, which granted civil rights for the people and created a *duma*, or popularly elected legislature. Many people were satisfied, but the Social Democrats rejected the Manifesto. The Social Democrats staged a violent uprising in December that was eventually put down. The following year, the government unveiled its new constitution. It left a great deal of power for the czar and not as much for the duma and the upper house of the legislature. Many members of the duma were unhappy and uncooperative. Nicholas dismissed that duma only to have a more radical one elected in 1907. Again, Nicholas dismissed the duma. Nicholas and his advisers rewrote the laws so that the propertied classes had more votes, and because of that legislation, the duma became much more loyal to the czar. Shortly thereafter, Peter Stolypin (1862–1911) introduced his "wager on the strong" legislation that encouraged modernization, especially among the peasants.

NOTE
The Slavic nationalism of the peoples who wanted an independent Slavic state was known as *Panslavism*.

THE CAUSES AND OUTBREAK OF WORLD WAR I (1914–1918)

World War I marked the beginning of the end for many European powerhouses, including the Austro-Hungarian Empire, the Ottoman Empire, Germany, and Russia. The causes of the Great War are very complicated and include nationalism, imperialism, militarism, and bitter rivalries between nations and military alliances.

The nineteenth century saw the rise of a nationalistic spirit across Europe that led individual countries to believe in their own sovereignty and superiority. But not all Europeans seeking their own independent state had achieved sovereignty. Slavic peoples in the Balkans and in the Austro-Hungarian Empire strongly desired their own states, free of outside influences. Many European leaders were growing fearful of the increasingly powerful influence of the socialists within their borders who threatened internal stability by staging strikes and revolts.

The strong sense of nationalism also fostered the tendency to look out only for a state's own interests and not the interests of the international community. It was precisely this that made imperialism such an important factor in the unrest prior to World War I. With most of the European powers scrambling to add foreign lands to their holdings, foreign lands were bound to become a point of contention. The industrialization of the nineteenth century had increased Europe's need to find new foreign markets for its goods as well as new sources of raw materials. As the majority of Africa was gobbled up by the hungry European imperial powers, nations began to argue over the land. In 1905 and in 1911, France and Germany almost went to war over Morocco. The brutality of the new imperialism also prompted some European nations to denounce the imperialistic actions of others, thus heightening tensions.

At the turn of the century, Germany possessed the most powerful army on the continent, and Britain controlled the most powerful navy. Germany rebuilt its navy and threatened Britain's naval supremacy. Both nations hurried to increase the size and power of their fleets and their armies in an attempt not to be outdone. The powers of Europe grew defensive and increased the production and storage of arms, further escalating the already high tensions. With the growing emphasis on military power came an increase in the influence of military leaders. These leaders often saw the world from a different perspective than did the political and diplomatic leaders of the era, and they exerted their influence upon those with political power. This militarism left Europe ready to go to war.

As the Great Powers amassed military weapons and technology, they grew increasingly defensive and perhaps a little paranoid. Nations sought strength in numbers, and they began forming alliances. During the nineteenth century, Otto von Bismarck worked hard to keep the peace by encouraging alliances. He had built Germany into a mighty nation, and he

TIP
Consider the differences between the old imperialism and the new imperialism. This would make for a great essay question.

didn't want that to be undone by a war. The alliances changed frequently, though, during the last years of the nineteenth century and the early years of the twentieth century. On the eve of the Great War, Europe was divided between two powerful alliances: the *Triple Entente* and the *Triple Alliance*. The Triple Entente, composed of Britain, France, and Russia, stemmed from the earlier *Entente Cordiale* between Britain and France and the later agreement between Britain and Russia. The Triple Entente hoped to check the power of the Triple Alliance between Germany, Austria, and Italy. With ties firmly in place, any aggression toward a nation who was part of an alliance meant aggression toward all the members of the alliance. The two alliances sat ready to provoke or be provoked into war.

NOTE
Austria's punitive measures against Serbia were simply an excuse to attack.

The spark that ignited the war came from the Balkans in 1914. On June 28, 1914, a Serbian nationalist named Gavrilo Princip (1895–1914) assassinated the heir to the Austro-Hungarian throne, Archduke Francis Ferdinand (1863–1914), and his wife while they were visiting Sarajevo. Sarajevo was the capital of the Austrian province of Bosnia. Princip operated with the cooperation of the Black Hand, a radical Serbian nationalist group with members in the army and in the government. Princip and the other Serbian nationalists sought their own state, independent of Austro-Hungarian control. The Austro-Hungarians, of course, resisted this movement in order to preserve their empire. Because Princip was loosely associated with the Serbian government, Austria issued an ultimatum to Serbia that would bring them under Austrian control. Germany offered a "blank check" to Austria, promising them basically anything they might need in order to crush the Serbians. Russia backed Serbia, and Austria knew this. Austria also knew that war with Serbia meant war with Russia, too. In order to remain sovereign, Serbia rejected the ultimatum. In response to Serbia and prodded by Germany, Austria declared war on Serbia on July 28, 1914.

Russia immediately began to mobilize its forces. Germany reacted to the Russians with an ultimatum of their own. Germany demanded that Russia cease mobilization within 12 hours. The Russians ignored the ultimatum, and Germany declared war on Russia on August 1, 1914. Germany immediately put into action the *Schlieffen Plan*, a military strategy that was based on a scenario of war with Russia and France, Russia's ally. The plan was to deploy some troops to Russia while the bulk of the forces went to France via Belgium. On August 2, Germany demanded that Belgium allow German troops to pass through Belgium into France. The next day, Germany declared war on France. In response to German aggression toward Belgium, a neutral nation, Britain declared war on Germany. German aggression toward Belgium also enraged the United States. After August 4, all the powers of Europe, except Italy, had become entangled in a war that would have unforeseen consequences on not only Europe but also on the world. Italy remained neutral until 1915, when it separated from the Triple Alliance and declared war on Austria-Hungary. Also in 1915, Bulgaria joined the Central Powers. The European nations each believed their cause was right and that they or their allies had been wronged. As a result, each nation eagerly entered the war and sent their troops to battle with great celebration.

THE WAR

At the outbreak of war, fighting began on three European fronts: the western, or Franco-Belgian, front; the eastern, or Russian, front; and the southern, or Serbian, front. When Turkey joined the war on the side of the Central Powers (Germany, Austria-Hungary) in November 1914, some fighting occurred in the Dardanelles as well. All nations involved in the war anticipated a short war, one in which all the troops would be home by Christmas. The war on the western front pitted the British and Belgian forces against the Germans in Belgium and the French forces against the Germans in France. In September 1914, the French government had left Paris for fear of German occupation. The Germans crossed the Marne River and ran into the French forces led by General Jacques Cesaire Joffre (1852–1931). The French held off the Germans at the First Battle of the Marne. After that battle, both sides dug in and held on. A war that was hoped to be quick had deteriorated to trench warfare.

The first trenches were just ditches created for soldiers to hide in for a small amount of time. Before long, though, huge trenches created by both Central and Allied forces stretched almost the entire length of the French border. The soldiers hid in the trenches and periodically emerged to run across the territory in between, known as *no man's land,* to attack enemy trenches. With the introduction of artillery fire, poisonous gas, and tanks, the trenches became death traps for the soldiers. The opposing sides remained entrenched in their positions, and neither side gained any significant amount of territory. Trench warfare accounted for an almost inconceivable number of World War I casualties—literally in the millions—and turned the Great War into an incredibly bloody war, the likes of which no one had predicted. Offensives launched at Verdun, the Somme, and Passchendaele were typical of the inefficient, inhumane warfare of World War I.

Although no fewer lives were lost in the east, the warfare of the eastern front proved to be markedly different from that on the western front. Because of the enormous size of the eastern theater, troops were much more mobile than in the west. Early in the war, the Russian armies won numerous victories over the Germans and Austro-Hungarians. However, as the war stalled in the west, Germany redirected its forces to the east to combat the Russians. Nearly bankrupt and running low on food and weapons, Russia suffered huge, demoralizing losses. These losses would contribute to the internal turmoil of Russia only a few years later. On the southern front, the British attacked the Turks. In an attack orchestrated by Winston Churchill (1874–1965), the British forces landed at Gallipoli in 1915. The British hoped to remove the Turks so that British forces could supply the Russians via the Black Sea. After months of losses against the fortified Turks, the British withdrew.

TIP
If you have the opportunity, you should read some (or all) of Erich Remarque's *All Quiet on the Western Front.* This book provides a first-hand look at the trench warfare of World War I.

The pivotal year in the war proved to be 1917. Russia, on the verge of revolution, sought peace with Germany. This would allow Germans to concentrate their efforts elsewhere and win the war—or so they thought. In 1915, German submarines sank a British passenger ship called the *Lusitania*, a ship carrying more than 120 Americans who lost their lives. The Americans issued a stern warning to Germany, and Germany agreed not to attack neutral ships. However, in 1917, Germany resumed its unrestricted submarine warfare. As a result, the United States entered the war against Germany. Although the United States did not immediately affect the war, they did eventually turn the tide.

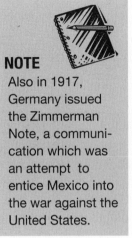

NOTE
Also in 1917, Germany issued the Zimmerman Note, a communication which was an attempt to entice Mexico into the war against the United States.

The Germans tried to organize an offensive that would end the war before the American troops arrived and made an impact. In 1918, the German forces advanced within 35 miles of Paris. Combined French and American forces repelled the Germans at the *Second Battle of the Marne*. Two million fresh troops landed in Europe, and allied forces began their march toward Germany. German General Ludendorff advised his government that all was lost. Germany created a new republic, and Kaiser William II capitulated. In November 1918, the republic signed an armistice with the Allies that ended the war.

World War I required of all its participants a new form of warfare called a *total war effort*. Total war meant that the entire population of a country was required to mobilize for the war effort. The governments of the nations realized that a quick war was out of the question. Therefore, the governments required the citizens to contribute in every imaginable way. Women went to work in factories, and children worked in the streets collecting all sorts of raw materials. The governments instituted price controls and rationing programs. The government also restricted the use of natural resources, such as coal. In order to keep spirits high on the home front, governments used propaganda. Governments created posters and movies to heighten morale and focus the citizens' attentions on the enemy and the task at hand. The enemies often were portrayed as monsters, and the citizens, to whom the propaganda was meant to appeal, were portrayed as heroes and heroines. In addition, governments censored information that entered and exited their borders to prevent undesirable information from upsetting the people on the home front.

THE TREATY OF VERSAILLES

In 1919, the Big Four met at Versailles to work out a peace settlement. President Woodrow Wilson (1856–1924) represented the United States, David Lloyd George (1863–1945) represented Britain, Georges Clemenceau (1841–1929) represented France, and Vittorio Emanuele Orlando (1860–1952) represented Italy. France, Britain, and the United States were the major players in peace talks; Germany had no say in the talks, and Russia was preoccupied with its own revolution. Wilson wanted to implement his *Fourteen Points* which included free trade, arms reductions, national self-

NOTE

After the war, many women experienced a new sense of freedom and independence. This spirit grew out of their time spent in the total war effort. Many women changed their style of dress, began smoking in public, and began acting more independently. Eventually, because of their contributions, women earned suffrage in many nations.

determination, and the establishment of an international peacekeeping organization called the *League of Nations*. Wilson's approach to the peace talks seemed idealistic compared to those of Lloyd George and Clemenceau. Because the British and the French suffered enormous loss of life and tremendous economic devastation, Lloyd George and Clemenceau sought a harsh and punitive resolution, almost revenge. They wanted immense reparations from Germany, and they wanted insurance that Germany would never again pose a threat to European nations. Ultimately, Britain and France won out over Wilson.

The Treaty of Versailles blamed Germany for World War I and required Germany to pay 132 billion gold marks in reparations. Germany was forced to give Alsace-Lorraine back to France. The treaty created an occupied, demilitarized zone along the Rhine to act as a buffer. Germany was forbidden from having an air force, and the German army and navy were severely restricted. Other treaties with Austria, Hungary, Bulgaria, and Turkey in 1919 redrew political boundaries. Czechoslovakia, Hungary, Romania, Serbia, Poland, Lithuania, Estonia, Latvia, and Finland were all created after the war. For many Europeans, the dream of an independent state was realized. At first glance, it may seem that the Treaty of Versailles accomplished a great deal. However, it failed miserably. The treaty failed to resolve the problems that led to the war in the first place. The United States eventually rejected the treaty, and Britain backed out of its defensive alliance with France. France felt isolated, Germany was resentful, and the League of Nations as Wilson envisioned it never came to fruition. The Treaty of Versailles was a quick fix that quickly unraveled.

THE IMPACT OF THE WAR

The war that was supposed to be over quickly soon became known as the "war to end all wars." The European powers, by hastily entering into a massive, multi-front war, devastated much of the continent. The war claimed more than 10 million lives, both military and civilian. Approximately twice that number of people suffered injury as a result of the war. It is safe to say that every French family between 1914–1918 either lost a family member or knew a family that lost someone. In addition to the incredible human carnage, entire cities, towns, and villages were decimated during the fighting. It was estimated that the total cost of the war topped $330 billion. The economies of Europe were virtually destroyed. Once the economic leaders of the world, the European nations found themselves in debt to other nations, primarily the United States, with virtually no means to repay. Psychologically, the men and women who participated in the war were scarred, and many found it very difficult to rejoin society. Europeans thought the twentieth century was going to be a century of prosperity and progress, but the war shook their belief in humanity, order, and reason. These doubts and fears manifested themselves in the art, writing, and philosophy of the early twentieth century.

THE RUSSIAN REVOLUTION

In 1915 alone, Russia lost 2 million soldiers in World War I. The under-equipped and under-funded Russian army continued to fight valiantly, though. To worsen matters, Russia's leadership was very poor. Public opinion began to call for a new government led by the duma and not by Czar Nicholas II. Foolishly, Nicholas dismissed the duma and left Russia to lead the troops on the front. Nicholas left his wife, Alexandra, in charge. In the czar's absence, Alexandra attempted to rule the way she had always encouraged Nicholas to rule, as an absolutist. Alexandra's chief adviser was a mystic named Gregori Rasputin who supposedly had the power to heal Alexandra's hemophiliac son. Under the influence of Rasputin, Alexandra dismissed and reappointed many of the top positions in the Russian government. In December 1916, amid rumors that Alexandra and Rasputin were lovers, Rasputin was assassinated. In March of the following year, riots broke out in Petrograd (formerly known as St. Petersburg). Nicholas sent orders for troops to put down the revolt, but the soldiers joined the rioters. The Duma created a provisional government to restore order, and Nicholas abdicated within days.

NOTE
Army Order No. 1 stripped officers of their military authority and gave the power to committees of common soldiers. This was intended to maintain order, but instead, army discipline fell apart.

From its creation, the new provisional government had to deal with the Petrograd Soviet. The soviets were councils of workers, and they began appearing in many towns and rural areas. The members of the soviets were generally socialists who were more radical than the provisional government. In April, with help of Germany, Vladimir Ulianov Lenin (1870–1924) arrived in Russia and immediately denounced the provisional government. Lenin was the leader of the Bolsheviks, a radical socialist party that advocated a violent working-class revolution in Russia led by professional revolutionaries. Lenin's opponents, the Mensheviks, believed that a bourgeois revolution must occur first in Russia before Russia could move toward socialism. After Lenin arrived, the Bolsheviks began convincing people to join their cause, and they worked toward a majority in the Petrograd Soviet. In the meantime, the provisional government tried desperately to deal with the peasants who had been waiting for the redistribution of lands. Many peasants had begun taking land for themselves. Also, because of the Petrograd Soviet's Army Order No. 1 (see sidebar), the military was in disarray.

After fleeing the country and then returning, Lenin, along with his avid supporter Leon Trotsky (1879–1940), convinced the Petrograd Soviet to make Trotsky the leader of a revolutionary group of military personnel. In November 1917, the revolutionaries seized government buildings and the provisional government. The Bolsheviks then declared Lenin the leader of their new government. Lenin and Trotsky provided outstanding leadership, leadership that the provisional government lacked. In addition, Lenin and Trotsky appealed to the masses and the workers. These things made Lenin and Trotsky successful in the revolution.

After assuming control, Lenin realized that Russia could not prevail in World War I. At a very high and unreasonable price, Lenin withdrew Russia from the war. He signed the Treaty of Brest-Lovik in 1918 and gave away a huge chunk of Russia. However, by doing so, Lenin saved Russia from certain disaster. Lenin created a one-party Communist government by dissolving the newly elected Constituent Assembly. This action made many realize that the republic they wanted was becoming a dictatorship. Popular opinion began to turn against Lenin's government. Led by military officers from different parts of Russia, the *Whites* rose up against the Bolsheviks, or *Reds*. However, the Reds defeated the Whites and won the civil war. The Whites failed because they were never well organized and because they had no clear-cut policy for people to rally behind. Above all, however, the Red army was simply superior.

The real accomplishment for Lenin and Trotsky was not the revolution but maintaining power and control. Under the leadership of Trotsky, the military was reorganized under a rigid system of discipline. The Bolsheviks nationalized everything from labor to banking. Especially during the civil war, the government instituted a *war communism,* or total war effort, in a civil war scenario. The secret police of the czar was reintroduced as the Cheka. The Cheka used terror to control Russia by hunting down and executing enemies of the state. The Russian Revolution proved to be one of the most significant events of the twentieth century because a one-party socialist dictatorship emerged in a powerful European country. Perhaps more importantly, this new government encouraged and advocated communist revolution around the world.

THE RISE OF STALIN

Lenin died in 1924 and left vacant the leadership of Russia. Two leading candidates vied for the position. One candidate was Trotsky, the leader of the Left Opposition. Trotsky believed that Russia needed to help spread communist revolution to other countries, and Trotsky wanted to return to the state-controlled war communism of the past. Trotsky's opponent and leader of the Right Opposition was Nikolai Bukharin (1888–1938). Bukharin believed that Russia needed to focus on the development of communism within Russia instead of spreading it into other nations. Bukharin also advocated the New Economic Policy, the policy with which Lenin replaced the old war communism.

As it turned out, neither man replaced Lenin. Rather, Joseph Stalin (1879–1953) became leader of Russia. Stalin's goal was to increase the Soviet's power. One of Stalin's first steps was the expulsion of Trotsky from the party. Two years later, Stalin expelled Bukharin from the party, too. In 1928, Stalin began his *Five-Year Plan* to further industrialize Russia. He planned to finance this plan through the collectivization of Russian farms. Stalin sent troops into the rural areas and forced the peasants to join the agricultural collectives. The peasants who refused to join were shot on sight.

Millions of these peasants, or *kulaks*, died because of Stalin's brutal policy. Within a decade, though, the Soviet Union rivaled the other industrial powers of Europe.

THE GREAT DEPRESSION

Although many people look to the Stock Market Crash of 1929 as the beginning of the Great Depression, its roots go farther back. During the Roaring Twenties, people spent money haphazardly. People extended their credit to the limit. Speculators and investors invested heavily in stocks and futures, hoping for a huge return. However, farm prices dropped in the post-war era. Stocks were overvalued and destined to plummet. When the market crashed in 1929, the world took notice. The speculators and investors lost everything. Purchasing declined, prices fell, production declined, and unemployment rose meteorically. The United States economy was failing. As a result, American banks began recalling loans from foreign countries. As European countries payed their loans, the gold supply of Europe was nearly depleted. In 1931, the most important bank in Austria, the Credit-Anstalt, collapsed. Prices worldwide fell, and investors dumped their goods to get cash. In Europe as in the United States, production slowed and unemployment rose. Also in 1931, Britain went off the gold standard. Shortly thereafter, nearly twenty other countries went off the gold standard, too. Nations introduced protective tariffs to protect their domestic markets. Against the advice of John Maynard Keynes (1883–1946), European governments reduced their spending. Keynes argued that governments should increase their spending through such programs as public works projects similar to Roosevelt's New Deal in the United States. The world finally began its slow road to recovery in 1933, but it wasn't until the coming of World War II that most nations made a full recovery. The desperation of many Europeans during this era made them look to anyone for leadership— even dictators.

FASCISM IN ITALY AND GERMANY

Although Italy and Germany developed different models of authoritarian governments, the government of choice for these two nations after World War I was fascism. First used by Mussolini in 1919, the word *fascism* comes from the word *fasces*, a bundle of sticks tied around an ax that was the ancient Roman symbol of civic unity and power. Fascism grew out of Italy's discontent following World War I and the growing threat, or at least the perceived threat, of the spread of communism. Fascism tended to be intensely nationalistic. There always was an enemy, either real or perceived, for fascists to defend or take offensive measures against. War was a noble cause for fascists. Fascism placed little or no value upon the individual and forced subordination of the individual to the state. Fascism disapproved of the modern parliamentary system. Instead, fascism manifested itself in single-party dictatorships. Fascist governments were unapologetically sexist and advocated the subordination of women to men and to the state. In some circumstances, especially in Germany, fascists were racist as well. The Germans, of course, harbored particular hatred for the Jews. More than just a political system, fascism represented economic policy as well. This applied much more in the case of Italy than in Germany, though. Unlike communism and socialism, fascism did not seek to eliminate classes, property, or private business.

In 1919, Benito Mussolini (1883–1945) created in Italy the *Fasci de Combattimento*, or League of Combat. Many of the members were disgruntled veterans who felt betrayed by the Treaty of Versailles; many Italian nationalists shared these sentiments, too. The members also feared the spread of socialism. In addition, the members of Mussolini's group had lost confidence in the parliamentary system. After the elections of 1919, the parliament, dominated by two uncooperative parties, proved itself to be incompetent as it became hopelessly deadlocked. Mussolini, being an opportunist, saw his chance to gain power for his party and for himself. In 1920 and 1921, Mussolini unleashed his *squadristi* on socialist offices and establishments where they used violence and fear to squelch socialist activity. Mussolini's activities brought attention to his *Fasci*. Mussolini's early rise to prominence was topped off by the threat of a march on Rome where he and his fascist blackshirts were going to seize control of the government. King Victor Emmanuel III (1869–1947, king 1900–1946) granted Mussolini the title of Prime Minister and virtually limitless power for one year.

Over the next few years, Mussolini and his men rigged elections, intimidated opponents, and terrorized dissenters. He instituted constitutional changes that eliminated nearly all hints of democracy. In 1925, after the murder of an Italian politician named Giacomo Matteotti threatened Mussolini's career, he turned Italy into a dictatorship. As a dictator, Mussolini implemented a secret police force and censored the media. State-sponsored propaganda filled the newspapers and airwaves. Mussolini encouraged the development of fascist youth organizations and used schools to indoctrinate the children. Mussolini passed laws to encourage women to stay at home and reproduce.

Mussolini wanted and tried desperately to create a totalitarian state. However, for all his efforts at terror and censorship, Mussolini basically failed. His state never developed into the authoritarian state of which he dreamed. Mussolini planned to help the workers and peasants but sided with big business. He never destroyed the monarchy, and he never completely controlled the military as he had hoped to do. Mussolini even sought the support of the Church by granting sovereignty to the Vatican. In the end, Mussolini's fascism paled in comparison to the fascist regime established by one of his admirers, Adolf Hitler.

The founder of the German fascist movement was none other than Adolf Hitler (1889–1945). Hitler was born in Austria and spent his early years in

NOTE

Mussolini once honored numerous men and women in a parade for their efforts in producing large numbers of children. For their efforts, the women were awarded gold medals!

Vienna where he was heavily influenced by the mayor of Vienna, Karl Lueger (1844–1910). It was in Vienna that Hitler began his hatred of Jews and Slavs, for Vienna was a hotbed of German nationalism and anti-Semitism. In 1913, Hitler moved to Munich and joined the German army. When Germany lost World War I, Hitler became convinced that Germany lost because of a Jewish and Communist conspiracy. In 1919, Hitler joined the German Workers' party, and by 1921, Hitler had total control of the party. In 1922 and 1923, membership in Hitler's party skyrocketed. As the Weimar Republic collapsed around him, Hitler decided to follow the example of Mussolini and lead a military uprising against the government. Hitler marched on Munich but ended up in prison. During his trial, Hitler gained attention and support by condemning the Republic. While in prison, Hitler wrote his autobiography *Mein Kampf*. Also while in prison, Hitler realized that he would have more political success by using legal means than by using military force.

Over the next five years, Hitler built the membership of his party up to approximately 100,000. In 1928, Hitler's Nazi party won only twelve seats in the *Reichstag*. As the Great Depression gripped Germany, Hitler seized the opportunity to further his cause by renouncing capitalism and advocating social programs for the middle- and lower-class workers. As the Depression worsened, Hitler's popularity grew. In 1930, the Nazi party won more than a hundred seats in the Reichstag. In 1932, the Nazis became the largest party in the Reichstag. Hitler's popularity continued to grow because he appealed to the masses and to the youth of Germany by using propaganda.

Germany faltered under the leadership of Chancellor Heinrich Bruning and President Paul von Hindenburg. Neither was able to work with the Nazi-dominated Reichstag. Therefore, in 1933, President Hindenburg asked Hitler to be chancellor. Hitler had achieved great political power, and he had done so legally. After his ascension, Hitler began his quest for dictatorship. The Reichstag building burned, and Hitler, who may have been responsible, blamed the Communists. Based on that accusation, Hitler persuaded Hindenburg to pass laws that virtually abolished personal freedoms. In the next election, when the Nazis failed to win a majority, Hitler outlawed the Communist party and arrested its representatives. The Reichstag then passed the Enabling Acts, legislation that made Hitler dictator, or *Fuhrer*, for four years. Hitler brought all state organizations under the control of the Nazi party, except for the military. To bring the SA under his control, Hitler had nearly 1,000 SA leaders arrested and executed. The army leaders swore their allegiance to Hitler, and the army, henceforth known as the SS, grew in numbers and reputation under the leadership of Heinrich Himmler (1900–1945). Throughout the 1930's, the military and the Gestapo targeted Jews and persecuted them, causing a mass exodus of German Jews.

Hitler enacted new policies and programs that spurred the economy and reduced unemployment in Germany. Whether or not the standard of living improved, though, is uncertain. Many people believed that their conditions

NOTE

Karl Lueger served as Viennese mayor from 1897 to 1910. He appealed to many middle-class people with his calls for "Christian socialism," which really amounted to anti-Semitic rhetoric.

were improving, but much of this feeling could be attributed to propaganda. The fact is that many of the lower classes did not achieve the status for which they had hoped or that Hitler had promised. There was some new potential for social advancement in Hitler's Germany, but there was no social revolution.

THE CAUSES AND OUTBREAK OF WORLD WAR II (1939–1945)

From the time Hitler rose to power, he planned to undo the Treaty of Versailles. Openly and defiantly, Hitler began the reconstruction of his military, which had been severely restricted by the Treaty. No one stopped Hitler from rearming, so Hitler took another defiant step. In 1936, German troops marched unopposed into the Rhineland. Hitler could have been stopped here, but he wasn't. The British and French wanted to avoid war at all costs, so they adopted a policy of appeasement to buy time and prevent war. Also in 1936, Hitler and Mussolini created the Rome-Berlin Axis. Hitler also helped the fascist Francisco Franco (1892–1972) achieve power in Spain. Hitler turned his sights to Austria and Czechoslovakia and marched into Austria unopposed in 1938. Hitler announced that he wanted Sudetenland, a Germanic area of Czechoslovakia, added to the German empire. Following their policy of appeasement, France and Britain agreed to the cession of Sudetenland. Hitler went on to occupy the rest of Czechoslovakia, too. In 1939, Hitler and Stalin signed a treaty of nonaggression, a move that stunned everyone. The final straw, though, was the German invasion of Poland in 1939. Two days after the invasion, France and Britain ended their appeasement by declaring war on Germany.

Hitler's army took Poland in four short weeks using the new *blitzkrieg* method of warfare, a method that involved tanks and planes. After a short period of down time, Germany attacked Denmark, Norway, Belgium, and then France. In a matter of just six weeks, Germany defeated the French army and occupied France. The French were unprepared for Germany's *blitzkrieg* but were entrenched just as in World War I. In a tremendous effort, the British staged a magnificent retreat at Dunkirk. The British used every available ship and boat to take more than 300,000 Allied soldiers from France back to Britain. A new French government, the *Vichy* government, was installed. Throughout the war, the Vichy government battled against French resistance forces and against the forces led by Charles de Gaulle (1890–1970). Hitler wanted to use France and Belgium as a launching pad for the invasion of Britain. He sent his air force, or *Luftwaffe*, on many raids into Britain, where German planes successfully attacked military sites. In one of the bigger German military blunders, though, Herman Goring (1893–1946) decided to demoralize Britain by attacking civilian targets instead of military targets. As a result, Britain increased its military production and recovered enough to repel the German attacks. Hitler changed his plan of invading Britain and turned to the Soviet Union. In June 1941, Hitler

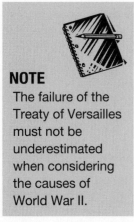

NOTE
The failure of the Treaty of Versailles must not be underestimated when considering the causes of World War II.

invaded Russia. They drove deep into Russia, basically all the way to Leningrad and Stalingrad. However, the Russians did not give in.

In December 1941, Japan attacked the U.S. base at Pearl Harbor, and the United States entered the war—now truly a World War. On the same day, Germany declared war on the United States. The *Axis Powers*, composed of Germany, Italy, and Japan, faced the *Allied Powers*, composed of the United States, Britain, and the Soviet Union. The Allies decided that they must take care of Europe first and then they would turn their attentions to the Pacific. The entry of the United States into the war marked one of the major turning points in World War II. The American troops made an instant impact, even in Africa where they helped drive out the Italians and the Germans. In 1943, the Allies knocked Italy out of the war. Then the Allies decided to invade Western Europe using Britain as a launching pad. On June 6, 1944, under the direction of General Dwight Eisenhower (1890–1969), the Allies landed on the beaches of Normandy in the famous D-Day invasion. A year later, the Allied forces finally crossed the Rhine and entered Germany. On the eastern front, the Russians moved through Romania, Hungary, Yugoslavia, and Poland before marching into Germany, where they met the Allied forces. Germany capitulated in May 1945, a day after Hitler committed suicide. In August, the United States dropped atomic bombs on Hiroshima and Nagasaki, Japan, a terrible act that ultimately brought the war to an end in the Pacific. World War II ended as the most violent conflict the world had ever seen. More than 50 million lives were lost during the war.

> **NOTE**
> The German *blitzkrieg*, which means "lightning," was a highly mobile attack. This was in stark contrast to the slow, inefficient warfare of World War I.

THE HOLOCAUST

Originally a term that described a religious ceremony in which an offering was consumed by fire, the term *Holocaust* has come to mean the all-out attack on European Jews by Hitler's regime. Beginning with the Night of Broken Glass, or *kristallnacht*, in 1938, when Jewish synagogues, businesses, and homes were attacked and destroyed, Hitler ruthlessly persecuted the Jews. When Germany occupied Poland in 1939, Polish Jews were moved into ghettos surrounded by barbed wire. As the Germans invaded the Soviet Union, they began executing Russian Jews on sight. As a part of Herman Goring's "final solution to the Jewish question," the Nazi's developed death camps, or concentration camps. These camps were equipped with gas chambers and incinerators to destroy the Jews. The worst of these camps was at Auschwitz, where more than a million Jews lost their lives. By the time the war ended and the camps were liberated, at least 6 million Jews and millions of Slavs, Communists, and homosexuals were dead as a result of the intense racial hatred of the Nazis.

IMPACT OF THE WAR

World War II left Europe physically, emotionally, and economically devastated. The end of the war brought with it the daunting task of rebuilding. The

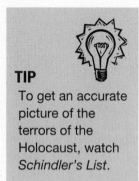

TIP
To get an accurate picture of the terrors of the Holocaust, watch *Schindler's List*.

two great wars of the first half of the twentieth century left everyone in the world looking for ways to prevent such a crisis from occurring again. In 1945, President Franklin Delano Roosevelt (1882–1945) suggested the League of Nations be replaced by a new international peacekeeping organization. In 1945, delegates met and created the United Nations, or UN, with its headquarters in New York. Another issue facing the world was how to deal with Germany after it had surrendered unconditionally. In February of 1945, the Big Three, which included Great Britain, the Soviet Union, and the United States, met in Yalta, a city in the Ukraine, to discuss post-war Germany. The Big Three decided to divide Germany into zones of British, French, American, and Soviet occupation. The Allies also agreed to let the Soviet Union keep and administer its Polish lands acquired in 1939. At Potsdam, later in 1939, the Big Three met again but with new U.S. President Harry Truman (1884–1972). The Allies agreed to each administer a zone in Germany. The participants became antagonistic, though, when the Soviet Union demanded reparations from Germany, but the United States wanted to rebuild the German economy instead. Tensions also mounted between East and West because of the Truman Doctrine that sought to stop the spread of Communism by granting military and economic aid to nations that were susceptible to Communist aggression. The Marshall Plan for the rehabilitation of the European economy also upset Stalin. In 1948, after the United States and Britain had agreed on an economic merger of their German zones, Stalin cut off the city of Berlin from western aid. In response, the United States and Britain staged the Berlin airlift in which supplies were dropped behind the Soviet blockades. In 1949, Britain, France, and the United States combined their zones and established the Federal Republic of Germany. The Soviets then created the German Democratic Republic, a Communist nation created from the Soviet-controlled eastern zone in Germany. The years following the war were filled with antagonistic meetings and discussions between the East and the West. This antagonism led to the icy relations over the next several decades known as the *Cold War*.

THE COLD WAR AND COMMUNISM AFTER WORLD WAR II

The roots of the Cold War lie in the post-war talks between the East and the West, between the United States and the Soviet Union in particular. President Truman wanted Eastern European nations to have free elections, but Stalin would not allow it. Stalin wanted only Communist nations on his western border, and free elections would end any chance of that happening. Truman was not willing to go to war to give those nations the freedoms he wanted for them. Therefore, Stalin got his way in eastern Europe. In response, Truman cut all aid to the Soviet Union and announced that the U.S. would not recognize any governments established against the will of the people. In 1946, Churchill proclaimed that an *iron curtain* had fallen over Europe, thus dividing it into two sides. The anti-Soviet mindset began to establish itself in the United States, and the Soviet Union launched a worldwide anticapitalism campaign. In 1949, the United States created the North Atlantic Treaty Organization, or NATO, as an anti-Soviet alliance of nations. Stalin strengthened his hold on eastern Europe and firmly divided Europe into two blocs, or groups of nations acting together. The Cold War intensified as Communism won out in China in 1949 and as the Stalin-backed North Korea invaded South Korea in 1950. In 1955, the Communist bloc set in stone its opposition to NATO by creating the *Warsaw Pact*. The Warsaw Pact united the Communist satellite states of eastern Europe, although it was dominated by the Soviet Union.

Even in the beginning, there were problems within the Communist bloc. Workers in East Germany demanded freedoms and better conditions. When their demands were not met, many fled to West Germany. To prevent further emigration, the Soviets constructed the Berlin Wall, the enduring symbol of the iron curtain of which Churchill spoke. Similar movements took place in Poland and Hungary, too. The Soviets, however, put down those movements. Hungary wanted out of the Warsaw Pact to establish its own independent government. The Soviet Union brutally ended Hungary's hopes of such a state. In 1953, Stalin died. The death of Stalin opened the door for change. Nikita Khrushchev (1894–1971) assumed power in the Soviet Union and almost immediately renounced the brutal actions of Stalin. Khrushchev argued in 1956 that Stalin's methods had strayed from the pure Marxist-Leninist communism. He announced that the Soviet Union would only follow policies in line with Marxism-Leninism. Khrushchev visited the United Nations in 1959 and relieved some tension, but when the Soviets shot down a U.S. U-2 spy plane, the tension again mounted. The tension almost erupted in 1962 over the Cuban Missile Crisis, and nuclear war was narrowly avoided. The Soviets stationed missiles in Cuba. Thankfully, President John F. Kennedy was able to diffuse the situation. Khrushchev was forced to retire in 1964 and was replaced by Leonid Brezhnev (1906–1982).

Brezhnev reinforced the position of the Soviet both at home and in the satellite states. In response to the unrest in Czechoslovakia in 1968, Brezhnev announced the Brezhnev Doctrine, which said that the Soviet Union would put down any unrest or uprising in any Communist state by the use of any means necessary. Events in Poland in 1980 tested the Brezhnev Doctrine. An electrician named Lech Walesa led the Solidarity movement in Poland, a labor movement that used protests and strikes to call for reforms. Solidarity had the support of millions of Polish workers and the Catholic Church under Polish Pope John Paul II. Supported by the Soviet Union, the Polish government arrested the Solidarity leaders and declared martial law. The martial law was lifted in 1982, and in 1988, the government began talks with Solidarity. In 1990, Lech Walesa was elected president of Poland.

Mikhail Gorbachev (b. 1931) became the leader of the Soviet Union in 1985 and sought some reforms in the Communist bloc. He opposed the Brezhnev Doctrine and found opposition in the old-school hard-line Communists. The four years after Gorbachev assumed power were filled with

NOTE
It should be noted that after the Cuban Missile Crisis, Kennedy appeared to be a masterful diplomat, while Khrushchev appeared to be a fool.

events that culminated in the monumental year of 1989. The Communist governments of Czechoslovakia, Bulgaria, Hungary, and Albania all collapsed. The following year, the Berlin wall came down, and East and West Germany were reunited. Romania followed a different path, though. The people of Romania rose up against the oppressive government of Nicolae Ceausescu (1918–1989) and executed both Nicolae and his wife in December, 1989. The people of the Soviet Union also wanted change. Gorbachev did not resist change, but he wanted the Communists to lead the reform movement. He accepted both *glasnost*, or openness, and *perestroika*, or economic restructuring. Nationalism swept through some of the Soviet states, and Gorbachev appointed hard-line Communists to deal with these problems. A last-ditch effort by the Communists was a coup attempt in 1991 that failed. Throughout 1991, the Soviet states left the Union, the Soviet Union fell apart, and Gorbachev resigned. In 1991, Boris Yeltsin (b. 1931) became the first popularly elected president of Russia. To this day, Russia struggles to adjust to its new political order.

THE END OF COLONIZATION AND IMPERIALISM

In 1947, India declared its independence from Britain, and other British holdings followed suit. Also in 1947, the British withdrew from Palestine and left the United Nations the task of determining the area's future. The UN divided Palestine into Arab and Jewish lands. The nation of Israel was born in 1948, but the Palestinian state never came to fruition. After a conflict with Egypt over control of the Suez Canal in 1956, the British Empire basically dissolved. Ghana, Kenya, Nigeria, Uganda, and Sierra Leone broke with Britain without any real incident. Rhodesia declared their independence in 1965 but did not earn their freedom until 1980 because of the large number of British who lived there. In 1949, the Netherlands granted independence to Indonesia. France lost Indochina, or Vietnam, and struggled to hold on to Algeria. After great internal turmoil over Algeria, France granted the nation its independence in 1962. The great colonial empires of the previous century had finally been dismantled.

ECONOMIC RECOVERY AFTER WORLD WAR II

After the war, the United States and the *Marshall Plan* paved the long road to economic recovery. Under the Marshall Plan, the United States invested more than 9 billion dollars in the reconstruction of Europe. The United States sent money and aid to Europe to help struggling nations avoid Communism. The Marshall Plan helped Europe move past subsistence and toward economic expansion. The economic growth, however, outpaced the increase in wages. As a result, many nations turned to socialist reform. Nations such as Britain nationalized industries and implemented pensions and employment insurance. The extremely high cost of such welfare systems, though, caused some nations to move away from extreme socialist policies. The nations still using socialist welfare programs have found it extremely challenging to remain competitive in the new global market. One of the key developments in the economic recovery of post-war Europe was the creation of an economic community. In 1951, France, Belgium, Holland, Italy, West Germany, and Luxembourg formed the European Coal and Steel Community. Six years later, the same six countries formed the European Economic Community or Common Market. In 1973, Britain, Ireland, and Denmark joined the Community. In 1979, the European Monetary System, or EMS, was established in order to move Europe toward an economic and monetary union, or EMU. In 1993, the Maastricht Treaty established the European Union out of the twelve members of the European Community and began working toward a common currency and a common banking system.

In 1999, the European Union (Belgium, Germany, Spain, France, Ireland, Italy, Luxembourg, the Netherlands, Austria, Portugal, and Finland) adopted the euro as the new currency for the Union. Greece joined these nations in 2001. The European Union began working toward the introduction of the euro as the official and only currency of its member states with 2002 as its target date. On January 1, 2002, the euro became the official and only currency used by the member states and by February 28, 2002, all national currency of the member states was removed from circulation. The euro can be used anywhere within the European Union and is not subject to moneychanging when consumers cross from one nation into another.

CONTEMPORARY EUROPE

Perhaps one of the most pressing issues in contemporary Europe is the situation in the former Yugoslavia. Yugoslavia managed to steer clear of the Eastern bloc under the strict leadership of Josip Tito (1892–1980). After Tito died, Slovenia and Croatia broke away from Yugoslavia and created their own independent states. Serbian President Slobodan Milosevic (b. 1941) responded with military force in an attempt to create a single Serb state. The war spread to Bosnia-Herzegovina in 1992 when it declared independence. The Serbs in Bosnia-Herzegovina refused to live under Bosnian Muslim rule. The Serbs seized land and began what has come to be known as ethnic cleansing. Ethnic cleansing, reminiscent of the Nazi Holocaust, involved the imprisonment, torture, and execution of those who were ethnically and religiously different. The war in Bosnia has resulted in hundreds of thousands of deaths and millions of refugees. In 1995, under the Dayton Accord, a tentative peace was established and then policed by U.S. and UN troops. Despite the tentative peace, fighting continued in the region as the factions continued to disagree about religion, politics, and geographical boundaries. Then, in 2001, Slobodan Milosevic was arrested in dramatic fashion and charged with war crimes. Milosevic faces charges relating to atrocities and war crimes allegedly committed in Croatia between 1991 and 1992, in Bosnia-Herzegovina between 1992 and 1995, and in Kosovo in 1999. Milosevic's trial began in February 2002. Even with Milosevic gone, tensions remain high in the Balkans.

NOTE
One of the greatest tragedies of the crisis in the Balkans was the destruction of Sarajevo. Once the beautiful host city of the 1984 Olympic Winter Games, the Bosnian capital is now in shambles from the constant fighting.

Another grave issue facing contemporary Europe is the ever-increasing threat of terrorist activity. On September 11, 2001, terrorists with anti-American agendas crashed two airplanes into the World Trade Center in New York City and a third airliner into the Pentagon in Washington, D.C. This attack caught the attention of all of Europe as many European citizens lost their lives in the attacks. In unprecedented fashion, European leaders joined together in condemnation of those responsible and in support of the investigation of terrorist activity. In the weeks and months that followed September 11, 2001, authorities from the United States and from European states began to uncover a tangled web of terrorist activity and conspiracy around the world, including Europe. Leading the way for Europe was Great Britain's Tony Blair.

THE MAJOR PLAYERS

Neville Chamberlain (1869–1940)—Neville Chamberlain was born in Birmingham, England, was educated there, and became mayor there in 1915. He worked his way up the political ladder and became Prime Minister in 1937. As Prime Minister, Chamberlain adopted a policy of appeasement toward Hitler in order to keep Britain out of war. In 1938, Chamberlain returned from the Munich Conference, having signed the Munich Pact, and claimed that he had achieved peace. Later, Chamberlain led his nation into war against Hitler. Although some historians have painted Chamberlain as a naïve and gullible politician, Chamberlain may deserve more credit because he did buy Britain some time before they faced imminent war.

Vladimir Ilich Lenin (1870–1924)—Vladimir Ilich Ulyanov was born to a government official in Simbirsk in 1870. In 1887, his brother was arrested and hanged for an attempt on the life of Czar Alexander III. Vladimir entered college but was expelled for being a troublemaker. After he was kicked out of college, he studied Marx's writings and became a self-proclaimed Marxist. He became a lawyer and moved to St. Petersburg in 1893 where he became involved with a labor organization. He, along with other leaders of the group, was arrested and put in jail. After his jail term, he fled to Siberia for a year. When he returned, he changed his name to Lenin to keep the authorities at bay. Lenin met Trotsky and began the development of his Communist philosophy. He wanted a revolution, and he believed that a band of professional revolutionaries would lead the workers against the czar. When World War I broke out, he opposed the war and said that the workers were fighting the war for the bourgeoisie. Lenin was not in Russia when the Revolution erupted in 1917. With the help of the Germans, Lenin returned to Russia and made a grand entrance. He became the leader of Russia, with the help of Trotsky, and he steered Russia toward socialism in a moderate, cautious manner. In 1921, Lenin initiated the New Economic Policy that allowed for a mixed economy of both nationalized and privatized industry and business. Regardless of the evaluation of Lenin as a philosopher or thinker, Lenin excelled as a leader. He should be remembered most as a revolutionary figure and as a leader whose greatest feat was simply maintaining control as long as he did.

Sir Winston Leonard Spencer Churchill (1874–1965) - Born into an aristocratic family, Churchill attended military college before serving in India and the Sudan. He quit his military duties to become a correspondent during the Boer War, where he was captured. After escaping his captors, Churchill became a national hero. He entered the political arena and worked his way up to the lord of the admiralty. During World War I, he almost ruined his career with the Gallipoli fiasco. He resigned the admiralty as a result. He continued his political career by serving in various positions. During the 1930s, Churchill criticized Chamberlain for his passive attitude toward Hitler. Churchill was one of the few who realized the danger of the Fuhrer. In 1940, Churchill became Prime Minister. During the war years, Churchill became one of the greatest leaders in British history. His fiery speeches and passionate quotes inspired the nation to dig in and fight against Hitler. Churchill's determination and will led the people of Britain from the brink of disaster to victory over the hated Germans. Churchill also played a major role in the peace talks and diplomatic meetings of wartime and post-war Europe. He will be remembered both as a leader and statesman, although he also won a Nobel Prize for literature in 1953.

Joseph Stalin (1879–1953)—Iosif Vissarionovich Dzhugashvili was born in Georgia in 1879 where he attended a church school as a youngster. As a devout Orthodox Christian, he began studying for the ministry. However, he soon became influenced by Marxist writings and abandoned his religious education. He joined the Russian Revolutionary movement against the monarchy and distributed Marxist propaganda. Eventually, he was arrested and exiled to Siberia. Unfortunately for the world, he escaped. Until 1917, he was arrested and exiled again several times, but each time he returned. Some time before 1912, he adopted the name Stalin, a Russian word meaning "man of steel." During the Russian Civil War, he led military efforts against the Whites. After the civil war, he worked in politics until Lenin's death in 1924 when he took control of the government. Stalin undid the New Economic Policy of Lenin and introduced his Five-Year Plan. He industrialized Russia and initiated the collectivization of agriculture. These processes cost millions of Russian lives. In the 1930s, he purged the party of thousands who he suspected of being disloyal or threatening. Late in the decade, the Great Purge included all of the Soviet Union, and historians estimate that somewhere between 2 and 7 million Soviets lost their lives during Stalin's Purge. Stalin signed a secret treaty with Hitler but suffered an attack on his nation by Germany in 1941, after which Stalin found himself somehow allied with Britain and the United States. After World War II, Stalin grabbed onto much of Eastern Europe and created many puppet governments there. Although he industrialized and modernized Russia, he did so at the expense of millions of lives. Some people consider Hitler the most abominable of all dictators, but

Stalin deserves serious consideration for that dubious honor.

Benito Mussolini (1883–1945)—Born and raised in Italy, Benito Mussolini began his career as a teacher and a journalist. When World War I began, he spoke out against it and then changed his mind and advocated Italy's entry into the war. He was kicked out of the Socialist party, but he created his own newspaper that was to become a primary instrument in the development of the Fascist party. His Fascist party grew to such an extent that Victor Emmanuel III asked Mussolini to head the government of Italy. Over the next four years, Mussolini turned Italy into a Fascist dictatorship. In his new state, workers were organized into party-controlled groups, unions and strikes were forbidden, and big business thrived. Mussolini used schools to recruit young fascists, and he encouraged women to have as many children as possible—also to increase the number of young potential fascists. Mussolini's foreign policy could be described as aggressive, with the takeover of Ethiopia and Albania and the aid to Franco in his struggle to rise in power in Spain. Despite Mussolini's attempts to be an authoritarian dictator, he never assumed total control of the army, and he never destroyed the monarchy. Near the end of World War II, Mussolini was dismissed and arrested. After the Germans helped him escape, they placed him in a puppet government in Northern Italy. In 1945, he and his mistress were shot and killed by Italians.

Adolf Hitler (1889–1945)—Adolf Hitler was born and raised in Austria. He never completed a high school program. In Vienna, he read incessantly and became fascinated by the words of the mayor of Vienna. He began to develop an intense racism and nationalism, a fondness of the individual, and disgust of the masses. In World War I, he left Austria and joined the German army but met with little success. In 1919, he joined the German Workers' Party, and by 1921, he was the head of the newly named National Socialist German Workers' Party, or Nazi party. He tried to exert power with a march, the way Mussolini had done, but his failed attempt landed him in prison. While in prison, he wrote *Mein Kampf*. After his release from prison, he tried a new legal approach to gaining power. He blamed the Great Depression and the loss of World War I on a Jewish-Communist plot against Germany. He promised a strong economy and national power. Millions of voters flocked to the Nazi party, especially young people. Hitler became chancellor in 1933 and immediately began his dictatorial regime. He used his secret police to control his opponents through violence and terror. He arrested those who opposed him as well as Jews and Slavs. He single-handedly instigated World War II through his ambitious and aggressive foreign policy. He wanted to create more living space for Germans by eliminating those subhuman races, such as the Jews and the Slavs. Fortunately for Europe, Hitler was not the military genius he thought he was. After a number of serious military blunders, Hitler realized that all was lost. In 1945 in a bunker, Hitler killed himself. He was a charismatic speaker who had the ability to control large numbers of people. His dynamic personality combined with his hatred of non-Germans made him one of the most dangerous of all dictators.

Charles De Gaulle (1890–1970)—Charles De Gaulle was born in France and was destined to be a leader. He attended a military school and then served in World War I, where he was injured several times. Between the wars, he wrote books on military tactics. During World War II, he formed a French resistance effort while in exile to combat the Germans. He commanded both the French forces fighting alongside the Allies and the French resistance forces in France. After the Second World War, he became president of the new government. He soon resigned, though, when the French people resisted his attempts to strengthen the presidency. In 1953, De Gaulle retired from politics. He came out of retirement in 1958 to lead the nation through a crisis created by the issue of Algerian independence. Soon, the Fifth Republic was created, and he was elected to be its president. He served as president until 1969. During his administrations, he led France through economic disasters, entered France in the European Economic Community, and pulled France out of NATO. He consistently stood by the United States during the Cold War, although he kept close ties with both China and the Soviet Union. He believed in a strong presidency, and he used his office to strengthen France's position in the world.

Nikita Sergeyevich Khrushchev (1894–1971)—Nikita Khrushchev was born to a Russian peasant family and received very little formal education. He did manual labor until he joined the Bolsheviks and served in the Red Army during the Russian Civil War. In 1929, he moved to Moscow and became affiliated with the Communist Party. He moved up through the party and became a member of the Party's highest bureau, the *Politburo*. He served during World War II and was in charge of the recovery efforts in the Ukraine after the war. When Stalin died in 1953, Khrushchev became the Party leader. Khrushchev denounced the methods of Stalin as too harsh. Although he predicted that the Soviet Union would eventually "bury" the United States, he sought nonviolent ways to compete with and coexist with non-Communist nations. However, it was Khrushchev who built the Berlin Wall and took the United States to the brink of war with the Cuban Missile Crisis. His politics caused the relations between China and the Soviets to deteriorate. He attempted to restructure the political system in the USSR by decentralizing some of the elements of the government. His colleagues removed him from office while he was on vacation in 1964 because he had failed to deliver on his promises.

Willy Brandt (1913–1992)—Herbert Ernst Karl Frahm was born in Lubeck in 1913. In 1933, he left Germany for Norway to escape the Nazis, whom he had opposed as a journalist, and he changed his name to Willy Brandt. He returned to West Germany after World War II and was elected to the legislature where he served until 1957. From 1957 to 1966, Brandt served as mayor of West Berlin. He served as

Chancellor of West Germany from 1966 until 1974 when it was discovered that an East German spy had been serving on his staff. In 1971, Brandt won the Nobel Peace Prize for his efforts to ease the East-West tensions with his policy of *Ostpolitik*. Under his policy, West Germany signed treaties of nonaggression with Poland and the Soviet Union.

Pope John Paul II (b. 1920)—Karol Wojtyla was born in Wadowice, Poland, in 1920. He studied poetry and drama as a young man and then prepared for priesthood. He eventually earned a Ph.D. and a Th.D. In 1978, he was elected to succeed Pope John Paul I as Pope John Paul II, the first non-Italian pope since the sixteenth century. Only three years later, he was shot in an unsuccessful assassination attempt. In his time as pope, Pope John Paul II has addressed the rivalry of the superpowers and the injustices of capitalism. He has opposed birth control, abortion, capital punishment, euthanasia, and genetic engineering. He became the first pope to visit the countries of the former Soviet Union, and he encouraged the establishment of democratic governments in eastern Europe. In recent months, Pope John Paul II has asked Jews and other groups for forgiveness for any injustices committed by the Church in the past. Pope John Paul II will be remembered as a tireless advocate of peace and mercy near the end of the tumultuous twentieth century.

Helmut Kohl (b. 1930)—Helmut Kohl was born in Ludwigshafen in 1930 and later attended university at Frankfurt and Heidelberg. In 1959, Kohl became active in politics as a member of the Christian Democratic Union, or CDU. He became national chairman of the CDU in 1973 and became Chancellor of West Germany in 1982. After the East German government collapsed in 1989, Kohl strongly advocated German reunification. East and West Germany united the following year, and Kohl became the first freely elected chancellor in fifty years.

Tony Blair (b.1953)—Born in Edinburgh in 1953 to a lawyer and politician, Anthony Charles Lynton Blair attended Fettes College and St. John's College at Oxford. At Oxford, Blair developed an interest in politics. Blair went to work as an apprentice for a prominent Labour Party member's law firm where he later earned a full-time position. Blair joined the Labour Party in 1976 but soon became dissatisfied with the direction of the party. Following "Britain's Winter of Discontent" in 1978, Margaret Thatcher's Tory Party moved British politics in a new, conservative direction and away from the traditional liberal Labour policy. Blair won a seat in Parliament in 1983, and by 1994, Blair had risen to such prominence that he was elected Labour Party Leader. He reformed the party's politics by placing a new emphasis on free enterprise. He also helped restructure party goals so that they were more in line with what modern Brits wanted. In 1997, Tony Blair upset the Tory Party and became the new Prime Minister by a huge majority vote. Blair won a second election in 2001 just months before the September 11 terrorist attacks shook the world. Blair immediately positioned Great Britain in a position of support for the United States and condemned those responsible for the attacks. Blair moved to the forefront again when he officially named known terrorist Osama Bin Laden as the perpetrator of the attacks.

CHRONOLOGY OF TWENTIETH-CENTURY EUROPE

1905—Revolution erupted in Russia.

1905–1910—Albert Einstein developed his theory of special relativity.

1914—Archduke Ferdinand was assassinated, thus igniting the Great War.

1914–1918—Europe engaged in World War I, or the Great War.

1919—The Treaty of Versailles ended World War I and planted the seeds for World War II.

1922—Benito Mussolini seized power in Italy.

1928—Stalin began the first of his Five-Year Plans.

1930—Audiences viewed the first talking movies.

1933—Adolf Hitler assumed the position of chancellor in Germany.

1936—Hitler and Mussolini supported Franco in the Spanish Civil War.

1939—Hitler and Stalin signed a secret nonaggression pact.

1939—Hitler invaded Poland and sparked World War II.

1939–1945—Europe, along with Japan and the United States, fought the Second World War.

1948—The Berlin airlift began dropping supplies in Berlin behind a Soviet blockade.

1948—Israel became a nation.

1957—The Russians launched their first Sputnik satellite into orbit.

1960—An American U-2 spy plane was shot down by the Soviets.

1961—The Berlin Wall was erected in Berlin.

1962—The Cuban Missile Crisis took the world to the brink of another world war.

1966—Indira Ghandi replaced Nehru Ghandi as prime minister of India.

1973—The Yom Kippur War was fought between Arabs and Israel.

TIP

Use this chronology to begin to frame the big picture. Chronologies are helpful when you are trying to see how a story unfolds; in this case, the story is that of Twentieth-Century Europe.

1986—A nuclear accident occurred in Chernobyl.

1989—East and West Germany were reunified.

1990—Mikhail Gorbachev received the Nobel Peace Prize.

1991—After numerous Soviet republics declared independence, the Soviet Union dissolved.

CAUTION
These questions are for review purposes only, not to predict the questions that will be on the AP exam.

SAMPLE ESSAY QUESTIONS

Now that you have reviewed the information about Twentieth-Century Europe, take a few moments to read through the sample essay questions that follow. The questions are intended to get you thinking about some of the ways the AP exam may test your knowledge of Twentieth-Century Europe. To completely answer the questions, you will need to draw upon the knowledge you gained during your own course of study in addition to your review with this book.

1. Trace the history of the two revolutions in Russia during the twentieth century. Discuss both the causes and effects of the revolutions.

2. Analyze and discuss the events that led to the outbreak of World War I.

3. Discuss the extent to which the political, philosophical, and economic events of the early twentieth century contributed to the development of the Age of Anxiety.

4. Discuss the extent to which the Treaty of Versailles contributed to the outbreak of World War II.

5. Contrast the warfare of World War I with that of World War II.

6. Compare and contrast the fascist regimes of Adolf Hitler and Benito Mussolini.

7. Trace the history of the Cold War from its beginnings to its "thaw."

8. Analyze and discuss the gradual movement toward a single economic community in Europe during the second half of the twentieth century.

9. Analyze and discuss the monumental events of 1989.

10. "The advancement of women's rights in the twentieth century had its roots in the total war effort of World War I." Assess the validity of this statement.

Enrichment Resources

OVERVIEW

Because every European History course is different, you may or may not be required to use sources outside the scope of your class. You can learn a great deal about European history from sources other than your textbook, and there is a plethora of primary and secondary sources available to you that can enrich your European History experience immeasurably. Primary sources, secondary sources, and even movies can add depth and meaning to your studies. If time permits during your studies, become familiar with as many of these outside sources as possible. The more of these sources you become acquainted with, the more likely you are to see the big picture of European history.

PRIMARY SOURCE READINGS

European history has provided you with a multitude of fascinating documents, some of which are listed for you here. The list is certainly not exhaustive, but many of the most important and most influential documents of the past 600 years are included. Although this list is too long for you to conquer in its entirety during the course of your studies, read as many of these documents as you can, even if you only read selections from the documents. These are the documents that shaped European history. Therefore, the more familiar you are with them, the better your understanding of European history will be.

RECOMMENDED PRIMARY SOURCE READINGS

Boccaccio, Giovanni - *The Decameron*

Burke, Edmund - *Reflections on the Revolution in France*

Calvin, John - *Institutes of the Christian Religion*

Castiglione, Baldassare - *The Book of the Courtier*

Churchill, Winston - Selected Speeches

Darwin, Charles - *Origin of the Species*

Descartes, René - *Discourse on Method*

NOTE

A primary source is generally defined as a source of information that is an eyewitness account or a source that is contemporary to a given event or time. For example, a letter, diary, journal, photograph, or newspaper article from Hawaii in mid-to-late December of 1941 would be a good example of a primary source of information concerning Hawaii after Japan attacked Pearl Harbor. Primary sources are invaluable to historians. Secondary sources are sources based on primary sources or other secondary sources and are not usually contemporary to the event or time. Examples of secondary sources of information on Hawaii after Japan attacked would include encyclopedia articles, textbook information, or CD-ROMs.

Diderot, Denis - *Encyclopedie*

Erasmus, Desiderius - *In Praise of Folly*

Freud, Sigmund - *Civilization and Its Discontents*

Hitler, Adolf - *Mein Kampf*

Hobbes, Thomas - *Leviathan*

Kant, Immanuel - *What is Enlightenment?*

Khrushchev, Nikita - *Secret Speech to Party Congress, February 25, 1956*

Kipling, Rudyard - *The White Man's Burden*

Lenin (Vladimir Ilyich Ulyanov) - *What is to be done?*

Locke, John - *Second Treatise on Government*; *Essay Concerning Human Understanding*

Luther, Martin - *95 Theses*; *On the Jews and their Lies*; *Against the Murderous, Thieving Hordes*

Machiavelli, Niccolo - *The Prince*

Malthus, Thomas - *Essay on the Principle of Population*

Marx, Karl and Frederick Engels - *The Communist Manifesto*

Mill, John Stuart - *On Liberty*; *Utilitarianism*

Mirandola, Pico della - *Oration on the Dignity of Man*

Montaigne, Michel de - *Essays*

Montesquieu, Charles de Secondat, baron de - *The Spirit of Laws*; *The Persian Letters*

More, Thomas - *Utopia*

Nietzsche, Friedrich - *The Will to Power*; *The Antichrist*

Robespierre - *The Terror Justified*

Rousseau, Jean-Jacques - *The Social Contract*

Smith, Adam - *The Wealth of Nations*

Voltaire - *Candide*

Weber, Max - *The Protestant Ethic and the Spirit of Capitalism*

Wiesel, Elie - *Night*; *Dawn*

Wollstonecraft, Mary - *A Vindication of the Rights of Woman*

Wordsworth, William. - *Lyrical Ballads*

Zola, Emile - *The Experimental Novel*

SECONDARY SOURCE READINGS

In addition to the many primary sources from European history, there exists a seemingly endless number of secondary sources that you can read to broaden your horizons. Don't worry—we won't list all of them for you. Instead, a small number of good secondary sources is listed. Any reading you could do in these sources would be beneficial.

SUGGESTED SECONDARY SOURCE READINGS

Brinton, Crane - *Anatomy of a Revolution*

Manchester, William - *A World Lit Only by Fire*

Shirer, William L. - *Rise and Fall of the Third Reich*

Strickland, Carol and John Boswell - *The Annotated Mona Lisa: A Crash Course in Art History from Prehistoric to Post-Modern*

Stromberg, Roland N. - *Modern European Intellectual History*

INTERNET RESOURCES

As you probably already know, you can find information on the Internet about nearly every topic imaginable. European history is no exception. Below are a few that may be helpful for you both during your course of study and while you are preparing for the AP exam.

http://www.collegeboard.com/ap/students/index.html—This is the College Board's official AP European History site. At this site, you can find official information about the course and the exam.

http://www.lib.utexas.edu/Libs/PCL/Map_collection/ Map_collection.html—The University of Texas has collected an extraordinary amount of maps, and many of those are historical maps of Europe.

http://historyplace.com/—This site contains many United States and World History exhibits and links.

http://www.fordham.edu/halsall/mod/modsbook.html—The Internet Modern History Sourcebook contains many full-length documents from modern European and American history. This is a great place to do primary source reading.

http://www.fordham.edu/halsall/sbook.html—The Medieval History Sourcebook contains many full-length documents from medieval European history. This is another great place to read primary sources.

http://historychannel.com/—This site was created by and is maintained by the History Channel. The History Channel site

TIP

If you are searching for a good secondary source of information that will enhance your AP European History experience and further prepare you for the exam, you should choose a source that deals with broad topics or entire eras, such as the ones listed here. Avoid reading secondary sources that are very specific or narrow in scope. For example, a secondary source about Japanese aircraft of World War II will probably not be very beneficial when you take the exam.

contains history exhibits, famous speeches, and more, including a listing of programming on the History Channel.

http://www.killeenroos.com/link/europe.htm—This site was created by students in Killeen Independent School District in Killeen, Texas. This site includes a multitude of links to European history sites on the Internet.

http://www.uflib.ufl.edu/hss/ref/history.html—The University of Florida Humanities and Social Sciences Electronic Reference timelines are a great place to look for chronologies.

http://www.lib.byu.edu/~rdh/eurodocs/homepage.html—Brigham Young University has made available at this site many full-length primary source documents from European history. Yet another great place to find primary source documents.

http://www.pbs.org/neighborhoods/history/—This site was created by and is maintained by PBS. In this particular area of the PBS site, you will find articles, biographies, exhibits, and links related to history.

http://history.hanover.edu/—This site, maintained by Hanover College Department of History, includes a historical text and image archive along with other history information and history links.

http://lcweb.loc.gov/—The Library of Congress maintains a very large Web site that contains many documents, archives, and exhibits on government, history, and more.

http://es.rice.edu/ES/humsoc/Galileo/—The Galileo Project by Rice University contains vast information on the life and times of Galileo.

http://www.academicinfo.net/histeuro.html—The Academic Info: Modern European History site contains numerous links to European history sites on the Internet.

HISTORICAL MOVIES

For many people, one of the most enjoyable ways to learn about history is to watch a movie about a person from another period or a film set against a historical backdrop. Granted, Hollywood often embellishes the facts of a story or uses the film medium to make a statement. Many movies, though, are very accurate portrayals of people and events from different eras in European history. We have listed for you many movies about European history subjects that would enhance what you have read about in your classes. For summaries and all sorts of information about these movies, you should check the Internet Movie Database found at http://www.imdb.com. When you get a chance, sit back with some popcorn, relax, and watch a good European history movie.

HISTORICAL MOVIES LIST

A Man for All Seasons
Amadeus
The Agony and the Ecstasy
All Quiet on the Western Front
Anne of the Thousand Days
Charge of the Light Brigade
Das Boot
The Diary of Anne Frank
Dr. Strangelove
Dr. Zhivago
El Cid
Elizabeth
Europa, Europa
Fire Over England
Gallipoli
Gandhi
Henry V
Immortal Beloved
Joan of Arc
Lady Jane
Last of the Mohicans
Lawrence of Arabia
The Madness of King George
Mary Queen of Scots
The Messenger
Michael Collins
Northwest Passage
Private Life of Henry VIII
Reds
Rob Roy
Saving Private Ryan
Schindler's List
Shakespeare in Love
War and Remembrance

CAUTION

Just because a movie is listed here does not imply that all information in the movie is factual or unbiased. Don't use information from a movie to answer an exam question unless you are absolutely sure of its accuracy.

Practice Tests

PART

3

PREVIEW

PRACTICE TEST 1

Answer Sheet

Section I

1. Ⓐ Ⓑ Ⓒ Ⓓ Ⓔ 17. Ⓐ Ⓑ Ⓒ Ⓓ Ⓔ 33. Ⓐ Ⓑ Ⓒ Ⓓ Ⓔ 49. Ⓐ Ⓑ Ⓒ Ⓓ Ⓔ 65. Ⓐ Ⓑ Ⓒ Ⓓ Ⓔ

2. Ⓐ Ⓑ Ⓒ Ⓓ Ⓔ 18. Ⓐ Ⓑ Ⓒ Ⓓ Ⓔ 34. Ⓐ Ⓑ Ⓒ Ⓓ Ⓔ 50. Ⓐ Ⓑ Ⓒ Ⓓ Ⓔ 66. Ⓐ Ⓑ Ⓒ Ⓓ Ⓔ

3. Ⓐ Ⓑ Ⓒ Ⓓ Ⓔ 19. Ⓐ Ⓑ Ⓒ Ⓓ Ⓔ 35. Ⓐ Ⓑ Ⓒ Ⓓ Ⓔ 51. Ⓐ Ⓑ Ⓒ Ⓓ Ⓔ 67. Ⓐ Ⓑ Ⓒ Ⓓ Ⓔ

4. Ⓐ Ⓑ Ⓒ Ⓓ Ⓔ 20. Ⓐ Ⓑ Ⓒ Ⓓ Ⓔ 36. Ⓐ Ⓑ Ⓒ Ⓓ Ⓔ 52. Ⓐ Ⓑ Ⓒ Ⓓ Ⓔ 68. Ⓐ Ⓑ Ⓒ Ⓓ Ⓔ

5. Ⓐ Ⓑ Ⓒ Ⓓ Ⓔ 21. Ⓐ Ⓑ Ⓒ Ⓓ Ⓔ 37. Ⓐ Ⓑ Ⓒ Ⓓ Ⓔ 53. Ⓐ Ⓑ Ⓒ Ⓓ Ⓔ 69. Ⓐ Ⓑ Ⓒ Ⓓ Ⓔ

6. Ⓐ Ⓑ Ⓒ Ⓓ Ⓔ 22. Ⓐ Ⓑ Ⓒ Ⓓ Ⓔ 38. Ⓐ Ⓑ Ⓒ Ⓓ Ⓔ 54. Ⓐ Ⓑ Ⓒ Ⓓ Ⓔ 70. Ⓐ Ⓑ Ⓒ Ⓓ Ⓔ

7. Ⓐ Ⓑ Ⓒ Ⓓ Ⓔ 23. Ⓐ Ⓑ Ⓒ Ⓓ Ⓔ 39. Ⓐ Ⓑ Ⓒ Ⓓ Ⓔ 55. Ⓐ Ⓑ Ⓒ Ⓓ Ⓔ 71. Ⓐ Ⓑ Ⓒ Ⓓ Ⓔ

8. Ⓐ Ⓑ Ⓒ Ⓓ Ⓔ 24. Ⓐ Ⓑ Ⓒ Ⓓ Ⓔ 40. Ⓐ Ⓑ Ⓒ Ⓓ Ⓔ 56. Ⓐ Ⓑ Ⓒ Ⓓ Ⓔ 72. Ⓐ Ⓑ Ⓒ Ⓓ Ⓔ

9. Ⓐ Ⓑ Ⓒ Ⓓ Ⓔ 25. Ⓐ Ⓑ Ⓒ Ⓓ Ⓔ 41. Ⓐ Ⓑ Ⓒ Ⓓ Ⓔ 57. Ⓐ Ⓑ Ⓒ Ⓓ Ⓔ 73. Ⓐ Ⓑ Ⓒ Ⓓ Ⓔ

10. Ⓐ Ⓑ Ⓒ Ⓓ Ⓔ 26. Ⓐ Ⓑ Ⓒ Ⓓ Ⓔ 42. Ⓐ Ⓑ Ⓒ Ⓓ Ⓔ 58. Ⓐ Ⓑ Ⓒ Ⓓ Ⓔ 74. Ⓐ Ⓑ Ⓒ Ⓓ Ⓔ

11. Ⓐ Ⓑ Ⓒ Ⓓ Ⓔ 27. Ⓐ Ⓑ Ⓒ Ⓓ Ⓔ 43. Ⓐ Ⓑ Ⓒ Ⓓ Ⓔ 59. Ⓐ Ⓑ Ⓒ Ⓓ Ⓔ 75. Ⓐ Ⓑ Ⓒ Ⓓ Ⓔ

12. Ⓐ Ⓑ Ⓒ Ⓓ Ⓔ 28. Ⓐ Ⓑ Ⓒ Ⓓ Ⓔ 44. Ⓐ Ⓑ Ⓒ Ⓓ Ⓔ 60. Ⓐ Ⓑ Ⓒ Ⓓ Ⓔ 76. Ⓐ Ⓑ Ⓒ Ⓓ Ⓔ

13. Ⓐ Ⓑ Ⓒ Ⓓ Ⓔ 29. Ⓐ Ⓑ Ⓒ Ⓓ Ⓔ 45. Ⓐ Ⓑ Ⓒ Ⓓ Ⓔ 61. Ⓐ Ⓑ Ⓒ Ⓓ Ⓔ 77. Ⓐ Ⓑ Ⓒ Ⓓ Ⓔ

14. Ⓐ Ⓑ Ⓒ Ⓓ Ⓔ 30. Ⓐ Ⓑ Ⓒ Ⓓ Ⓔ 46. Ⓐ Ⓑ Ⓒ Ⓓ Ⓔ 62. Ⓐ Ⓑ Ⓒ Ⓓ Ⓔ 78. Ⓐ Ⓑ Ⓒ Ⓓ Ⓔ

15. Ⓐ Ⓑ Ⓒ Ⓓ Ⓔ 31. Ⓐ Ⓑ Ⓒ Ⓓ Ⓔ 47. Ⓐ Ⓑ Ⓒ Ⓓ Ⓔ 63. Ⓐ Ⓑ Ⓒ Ⓓ Ⓔ 79. Ⓐ Ⓑ Ⓒ Ⓓ Ⓔ

16. Ⓐ Ⓑ Ⓒ Ⓓ Ⓔ 32. Ⓐ Ⓑ Ⓒ Ⓓ Ⓔ 48. Ⓐ Ⓑ Ⓒ Ⓓ Ⓔ 64. Ⓐ Ⓑ Ⓒ Ⓓ Ⓔ 80. Ⓐ Ⓑ Ⓒ Ⓓ Ⓔ

Master the AP European History Test

Practice Test 1

Section I of this examination contains 80 multiple-choice questions. Therefore, please be careful to fill in only the ovals that are preceded by numbers 1 through 80 on your answer sheet.

GENERAL INSTRUCTIONS

INDICATE YOUR ANSWERS TO QUESTIONS IN SECTION I ON THE SEPARATE ANSWER SHEET. No credit will be given for anything written in this examination booklet, but you may use the booklet for notes or scratch work. After you have decided which of the suggested answers is best, COMPLETELY fill in the corresponding oval on the answer sheet. Give only one answer to each question. If you change an answer, be sure that the previous mark is erased completely.

Example:

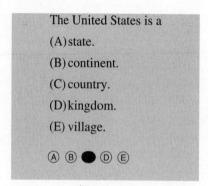

The United States is a

(A) state.

(B) continent.

(C) country.

(D) kingdom.

(E) village.

Many candidates wonder whether or not to guess the answers to questions about which they are not certain. In this section of the examination, as a correction for haphazard guessing, one fourth of the number of questions you answer incorrectly will be subtracted from the number of questions you answer correctly. It is improbable, therefore, that mere guessing will increase your score significantly; it may even lower your score, and it does take time. If, however, you are not sure of the best answer but have some knowledge of the question and are able to eliminate one or more of the answer choices as wrong, your chance of getting the right answer is improved, and it may be to your advantage to answer such a question.

Use your time effectively, working as rapidly as you can without losing accuracy. Do not spend too much time on questions that are too difficult. Go on to other questions and come back to the difficult ones later if you have time. It is not expected that everyone will be able to answer all multiple-choice questions.

SECTION I—MULTIPLE CHOICE

80 Questions • Time—55 Minutes

Directions: Each of the questions or incomplete statements below is followed by five suggested answers or completions. Select the one that is best in each case, and then fill in the corresponding oval on the answer sheet.

1. "A prince therefore who desires to maintain himself must learn to be not always good, but to be so or not as necessity may require." This statement is typical of the writings of which of the following?

    (A) Castiglione

    (B) Erasmus

    (C) Machiavelli

    (D) Petrarch

    (E) Boccaccio

2. On the issue of salvation, Martin Luther differed from the Catholic Church in that he believed

    (A) salvation was obtained through good works alone.

    (B) salvation was obtained through good works and faith.

    (C) salvation was predetermined by God.

    (D) salvation was available only through the Church.

    (E) salvation could be obtained through faith alone.

3. Women were frequently tried and executed as witches for all of the following reasons EXCEPT

    (A) their repeated acts of violence.

    (B) their neighbors suspected the women of witchcraft.

    (C) their communities feared the women worshipped the Devil.

    (D) their neighbors feared the women engaged in sexual activities with the Devil.

    (E) the prevailing misogyny of the period.

4. King Louis XIV of France provides perhaps the best example of the form of government known as

    (A) despotism.

    (B) absolutism

    (C) constitutional monarchy.

    (D) fascism.

    (E) representative democracy.

5. The intellectuals that dominated the thought of the Enlightenment were known as

   (A) scholastica.

   (B) philosophes.

   (C) Encyclopedie.

   (D) Romantics.

   (E) empiricists.

6. The Industrial Revolution, which began in the late eighteenth century, began in

   (A) France.

   (B) Germany.

   (C) Russia.

   (D) the Low Countries.

   (E) Great Britain.

7. The event that triggered the outbreak of World War I was

   (A) Germany's return to unrestricted submarine warfare.

   (B) the collapse of the Three Emperor's League.

   (C) the assassination of Archduke Francis Ferdinand.

   (D) the Bloody Sunday massacre.

   (E) failure of the Treaty of Versailles.

8. During World War II, the Alliance of Germany, Italy, and Japan was known as

   (A) the Entente Cordiale.

   (B) the Allied Powers.

   (C) the Triple Alliance.

   (D) the Axis Powers.

   (E) the Eastern Bloc.

9. The Supremacy Act of 1534

   (A) declared the king the official head of the Church of England.

   (B) revoked the Edict of Nantes.

   (C) declared the Pope the supreme religious figure in England.

   (D) declared the Bible the supreme source of religious authority.

   (E) closed the monasteries and led to a more equitable distribution of land in England.

10. Generally speaking, after the Thirty Years' War,

    (A) the Holy Roman Empire was strengthened.

    (B) the German princes were granted sovereignty and the Holy
        Roman Empire collapsed.

    (C) Calvinism was prohibited throughout Germany.

    (D) the pope was allowed to intervene in German religious affairs.

    (E) Germany was unified.

11. The Glorious Revolution (1688–1689) was significant because

    (A) William and Mary led a successful revolt among the
        English peasants.

    (B) it reinstated the idea of the divine right of kings.

    (C) the Parliament was suppressed by royal authority.

    (D) of the excessive violence necessary to succeed in its attempt to
        overthrow the king.

    (E) the idea of divine right was destroyed, and one monarch was
        replaced by another with minimal bloodshed.

12. This painting most likely depicts

    (A) the trial of an alleged witch.

    (B) the licensing of a prostitute in early modern Europe.

    (C) an anatomy lesson during the Scientific Revolution.

    (D) the examination of a native from the New World during the Age
        of Exploration and Expansion.

    (E) the public ostracizing of a woman who posed nude for a painting
        during the Renaissance.

13. The phrase "I am the state" best characterizes the reign of
    (A) William and Mary.
    (B) Louis XIV.
    (C) Victor Emmanuel III.
    (D) Otto von Bismarck.
    (E) Helmut Kohl.

14. The philosopher who first doubted all but the power of his own reason and deduced the existence of God was
    (A) René Descartes.
    (B) Blaise Pascal.
    (C) Sir Francis Bacon.
    (D) Sir Isaac Newton.
    (E) Baruch Spinoza.

15. The industry that paved the way for the Industrial Revolution was the
    (A) steel industry.
    (B) agricultural industry.
    (C) textile industry.
    (D) luxury goods industry.
    (E) shipbuilding industry.

16. The Tennis Court Oath symbolized
    (A) the resolve of the National Assembly to create a new constitution.
    (B) the desire of the National Assembly to behead the king and queen.
    (C) the resolve of the First and Second Estates to resist change.
    (D) the resolve of the monarchy to resist change.
    (E) the determination of Robespierre to eliminate all enemies of the state.

17. An experimental utopian socialist society was built in New Harmony, Indiana, in the 1820s by
    (A) Robert Owen.
    (B) Karl Marx.
    (C) Friedrich Engels.
    (D) Thomas More.
    (E) Flora Tristan.

18. Strides were made in nineteenth-century health care by

    (A) returning to traditional methods of treatment and prevention.

    (B) practicing methods formerly used by midwives and rural health-care professionals.

    (C) mixing religion and science to prove a holistic approach to medicine.

    (D) reviving classical ideas about health and sickness.

    (E) employing rational methods of treating and preventing diseases.

19. Popular unrest, mass exodus, and mass demonstrations against the repressive measures of Erich Honecker in 1989 led to

    (A) retaliatory measures by Honecker's secret police.

    (B) intervention into East German affairs by the United States.

    (C) the strengthening of the East German government.

    (D) the arrest of Solidarity leaders, including Lech Walesa.

    (E) the collapse of the Communist Party and the destruction of the Berlin Wall.

20. The English Star Chamber was

    (A) the first astronomer's observatory of the Scientific Revolution.

    (B) a court designed to end the influence of powerful nobles on the English courts.

    (C) a room for the torture of Protestants under the control of Bloody Mary Tudor.

    (D) the room designated for the trial of those suspected of witchcraft.

    (E) established to increase the power of the English nobility.

21. Calvinists in France were known as

    (A) Anabaptists.

    (B) Trinitarians.

    (C) Unitarians.

    (D) Huguenots.

    (E) Presbyterians.

22. The eighteenth-century European family household typically

    (A) was a nuclear family.

    (B) included grandparents and great-grandparents.

    (C) included three to five other families.

    (D) consisted of ten to twelve family members.

    (E) consisted of an unmarried couple.

European Emigrants, 1851-1960

Nations of Origin

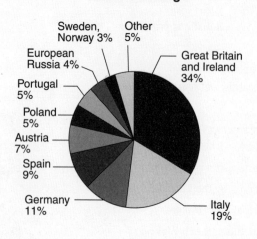

Nations of Destination

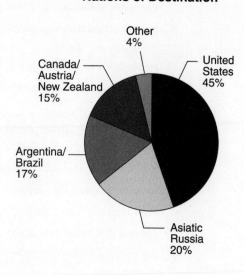

23. This graph illustrates

    (A) the economic impact of the Great Depression.

    (B) the devastating effects of the bubonic plague.

    (C) the pattern of the Great Migration.

    (D) the rise of capitalism.

    (E) national participation in World War II.

24. Adolf Hitler learned from Benito Mussolini's example that

    (A) he should establish fascist government through a military coup.

    (B) fascism did not have to be violent.

    (C) he should first gain political power through legal measures before establishing a totalitarian state.

    (D) women were not inferior to men.

    (E) Jews, Catholics, and homosexuals should be eliminated.

25. "Man is nothing else but what he makes of himself." This statement is the first principle of

    (A) abstract expressionism.

    (B) transcendentalism.

    (C) existentialism.

    (D) atheism.

    (E) postmodernism.

26. In response to the German Peasant Revolts of 1524–1525, Luther

    (A) encouraged the peasants to seek political freedom similar to their spiritual freedom.

    (B) encouraged the princes to crush revolts.

    (C) encouraged the princes to grant the peasants' wishes.

    (D) encouraged the peasants to peacefully petition the princes with their desires.

    (E) encouraged the papacy to grant the peasants' wishes.

27. This illustration most likely depicts

    (A) the destructive power of witches.

    (B) the devastating results of total war.

    (C) the aftermath of the Great Lisbon Earthquake.

    (D) the effects of nuclear warfare.

    (E) the nuclear disaster at Chernobyl.

28. During the presidential elections of 1848 in France, a war veteran spoke of whom when he said, "Why shouldn't I vote for this gentleman? I, whose nose was frozen near Moscow?"

    (A) Louis XVI

    (B) Louis-Philippe

    (C) Louis Napoleon

    (D) Richard Dreyfus

    (E) Louis XIV

29. The leader of the group known as the Red Shirts was

    (A) Victor Emmanuel III.

    (B) Giuseppe Mazzini.

    (C) Camillo de Cavour.

    (D) Giuseppe Garibaldi.

    (E) Benito Mussolini.

30. One of the outstanding new developments of Romantic music by musicians such as Franz Liszt was

    (A) the use of music to express a literary or pictorial concept or idea.

    (B) the use of random, atonal music.

    (C) the cold, unemotional use of music.

    (D) the return to traditional forms.

    (E) the removal of the piano from the orchestra.

31. By the early twentieth century, art and literature began to reflect many people's notions that

    (A) the world needed to return to religion to restore hope and order.

    (B) reality was to be perceived according to a few universal truths.

    (C) the purpose of art and literature was to recreate reality as accurately as possible.

    (D) the reason and rationality of the past was to be necessary for man's progression in the future.

    (E) reality may not be what they had once believed, especially in light of the new physics and new psychology.

32. In the years prior to World War I, the entity most perceived by Austria-Hungary as a threat to its empire was

    (A) Russia.

    (B) Germany.

    (C) France.

    (D) Serbia.

    (E) the Ottoman Empire.

33. All of the following are tenets of John Calvin's theology EXCEPT

    (A) perseverance of the saints.

    (B) total depravity of man.

    (C) unconditional predestination.

    (D) infallibility of the Church.

    (E) limited atonement.

34. All of the following were true of the Council of Trent (1545–1563) EXCEPT

    (A) authority of local bishops was increased.

    (B) the selling of church offices was restricted.

    (C) no doctrinal concessions were made to the Protestants.

    (D) steps were taken to enhance the image and abilities of local parish priests.

    (E) the rules requiring priests to remain celibate were relaxed and, in some cases, revoked.

35. The Peace of Utrecht (1713–1714)

    (A) established the dominance of France after the War of the Spanish Succession.

    (B) laid the foundations for the French dominance of Europe during the eighteenth century.

    (C) established a balance of power in Europe and ended French dominance.

    (D) established Catholicism as the one true religion in the Nether lands.

    (E) greatly reduced the holdings of Great Britain in North America.

36. Sir Francis Bacon advocated

    (A) reliance on scholastic traditions and knowledge from antiquity.

    (B) the understanding of nature through mathematical laws.

    (C) deductive reasoning.

    (D) examination of empirical evidence.

    (E) the idea that most truth had already been discovered.

37. In the time during and after the French Revolution, the French Catholic clergy were alienated most by

    (A) the elimination of tax exemptions for the First Estate.

    (B) the state's seizure of Church property.

    (C) the Declaration of the Rights of Man and the Citizen.

    (D) the involvement of women in the revolutionary activities.

    (E) the Civil Constitution of the Clergy.

38. John Wesley's ministry primarily involved

    (A) writing pamphlets and tracts.

    (B) preaching in open fields.

    (C) teaching in universities.

    (D) preaching hellfire and brimstone sermons from the pulpit.

    (E) caring for the sick in the slums of the urban areas.

39. The two major factors in the onset of the Great Depression were

(A) the collapse of the American stock market and the slowing of national economies.

(B) the slowing of national economies and the rise in unemployment.

(C) the collapse of the American stock market and the collapse of the Credit-Anstalt.

(D) the collapse of the Credit-Anstalt and the rise of unemployment.

(E) the skyrocketing unemployment rate worldwide and the secret treaties between European powers.

40. The Edict of Nantes, issued by Henry IV in 1598, effectively

(A) outlawed Protestantism in France.

(B) restricted Protestantism to rural areas of France.

(C) granted religious freedom to Protestants in France.

(D) ended papal authority in France.

(E) ignited the French Wars of Religion.

41. The building in the picture was most likely constructed to

(A) honor the gods represented by the statues around the fountain.

(B) intimidate and impress foreign dignitaries.

(C) provide safety and protection.

(D) recreate classical architecture.

(E) serve as a public works project that would provide jobs for the unemployed.

42. The dominance of Napoleon helped inspire in subjugated lands feelings of

   (A) loyalty to Napoleon.

   (B) intense religious revival.

   (C) nationalism.

   (D) respect for the Catholic Church.

   (E) a deep appreciation for French culture.

43. "I grieve, when on the darker side

   Of this great change I look; and there behold

   Such outrage done to nature as compels

   The indignant power to justify herself."

   This poem is most characteristic of

   (A) Michel de Montaigne.

   (B) Miguel de Cervantes.

   (C) Vaclav Havel.

   (D) Friedrich Nietzsche.

   (E) William Wordsworth.

44. The German Schlieffen Plan during World War I called for

   (A) German troops to maintain a defensive position in case of an attack by Russian forces.

   (B) German troops to be positioned for a battle on both the eastern and western fronts.

   (C) Germany to be allied with Russia in case Austria-Hungary attacked the Balkans.

   (D) a total war effort on the homefront.

   (E) the unconditional surrender of Germany's enemies.

45. Joseph Stalin's five-year plans were designed to

   (A) turn Russia into an industrial power.

   (B) make Russia the world's leading agricultural producer.

   (C) put Russian astronauts in orbit before the Americans.

   (D) empower the kulaks.

   (E) spread Communism to capitalist nations within five years.

46. The Dayton Accords of 1995

    (A) split Bosnia into two separate states.

    (B) authorized NATO forces to use force in Chechnya if needed.

    (C) decelerated the international nuclear arms race.

    (D) granted significant amounts of financial aid to Russia and states of the former Soviet Union.

    (E) created the European Union.

47. In the mid-eighteenth century, the leading banking center of Europe was

    (A) Florence.

    (B) Milan.

    (C) Amsterdam.

    (D) Vienna.

    (E) Prague.

48. The family that ruled Russia from the 1600s until 1917 was the

    (A) Muscovites.

    (B) Hohenzollerns.

    (C) Romanovs.

    (D) Brezhnevs.

    (E) Habsburgs.

49. The philosophy of the *philosophes* conflicted with the theology of the Church because

    (A) the *philosophes* believed that humanity could not be improved and the Church did.

    (B) the *philosophes* were not concerned with matters of this world but matters of the world beyond this one.

    (C) the *philosophes* disapproved of the scientific study of humanity as advocated by the Church.

    (D) the *philosophes* believed the Church was too open to new ideas.

    (E) the *philosophes* believed that humanity was not depraved and could be improved, as opposed to the view of the Church.

50. Prior to the French Revolution, the First Estate owned approximately what percent of the land of France?

    (A) 10 percent

    (B) 25 percent

    (C) 50 percent

    (D) 75 percent

    (E) 90 percent

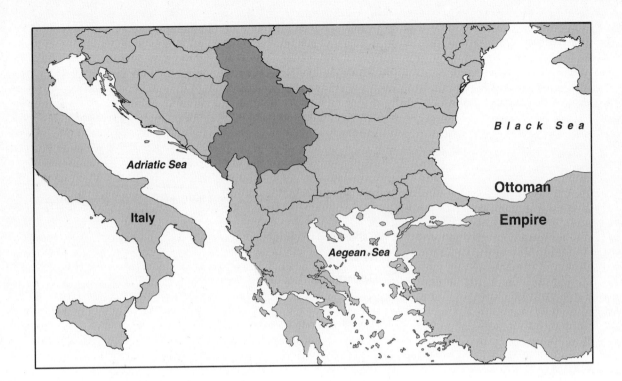

51. This map most likely depicts

    (A) the Ottoman Empire prior to the Crimean War.

    (B) the Ottoman Empire after the Crimean War.

    (C) the Balkans in 1914.

    (D) the Balkans in 1995.

    (E) Germany prior to 1871.

52. Hitler's hatred of the Jews was no secret, but Hitler also despised

    (A) the Anglo-Saxon European.

    (B) the Scandinavians.

    (C) the Italians.

    (D) the French.

    (E) the Slavs.

53. The reduction of international tension through diplomacy and trade is best defined as

    (A) perestroika.

    (B) solidarity.

    (C) glastnost.

    (D) appeasement.

    (E) détente.

54. The issue that drove a wedge between the French people in 1954 and nearly cost Charles de Gaulle his country was

(A) the independence of Algeria.

(B) the independence of Morocco and Tunisia.

(C) the destalinization of the Soviet Union.

(D) the Dreyfus Affair.

(E) the youth revolt in Paris.

55. The two thinkers who were the most influential forerunners of the Enlightenment were

(A) Galileo and Copernicus.

(B) Newton and Galileo.

(C) Descartes and Locke.

(D) Descartes and Newton.

(E) Newton and Locke.

56. The phrase *enlightened absolutism* is most often associated with

(A) Louis XIV and Frederick William I of Prussia.

(B) Charles V and Catherine the Great.

(C) Catherine the Great and Joseph II of Austria.

(D) William and Mary of England.

(E) Joseph I and Joseph II of Austria.

57. The Frenchman Joseph de Maistre would most likely agree that

(A) society was an agreement between the governed and the government.

(B) only an absolute monarch could maintain control and order in the wake of events like the French Revolution.

(C) the government's key function was the preservation of its citizens' basic natural rights.

(D) absolute monarchs had no place in the eighteenth and nineteenth centuries.

(E) democracy was superior to monarchy.

58. All of the following were true of Camillo de Cavour EXCEPT

(A) he favored a constitutional government in Italy.

(B) he encouraged economic development by expanding industry.

(C) he encouraged economic development by building railroads and canals.

(D) he spent large amounts of money to build and equip a large army.

(E) he enlisted the help of Austria to declare war on Napoleon III.

59. The nineteenth century concept of the germ theory

    (A) inspired the germ warfare used in the twentieth century.

    (B) was incorrect in asserting that germs were non-living organisms.

    (C) was developed by Marie Curie and ultimately won her the Nobel Prize.

    (D) implied that diseases were caused by living organisms.

    (E) had no impact in hospital treatment and surgical procedures.

60. The most significant decision made at the Teheran Conference in 1943 was

    (A) to partition Germany after the war.

    (B) to drop an atomic bomb on Japan.

    (C) to invade Normandy.

    (D) to build a wall in Berlin after the war.

    (E) to invade Germany from the east and west.

61. The Labour Party, which defeated Churchill's Conservative Party after World War II, created in Britain what was best described as

    (A) a democracy.

    (B) a republic.

    (C) a capitalist state.

    (D) a communist state.

    (E) a welfare state.

62. The Hohenzollerns were

    (A) representatives in the *Reichstag*.

    (B) representatives in the duma.

    (C) rulers of Prussia known for their social fairness and economic freedoms.

    (D) rulers of Prussia known for their weak military and poor administration.

    (E) rulers of Prussia characterized by military strength and discipline.

63. All of the following were reforms of Peter the Great EXCEPT

    (A) secularization of the Russian church.

    (B) replacement of the government ministers with bureaus to more effectively manage taxes and economic affairs.

    (C) establishment of new industries in Russia.

    (D) the elimination of all Western ideas and influences in Russia.

    (E) the subordination of the *boyars*.

64. All of the following are true of deism EXCEPT
  (A) it is emotional and irrational.
  (B) it is tolerant.
  (C) it allows for and encourages virtuous living.
  (D) it is reasonable.
  (E) it is empirical.

65. Napoleon's armies were significant because
  (A) of their sheer numbers and strength.
  (B) Napoleon successfully used mercenaries to win numerous battles.
  (C) they were not composed of conscripts.
  (D) they successfully fought for someone in whom they did not believe and for a nation to whom they were not loyal.
  (E) they were trained abroad and then brought back to France for battle.

66. The government of France after the July Revolution of 1830 could best be described as
  (A) mutually beneficial to the upper and lower classes.
  (B) beneficial only to the upper middle class.
  (C) beneficial only to the workers.
  (D) one of near-miraculous economic prosperity.
  (E) an absolute monarchy.

67. Turner, Friedrich, and Delacroix were painters of which of the following movements?
  (A) Romanticism
  (B) Neoclassicism
  (C) Impressionism
  (D) Dadaism
  (E) Cubism

68. All of the following can be said of Russian peasants after Czar Alexander II emancipated them in 1861 EXCEPT
  (A) they could own property.
  (B) they could marry freely.
  (C) they were completely free.
  (D) they could bring cases before the courts.
  (E) they could purchase land that had been made available to them.

69. Although the ostensible cause for the removal of Khrushchev from office was his deteriorating health, the real reason for his removal was

    (A) his renunciation of Stalin.

    (B) his failed economic policies.

    (C) his increased contact with the Western world.

    (D) his personality.

    (E) the abuse and corruption he practiced while he was in office.

70. Through the teachings and work of John Knox, the ideas of John Calvin spread to Scotland in the form of

    (A) Anglicanism.

    (B) Methodism.

    (C) Anabaptism.

    (D) Presbyterianism.

    (E) Catholicism.

71. The Prussian leader during the eighteenth century who was obsessed with all things military was

    (A) Frederick William I.

    (B) Franz Joseph.

    (C) Catherine the Great.

    (D) Peter the Great.

    (E) Maria Theresa.

72. "The ordinary means therefore to increase our wealth and treasure is by Foreign Trade wherein we must ever observe this rule; to sell more to strangers yearly than we consume of theirs in value." This statement best explains which of the following?

    (A) Imperialism

    (B) Socialism

    (C) Communism

    (D) Mercantilism

    (E) Protectionism

73. The declaration of Notre Dame Cathedral as a Temple of Reason and the renaming of the days and months were measures taken by the Republic of Virtue to

    (A) make the common people forget their old way of life.

    (B) dechristianize the republic.

    (C) satisfy the demands of the *sans-culottes*.

    (D) unite the provinces with the revolutionary forces of the capital.

    (E) unite both the clerical and secular factions of the republic.

74. Women tended to be especially oppressed in
    (A) Russia under Lenin.
    (B) Russia under Stalin.
    (C) Germany under the Weimar Republic.
    (D) Italy under Mussolini.
    (E) France under de Gaulle.

75. One of the main reasons for the success of Lech Walesa's Solidarity movement was
    (A) the enormous amount of funding it received from the United Nations.
    (B) the large military following Walesa amassed.
    (C) the support of other Eastern bloc governments.
    (D) the support of the Catholic Church.
    (E) the support of the Polish government.

76. The English Game Laws were examples of
    (A) legislation designed to reduce the economic burden of the peasantry.
    (B) laws that enabled Parliament to produce revenue by charging the peasants for hunting licenses.
    (C) legislation that banned medieval tournaments.
    (D) legislation that allowed hunting on the king's land only in order to feed families and not for profit.
    (E) class legislation that benefited only the gentry.

77. The last great outbreak of which of the following diseases took place in France in 1720?
    (A) Smallpox
    (B) Dysentery
    (C) Bubonic plague
    (D) Influenza
    (E) Typhus

78. In response to the revolutionary activities in France, many European governments

    (A) ignored the events.

    (B) offered to lend assistance to the revolutionaries.

    (C) instituted repressive domestic policies to prevent the spread of the revolutionary fervor.

    (D) did not see the danger in the ideas of the revolutionaries in France.

    (E) signed treaties of nonaggression with both the old regime and the revolutionary forces.

79. The significant increase in crime rates across Europe in the early nineteenth century is most likely attributable to

    (A) the collapse of governments across Europe.

    (B) the inefficiency of local justice under the absolute rulers of Europe.

    (C) the increase in wealth due to industrialization and the jealousy of the few poor who remained.

    (D) the undesirable living conditions of the increasingly large number of poor as a result of urban overcrowding.

    (E) the increased number of secret political societies and student groups.

80. Between 1871 and 1914, the two European countries LEAST likely to rally were

    (A) France and Great Britain.

    (B) Austria-Hungary and Russia.

    (C) Germany and Italy.

    (D) France and Germany.

    (E) Great Britain and Russia.

SECTION II—FREE RESPONSE

Time—2 hours and 10 minutes

Percent of Total Grade—50

GENERAL INSTRUCTIONS

Reading Period—15 minutes: All students should read and plan their answer to Part A, Question 1, the document-based essay question. If time permits, they may also read the essay questions in Part B.

Part A Suggested writing time—45 minutes: All students must answer Question 1.

Part B Suggested planning and writing time—35 minutes: Answer ONE question from Group 1; 35 minutes: Answer ONE question from Group 2.

Section II of this examination requires answers in essay form. The supervisor will announce the time for starting and ending the reading period. To help you use your time efficiently, the supervisor will also announce the time at which the writing for Part A should be completed. Be careful not to exceed the writing time suggested for Part A. If you do so, you may endanger your grade on the whole examination. If you finish writing Part A before time is announced, you may go on to plan and write Part B. If you finish the examination in less than the time allotted, you may go back and work on either Part A or Part B. Keep in mind that in an essay, you should pay attention to the organization of your material, the validity and clarity of your general statements, and the intelligent and appropriate use of facts to support your generalizations.

You should write your answers with a pen, preferably one with black or dark blue ink. Be sure to write CLEARLY and LEGIBLY. Cross out any errors you make.

The questions for Section II are printed in the green insert. Use the green insert to organize your answers and for scratchwork, but *write your answers in the pink booklet.* Number each answer as the question is numbered in the examination. Do not skip lines. Begin each answer on a new page in the pink booklet.

After you have completed the examination, circle Question 1 and the numbers of the two questions you answered in Part B.

PART A

Suggested Writing Time—45 minutes

Percent of Section II Score—45

Directions: The following question is based on the accompanying documents 1–13. (Some of the documents have been edited for the purpose of this exercise.) Write your answer on the lined pages of the pink essay booklet.

This question is designed to test your ability to work with historical documents. As you analyze the documents, *take into account both the sources of the documents and the authors' points of view*. Write an essay on the following topic that integrates your analysis of the documents. **Do not simply summarize the documents individually**. You may refer to relevant historical facts and developments not mentioned in the documents.

1. Analyze and discuss the issue and the positions held by the two sides involved in the debate over Galileo's support of the Copernican theory of the universe.

Historical Background: In 1543, Nicolaus Copernicus published *On the Revolution of Heavenly Bodies* in which he explained that the reason for planetary motion was the central location of the sun and not of the earth. In 1609, Galileo Galilei created a telescope and claimed to have found evidence that supported the Copernican theory.

Document 1

From the *King James Bible*

Then spake Joshua to the Lord in the day when the Lord delivered up the Amorites before the children of Israel, and he said in the sight of Israel, Sun stand thou still upon Gibeon; and thou, Moon, in the valley of Ajalon. And the sun stood still, and the moon stayed, until the people had avenged themselves upon their enemies. Is not this written in the book of Jashar? So the sun stood still in the midst of heaven, and hastened not to go down about a whole day. *(Joshua, 10:12-13)*

The sun also ariseth, and the sun goeth down, and hasteth to its place where it ariseth again. *(Ecclesiastes I:5)*

Behold, I will bring again the shadow of the degrees which is gone down in the sun dial of Ahaz, ten degrees backward. So the sun returned ten degrees, by which degrees it was gone down. *(Isaiah 38:8)*

Document 2

From a Consultant's Report on Copernicanism in February 1616

Proposition to be assessed:

(1)   The sun is the center of the world and completely devoid of local motion. Assessment: All said that this proposition is foolish and absurd in philosophy, and formally heretical since it explicitly contradicts many places the sense of Holy Scripture, according to the literal meaning of the words and according to the common interpretation and understanding of the Holy Fathers and the doctors of theology.

(2)   The earth is not the center of the world, nor motionless, but it moves as a whole and also with diurnal motion. Assessment: All said that this proposition receives the same judgment in philosophy and that in regard to theological truth it is at least erroneous in faith.

Document 3

Cardinal Bellarmine's observations about the Church

. . . the Council [of Trent] prohibits interpreting Scripture contrary to the common agreement of the Holy Fathers; and if [you] would read not only all their works but also the modern commentaries. . . you will find that all agree in expounding literally that the Sun is in the heavens and travels swiftly around the Earth, while the Earth is far from the heavens and remains motionless in the center of the world. Now consider, with your sense of prudence, whether the Church could support giving Scripture a meaning contrary to the Holy Fathers and to all the Greek and Latin expositors.

Document 4

A statement from Cardinal Bellarmine on Galileo's ideas

I say that if a real proof be found that the sun is fixed and does not revolve round the earth, but the earth round the sun, then it will be necessary, very carefully, to proceed to the explanation of the passages of Scripture which appear to be contrary, and we should rather say that we have misunderstood these than pronounce that to be false which is demonstrated. But I will not believe that there is such a demonstration, until it is shown to me.

Document 5

From a letter from Cardinal Bellarmine to Foscarini

I say that, as you know, the Council prohibits interpreting Scripture against the common consensus of the Holy Fathers; and if Your Paternity wants to read not only the Holy Fathers, but also the modern commentaries on Genesis, the Psalms, Ecclesiastes, and Joshua, you will find all agreeing in the literal interpretation that the sun is in heaven and turns around the earth with great speed, and that the earth is very far from heaven and sits motionless at the center of the world.

Document 6

From a report issued by theological consultants to the Inquisition in 1616

. . . foolish and absurd in philosophy, and formally heretical since it explicitly contradicts in many places the sense of Holy Scripture, according to the literal meaning of the words and according to the common interpretation and understanding of the Holy Fathers and the doctors of theology. . .

Document 7

From the sentencing hearing of Galileo's trial

Furthermore, so that this serious and pernicious error and transgression of yours does not remain completely unpunished, and so that you will be more cautious in the future and an example for others to abstain from similar crimes, we order that the book *Dialogue* by Galileo Galilei be prohibited by public edict.

We condemn you to formal imprisonment in this Holy Office at our pleasure. As a salutary penance we impose on you to recite the seven penitential Psalms once a week for the next three years. And we reserve the authority to moderate, change, or condone wholly or in part the above-mentioned penalties and penances.

Document 8

From the Jesuits on Galileo

If Galileo had only known how to retain the favor of the fathers of this college, he would have stood in renown before the world; he would have been spared all his misfortunes, and could have written about everything, even about the motion of the earth.

Document 9

From Galileo's *Considerations on the Copernican Theory* in 1615

Let us now see in what kind of hypothesis Copernicus places the earth's motion and sun's stability. There is no doubt whatever…that he places them among the primary and necessary suppositions about nature.

We should therefore understand clearly that Copernicus takes the earth's motion and sun's stability for no other reason and in no other way than to establish it, in the manner of the natural philosopher, as a hypothesis of the primary sort.

Document 10

From Galileo on the Church's attacks on the Copernican theory

Consider now those who persist in wanting to say that as an astronomer Copernicus considered the earth's motion and the sun's stability only a hypothesis that is more adequate to save celestial appearances and to calculate the motions of planets, but that he did not believe it to be true in reality and in nature. With all due respect, these people show that they have been too prone to believe the word of someone who speaks more out of whim than out of experience with Copernicus's book or understanding the nature of this business. For this reason they talk about it in a way that is not altogether right.

Document 11

From Galileo on the Church's attack on him

Finally, now that one is discovering how well-founded upon clear observations and necessary demonstrations this doctrine is, some persons come along who, without having seen the book, give its author the reward of so much work by trying to have him declared a heretic; this they do only in order to satisfy their special animosity, groundlessly conceived against someone else [Galileo, himself] who has no greater connection with Copernicus than the endorsement of his doctrine.

Document 12

From Galileo

If the earth de facto moves, we cannot change nature and arrange for it not to move. But we can rather easily remove the opposition of Scripture with the mere admission that we do not grasp its true meaning. Therefore, the way to be sure not to err is to begin with astronomical and physical investigations, and not with scriptural ones.

Document 13

From Galileo's book *Dialogue Concerning the Two Chief World Systems* in 1632

Take care, theologians, that in wishing to make matters of faith of the propositions attendant on the motion and stillness of the Sun and the Earth, in time you probably risk the danger of condemning for heresy those who assert the Earth stands firm and the Sun moves; in time, I say, when sensately or necessarily it will be demonstrated that the Earth moves and the Sun stands still.

PART B

Suggested Planning and Writing Time—70 minutes

Percent of Section II Score—55

> Directions: You are to answer TWO questions, one from each group of three questions below. Make your selections carefully, choosing the questions that you are best prepared to answer thoroughly in the time permitted. You should spend 5 minutes organizing or outlining each essay. In writing your essays, *use specific examples to support your answer*. Write your answers to the questions on the lined pages of the pink essay booklet. If time permits when you finish writing, check your work. Be certain to number your answers as the questions are numbered below.

Group 1

Choose ONE question from this group. The suggested writing time for this question is 30 minutes. *You are advised to spend 5 minutes planning your answer in the space provided.*

2. Evaluate the art of the Renaissance as a reflection of the values and ideals of the Renaissance era.

3. Compare and contrast the general trends in the feudalism of eastern and western Europe prior to, during, and after the Black Death.

4. Analyze and discuss the economic and social consequences of the Industrial Revolution. Include a treatment of the major developments of the Industrial Revolution and the consequences of those developments.

Group 2

Choose ONE question from this group. The suggested writing time for this question is 30 minutes. *You are advised to spend 5 minutes planning your answer in the space provided.*

5. "The second half of the nineteenth century could be accurately called the Age of Nationalism." Assess the validity of this statement.

6. Discuss the causes of the Russian Revolution as well as the long-term effects of the Revolution not only in Russia but also in the rest of Europe.

7. Analyze and discuss the extent to which the events following World War I contributed to the outbreak of World War II.

Answers and Explanations

Quick-Score Answers

1. C	11. E	21. D	31. E	41. B	51. C	61. E	71. A
2. E	12. A	22. A	32. D	42. C	52. E	62. E	72. D
3. A	13. B	23. C	33. D	43. E	53. E	63. D	73. B
4. B	14. A	24. C	34. E	44. B	54. A	64. A	74. D
5. B	15. C	25. C	35. C	45. A	55. E	65. A	75. D
6. E	16. A	26. B	36. D	46. A	56. C	66. B	76. E
7. C	17. A	27. C	37. E	47. C	57. B	67. A	77. C
8. D	18. E	28. C	38. B	48. C	58. E	68. C	78. C
9. A	19. E	29. D	39. A	49. E	59. D	69. B	79. D
10. B	20. B	30. A	40. C	50. A	60. A	70. D	80. D

1. **The correct answer is (C).** Machiavelli's *The Prince* illustrated his view of humanity by instructing the prince, or ruler, that he should manipulate people as necessary in order to obtain and maintain power.

2. **The correct answer is (E).** Martin Luther believed that faith was the means by which man received God's grace and that there was nothing man could do to earn that grace.

3. **The correct answer is (A).** Women were usually tried as witches because of the suspicions and fears of others. Historians agree that those accused of witchcraft were rarely guilty of anything worse than having an unexplainable illness or being in the wrong place at the wrong time.

4. **The correct answer is (B).** Louis XIV exemplified absolutism through his command of the state's economy, control of the state's religion, maintenance of a permanent standing army, and claim of rule by divine right.

5. **The correct answer is (B).** The Enlightenment reached its zenith in France, and *philosophe* is the French word for philosopher. The *philosophes* were not only the most influential Enlightenment thinkers but also some of the most influential thinkers in European history.

6. **The correct answer is (E).** Because of the available natural resources, the abundance of rivers and canals, agricultural surplus, and the growing market in the Americas, the Industrial Revolution first appeared in Great Britain.

7. **The correct answer is (C).** On June 28, 1914, a Serbian nationalist assassinated Archduke Francis Ferdinand, the heir to the Austro-Hungarian throne. Austria-Hungary presented Serbia with a punitive ultimatum and then invaded; this was the first act of World War I.

8. **The correct answer is (D).** In 1936, Italy and Germany joined in an alliance, and Japan joined the alliance soon after. These nations became known as the Axis Powers, taking the name from the original Rome-Berlin Axis of Italy and Germany.

9. **The correct answer is (A).** Henry VIII used the Reformation Parliament to legalize the Reformation in England. The Supremacy Act of 1534, passed by the Reformation Parliament, made the king the head of the Church of England.

10. **The correct answer is (B).** The Peace of Westphalia, which ended the Thirty Years' War, recognized the independence of the German princes. Each ruler was free to rule his own territory as he wished, thus effectively destroying the Holy Roman Empire.

11. **The correct answer is (E).** William and Mary accepted the throne, after a mostly nonviolent revolution, on the condition that Parliament maintained supremacy over the crown. Therefore, the divine right of kings was effectively abolished in England.

12. **The correct answer is (A).** This painting depicts a witch trial where several people are accusing a man of witchcraft.

13. **The correct answer is (B).** As an absolutist who claimed the divine right of kings, Louis XIV said, "*L'etat, c'est moi*" or "I am the state."

14. **The correct answer is (A).** René Descartes believed in the power of human reason, and he believed that through human reason, he could deduce the existence of God.

15. **The correct answer is (C).** The textile industry not only paved the way for the Industrial Revolution but also provided the best example of an industry increasing to meet the rising demand of consumers.

16. **The correct answer is (A).** In 1789, the National Assembly convened on an indoor tennis court and vowed not to disband until a new constitution had been created.

17. **The correct answer is (A).** Robert Owen built upon his success in New Lanark, Scotland, and unsuccessfully attempted to create a self-sufficient utopian society in Indiana.

18. **The correct answer is (E).** Through the work of such pioneers as Louis Pasteur, the medical community began to approach medicine in a more scientific and rational manner during the nineteenth century.

19. **The correct answer is (E).** In 1989, the Berlin Wall came down after Honecker's government gave in to the popular demands voiced during several mass demonstrations.

20. **The correct answer is (B).** The Court of the Star Chamber was created by Parliament to end the influence of powerful nobles who intimidated lawyers and judges.

21. **The correct answer is (D).** The French Calvinists were known as Huguenots.

22. **The correct answer is (A).** Family households in Europe, particularly north-western Europe, tended to be a nuclear family of no more than five to six members, including children and excluding extended family members. This applied to families other than those who were very wealthy.

23. **The correct answer is (C).** This graph indicates the origins and destinations of those who participated in the Great Migration in the late nineteenth and early twentieth centuries.

24. **The correct answer is (C).** To take over the German government, Hitler tried a military show of force, but that landed him in jail. He then resolved to do as Mussolini and achieve a high governmental position legally.

25. **The correct answer is (C).** This statement by existentialist Jean-Paul Sartre is existentialism in a nutshell.

26. **The correct answer is (B).** The German peasantry thought that Luther's message of spiritual freedom also applied to political freedom. Luther proved rather unsupportive of the peasants and encouraged the princes to crush the un-Christian revolts.

27. **The correct answer is (C).** This illustration shows the destruction of Lisbon by the earthquake that struck the city and destroyed many of its inhabitants in 1755. The earthquake sparked a heated theological and philosophical debate on its causes.

28. **The correct answer is (C).** Louis Napoleon, later Napoleon III, won a landslide victory in the elections of 1848 largely on the popularity of his uncle's name.

29. **The correct answer is (D).** Giuseppe Garibaldi led the thousand-man army known as the Red Shirts and took Sicily even though his men were outnumbered.

30. **The correct answer is (A).** Franz Liszt referred to his works as symphonic poems because they were intended to depict particular literary or pictorial ideas or images.

31. **The correct answer is (E).** The new physics and new psychology made many people question reality and question such traditional values as religion and reason. The art of the early twentieth century reflected this new skepticism.

32. **The correct answer is (D).** Serbia sought an independent nation, which threatened the security and stability of the Austro-Hungarian Empire prior to World War I.

33. **The correct answer is (D).** John Calvin's theology is summed up in TULIP: **T**otal depravity of man, **U**nconditional predestination, **L**imited atonement, **I**rresistible grace, and **P**erseverance of the saints.

34. **The correct answer is (E).** The Council of Trent (1545–1563) upheld the Church tradition of celibacy among its clergy.

35. **The correct answer is (C).** The Peace of Utrecht, several treaties in 1713 and 1714, established a balance of power in Europe by ending the expansion and dominance of Louis XIV. The Peace also made way for the dominance of Great Britain during the eighteenth century.

36. **The correct answer is (D).** Bacon advocated inductive reasoning, which is the examination of empirical evidence. Bacon sought to break with tradition, ask new questions, and find new answers.

37. **The correct answer is (E).** The Civil Constitution of the Clergy required the clergy to declare allegiance to the state and allowed the state to appoint Church officials.

38. **The correct answer is (B).** John Wesley felt that his place was not in the pulpit, so he took his message to the open fields of rural England.

39. **The correct answer is (A).** After the Great War, national economies slowed drastically. Then in 1929, the American stock market crashed. These two factors combined to send shockwaves around the world.

40. **The correct answer is (C).** The Edict of Nantes granted Calvinists the freedom to worship in public, the right of assembly, the right to hold public offices, and more.

41. **The correct answer is (B).** The building in the picture is the palace of Louis XIV at Versailles. An absolutist, Louis used his architecture to flaunt his wealth and power in order to impress and intimidate foreign dignitaries.

42. **The correct answer is (C).** In many lands, especially Germany, Napoleon's conquests inspired feelings of nationalism in the people. This nationalism eventually led to the downfall of Napoleon's empire.

43. **The correct answer is (E).** These are the words of the Romantic poet William Wordsworth. As in this poem, Romantics often lamented the destruction of the natural world at the hands of industrialization.

44. **The correct answer is (B).** According to the Schlieffen Plan, German troops were to be allocated for war against Russia in the east and France in the west.

45. **The correct answer is (A).** Stalin's five-year plan did indeed transform Russia into a leading industrial nation in a very short amount of time.

46. **The correct answer is (A).** The Dayton Accords created a Serb republic and a Muslim-Croat confederation in Bosnia.

47. **The correct answer is (C).** Amsterdam replaced the Italian and German cities as the leading banking center of Europe in the mid-eighteenth century. It remained so until the late eighteenth century.

48. **The correct answer is (C).** Michael Romanov was elected czar in 1613, and his family ruled Russia until 1917.

49. **The correct answer is (E).** The Church, in the opinion of the *philosophes*, was too restrictive. In addition, the Church maintained the depravity of man. The *philosophes*, however, believed that the human condition could be improved.

50. **The correct answer is (A).** Although the First Estate numbered only a little more than 100,000 people, it owned approximately 10 percent of French land.

51. **The correct answer is (C).** This represents the Balkans in 1914, just prior to the outbreak of World War I.

52. **The correct answer is (E).** Hitler hated the Slavs, and many Slavs lost their lives in Hitler's concentration camps and from Nazi bullets.

53. **The correct answer is (E).** The beginning of the end of the Cold War was marked by an era known as détente. It was an era of renewed diplomacy, trade, and cultural exchange.

54. **The correct answer is (A).** After Morocco and Tunisia had been granted their independence by the French, Algiers launched a war to win its independence. This war divided the French people, so de Gaulle granted Algeria independence.

55. **The correct answer is (E).** Sir Isaac Newton, with his emphasis on the power of the mind, along with John Locke, and his belief that the human condition could be improved, paved the way for the thought of the Enlightenment.

56. **The correct answer is (C).** Catherine the Great of Russia and Joseph II of Austria, along with Frederick II of Prussia, were referred to as enlightened absolutists because they seemed to have embraced the philosophy of the *philosophes* and tried to practice it.

57. **The correct answer is (B).** Joseph de Maistre believed that monarchy was an institution sanctioned by God. Therefore, he believed that monarchy held the key to order in light of the French Revolution.

58. **The correct answer is (E).** Camillo de Cavour reached an agreement with Napoleon III to ensure Italy would have help in case Austria attacked. Although France helped at first, Napoleon III eventually withdrew.

59. **The correct answer is (D).** Louis Pasteur's germ theory implied that diseases were caused by germs or living organisms. This discovery led not only to improved health care conditions but also to advancements in the production of beer, wine, and milk.

60. **The correct answer is (A).** Stalin, Roosevelt, and Churchill met in Teheran and agreed to divide Germany into zones of influence after the war ended. Other major issues were put on hold until after the war.

61. **The correct answer is (E).** The Labour Party enacted a number of social welfare reforms that provided for the British people, thus creating a welfare state.

62. **The correct answer is (E).** The Hohenzollerns ruled Prussia by subordinating all classes of people and by establishing strict discipline in their military. They were known for their superior administration.

63. **The correct answer is (D).** Peter the Great actually tried to implement Western ideas in Russia. He sent his men to the West to be trained and tried to attract Western engineers and craftsmen to Russia.

64. **The correct answer is (A).** Deism and the deists are both reasonable and rational. Therefore, deism is necessarily unemotional. Many of the *philosophes* were deists.

65. **The correct answer is (A).** Napoleon amassed an army that was larger than any army that Europe had ever seen.

66. **The correct answer is (B).** Louis-Philippe, known as the bourgeois monarch, basically eliminated working class Frenchmen from the political process. Voting qualifications remained such that only the wealthy could vote.

67. **The correct answer is (A).** The Romantic painters such as Turner, Friedrich and Delacroix often painted bright, vivid paintings full of emotion and feeling.

68. **The correct answer is (C).** Although each of the other statements was true of the Russian peasants, they were not completely free. They found themselves severely limited by available land, and they were often subjected to the rule of the village commune.

69. **The correct answer is (B).** Khrushchev made numerous economic promises, but he never was able to improve the Soviet economy. Therefore, he was removed from office while he was on vacation.

70. **The correct answer is (D).** John Knox founded the Presbyterian Church in Scotland after spending time with Calvin.

71. **The correct answer is (A).** Frederick William I, King of Prussia, was obsessed with the military. Always in a military uniform, Frederick built one of the greatest armies of eighteenth-century Europe but tried to avoid conflict throughout his reign.

72. **The correct answer is (D).** This statement by Thomas Mun is one of the earliest statements of mercantilist philosophy. Mun clearly advocates a favorable balance of trade, a must for a mercantilistic economy.

73. **The correct answer is (B).** In an effort to de-Christianize the French Republic of Virtue, the National Convention renamed the days and months of the calendar, closed churches, renamed the Notre Dame Cathedral, and introduced the Cult of the Supreme Being.

74. **The correct answer is (D).** Mussolini did not believe in the emancipation of women. Rather, he believed that women should stay at home and have children. Women had no rights under Mussolini.

75. **The correct answer is (D).** The pope, who happened to be Polish, offered the support of the Catholic Church to Walesa and his Solidarity movement.

76. **The correct answer is (E).** The Game Laws prohibited anyone other than landowners from hunting deer, pheasants, and other animals. The landowners who passed the legislation were also the ones who collected the fines from those caught poaching.

77. **The correct answer is (C).** The bubonic plague struck one final time in a major outbreak in southern France in 1720.

78. **The correct answer is (C).** Other European nations realized the danger and potential of the ideas and events of the French Revolution. Therefore, these governments instituted repressive policies within their borders to guard against the infiltration of revolutionary thoughts, etc.

79. **The correct answer is (D).** As people flocked from the countryside into the cities, the urban areas became overcrowded. The overcrowding led to poor living conditions. These conditions prompted many of the urban poor to resort to crime as a means of survival.

80. **The correct answer is (D).** Although there were attempts at rapprochements, especially during the presidency of Jules Ferry, the wounds that remained from the war of 1870–1871 were too great to permit an alliance between these two countries.

FREE-RESPONSE QUESTIONS ANSWER GUIDE

1. Analyze and discuss the issue and the positions held by the two sides involved
    in the debate over Galileo's support of the Copernican theory of the universe.

Answer Guide:

Hopefully, you remembered to take notes on the documents and organize the
documents using a chart. If you did, then writing this essay should not have felt
impossible. The most important part of answering this question is the development
of your thesis. Your thesis should be clear and concise. It should tell the
reader exactly what you are going to say in your essay. In short, your thesis
should clearly sum up your argument.

For this particular question, your thesis should deal first with the issue of
whether or not the Copernican theory is valid and whether or not it contradicts
the Scriptures. Second, your thesis should identify the position held by the
Church, that the Copernican theory is invalid and contradicts the Bible, and the
position held by Galileo, that the Copernican theory is valid and that it does not
necessarily contradict the Bible.

The next step is the body of the essay. Your essay should offer a clear,
organized argument that supports your thesis. The body of your essay should
include some historical background of the controversy over the Copernican
theory. Your essay should outline the position of the Church against the
Copernican theory based upon the Scriptures from Document 1. Your essay
should also point out that the Church believed that the Scriptures were to be
taken literally; thus, the Copernican theory was invalid. As illustrated by
Document 2, the Church had already established its official position of the
Copernican theory; it denounced the theory as false and erroneous. Furthermore, the Copernican theory, especially as supported by Galileo, was heretical
because it contradicted the Scriptures. Any contradiction of the Scriptures, as
illustrated in Document 3 and Document 6, was considered an interpretation of
the Scriptures. The Council of Trent strictly forbade interpretation of the
Scriptures by laymen. The Church, by edict, officially prohibited Galileo's
book in Document 7. Your essay should point out that the Church perceived
Galileo's work as a threat and that was why his work was prohibited. Your
essay should also address the words of Cardinal Bellarmine. In Document 5,
Bellarmine supports and reiterates the Church view that a reinterpretation of the
Scriptures was forbidden. Your essay should also illustrate that Bellarmine
used not only the Scriptures but also the writings of the Church fathers to
disprove the Copernican theory. In Document 4, Bellarmine seems to allow the
slight possibility that Galileo was correct. However, as your essay should state,
Bellarmine is quick to say that such evidence would indicate a misunderstand-
ing of the Scriptures and not that the Scriptures were false. Also, Bellarmine
qualifies his statement by saying that his mind would not be changed until he
saw proof. All or most of these points should be included in your essay.

On the other side of the issue are Galileo and his position. A good essay
will point out that in Documents 9 and 10, Galileo not only clearly establishes
Copernicus' views on a heliocentric universe but also argues, in Document 9,

that Copernicus did so only for scientific reasons. In other words, Copernicus did not mean to offend the Church in his writings. In Document 12, Galileo takes care to note that a heliocentric universe simply means that the Scriptures have been misunderstood, not that the Scriptures have been rendered false. He argues furthermore that a decision on the issue should begin with a scientific observation rather than a Scriptural observation, implying that the issue is a scientific issue and not a religious issue. Your essay should illustrate that concerning the Church's attacks on Galileo, Galileo claims in Document 11 that some of the people involved have not even read his work but rather are attacking him based solely on his association with the Copernican theory. In Document 13, Galileo stands by his belief that the earth moves and the sun stands still. He also warns the Church that they are likely to condemn for heresy those who believe in the Copernican theory simply because the Church wants to make a scientific issue a matter of faith. As a final note, your essay might mention that Document VIII by the Jesuits seems to indicate that Galileo's support of the Copernican theory might have been more well received by the Church had his methodology been different. If your essay includes most or all of these points, you are well on your way to a good, solid essay. In addition, any extra historical information you can add to your essay will enhance the overall quality of your essay. Use the rubric in Chapter 2 to further evaluate your essay.

2. Evaluate the art of the Renaissance as a reflection of the values and ideals of the Renaissance era.

Answer Guide:

Your essay should give some historical background, including perhaps a brief treatment of society, politics, economics, and religion, on both the Renaissance and the art of the Renaissance. You should discuss the humanistic and classical values of the period. In addition, you should discuss the ways in which Renaissance art digressed from the medieval tradition and adopted the humanistic and classical values of the Renaissance. For example, you could mention the glorification of the human body as a classical ideal and give examples of Renaissance art that embodied that ideal. You could also include a discussion of such classical characteristics as realism, perspective, balance, and proportion. Your essay should address the increasingly secular style of art as well as the increasingly secular patronage of the era. Be sure your essay uses historical facts to support your argument. Finally, make sure your essay has a clear, organized thesis and an organized body that supports your thesis.

3.   Compare and contrast the general trends in the feudalism of eastern and western Europe prior to, during, and after the Black Death.

Answer Guide:

Your essay should indicate that prior to the plague, the serfdom of the east and west were very similar. Likewise, during the plague, both the east and the west experienced a decline in population, a decline in the economy, and a labor shortage. Your essay should stress that the status of the peasants in the west improved after the plague. Some of the peasants' demands were met, and serfdom began to disappear. Some peasants even gained minimal amounts of political power. Strong monarchies that decreased the power of the nobility increased the power of the lower and middle classes. An excellent essay would mention an example such as the French absolutism. In the east, the nobles reacted by taking away land and power from the peasants and restricting their movements. The nobility also increased the work duties of the peasants. A stronger nobility meant a weaker monarchy. Your essay should point out that these restrictions prevented the peasants from effectively revolting as they did in the west. Therefore, serfdom remained for a much longer period of time in the east. Be sure your essay uses historical facts to support your argument. Finally, make sure your essay has a clear, organized thesis and an organized body that supports your thesis.

4.   Analyze and discuss the economic and social consequences of the Industrial Revolution. Include a treatment of the major developments of the Industrial Revolution and the consequences of those developments.

Answer Guide:

Your essay should discuss the historical background of the Industrial Revolution and the predecessor to the Revolution, the putting-out system or the cottage industry. Your essay should also include the causes of the Industrial Revolution. Be sure your essay includes a discussion of such inventors as Hargreaves and Arkwright and their inventions. Your essay should also include a discussion of industrial innovations by the likes of Watt and Stephenson. The most thorough part of your essay should be a discussion of the economic and social consequences of the Industrial Revolution. Your essay should discuss such things as employment opportunities, the changes in standards of living, the changes in wages, and the changes in the national economies. Your discussion of social consequences should include information about living and working conditions, the sexual division of labor, the emergence of a new class, and urban problems that emerged as a result of the Industrial Revolution. A discussion of the emergence of the labor movement would be excellent. Be sure your essay uses historical facts to support your argument. Finally, make sure your essay has a clear, organized thesis and an organized body that supports your thesis.

5.   "The second half of the nineteenth century could be accurately called the Age of Nationalism." Assess the validity of this statement.

Answer Guide:

Your essay should begin with some historical background, perhaps including a discussion of the Revolutions of 1848. Your essay should also include a discussion of the basic tenets of nationalism, including the desire for a nation based upon common historical, cultural, geographic, or linguistic heritage. Your essay must include a discussion of the unification of Italy and the key players in that nationalistic movement, such as Cavour and Garibaldi. Your essay must also include a discussion of the unification of Germany and the key players in that nationalistic movement, such as Bismarck. An excellent essay would also include the nations of France and/or Great Britain. Be sure your essay uses historical facts to support your argument. Finally, make sure your essay has a clear, organized thesis and an organized body that supports your thesis.

6.   Discuss the causes of the Russian Revolution as well as the long-term effects of the Revolution not only in Russia but also in the rest of Europe.

Answer Guide:

Your essay should begin with the historical background of the Russian Revolution, including a discussion of the Russian condition prior to the Revolution. Your essay should outline the Revolution of 1905 and its causes and effects. You should include in your discussion of the causes a treatment of the failing effort in World War I, poor leadership, the social and economic conditions on the eve of the Revolution, and the popular unrest in February and March of 1917. Your essay should discuss the rise to power of Trotsky and Lenin and the eventual triumph of the Bolsheviks. The effects of the Revolution for Russia included the establishment of a Communist government and the implementation of Lenin's NEP. The long-term effects for both Russia and the rest of Europe included the rise and spread of Communism that led to icy relations between Russia (and eventually the USSR) and the West. Be sure your essay uses historical facts to support your argument. Finally, make sure your essay has a clear, organized thesis and an organized body that supports your thesis.

7.   Analyze and discuss the extent to which the events following World War I
     contributed to the outbreak of World War II.

Answer Guide:

Your essay should first discuss the attitude and emotions of Europe after World
War I. Also, your essay must cover the failure of the Treaty of Versailles.
Specifically, discuss the war-guilt clause, the reparations, and the dismantling
of German lands. The continued dispute over Alsace-Lorraine and Poland and
the demilitarization of Germany should also be included. Your essay should
address the resentment of Germany and the suspicions of France and Great
Britain. Your essay must include a discussion on the failure of the United States
and the League of Nations. Finally, your essay must include a discussion of the
policy of appeasement while Hitler began his conquest of Europe prior to
World War II. Be sure your essay uses historical facts to support your argument.
Finally, make sure your essay has a clear, organized thesis and an organized
body that supports your thesis.

PRACTICE TEST 2

Answer Sheet

Section 1

1. Ⓐ Ⓑ Ⓒ Ⓓ Ⓔ 17. Ⓐ Ⓑ Ⓒ Ⓓ Ⓔ 33. Ⓐ Ⓑ Ⓒ Ⓓ Ⓔ 49. Ⓐ Ⓑ Ⓒ Ⓓ Ⓔ 65. Ⓐ Ⓑ Ⓒ Ⓓ Ⓔ

2. Ⓐ Ⓑ Ⓒ Ⓓ Ⓔ 18. Ⓐ Ⓑ Ⓒ Ⓓ Ⓔ 34. Ⓐ Ⓑ Ⓒ Ⓓ Ⓔ 50. Ⓐ Ⓑ Ⓒ Ⓓ Ⓔ 66. Ⓐ Ⓑ Ⓒ Ⓓ Ⓔ

3. Ⓐ Ⓑ Ⓒ Ⓓ Ⓔ 19. Ⓐ Ⓑ Ⓒ Ⓓ Ⓔ 35. Ⓐ Ⓑ Ⓒ Ⓓ Ⓔ 51. Ⓐ Ⓑ Ⓒ Ⓓ Ⓔ 67. Ⓐ Ⓑ Ⓒ Ⓓ Ⓔ

4. Ⓐ Ⓑ Ⓒ Ⓓ Ⓔ 20. Ⓐ Ⓑ Ⓒ Ⓓ Ⓔ 36. Ⓐ Ⓑ Ⓒ Ⓓ Ⓔ 52. Ⓐ Ⓑ Ⓒ Ⓓ Ⓔ 68. Ⓐ Ⓑ Ⓒ Ⓓ Ⓔ

5. Ⓐ Ⓑ Ⓒ Ⓓ Ⓔ 21. Ⓐ Ⓑ Ⓒ Ⓓ Ⓔ 37. Ⓐ Ⓑ Ⓒ Ⓓ Ⓔ 53. Ⓐ Ⓑ Ⓒ Ⓓ Ⓔ 69. Ⓐ Ⓑ Ⓒ Ⓓ Ⓔ

6. Ⓐ Ⓑ Ⓒ Ⓓ Ⓔ 22. Ⓐ Ⓑ Ⓒ Ⓓ Ⓔ 38. Ⓐ Ⓑ Ⓒ Ⓓ Ⓔ 54. Ⓐ Ⓑ Ⓒ Ⓓ Ⓔ 70. Ⓐ Ⓑ Ⓒ Ⓓ Ⓔ

7. Ⓐ Ⓑ Ⓒ Ⓓ Ⓔ 23. Ⓐ Ⓑ Ⓒ Ⓓ Ⓔ 39. Ⓐ Ⓑ Ⓒ Ⓓ Ⓔ 55. Ⓐ Ⓑ Ⓒ Ⓓ Ⓔ 71. Ⓐ Ⓑ Ⓒ Ⓓ Ⓔ

8. Ⓐ Ⓑ Ⓒ Ⓓ Ⓔ 24. Ⓐ Ⓑ Ⓒ Ⓓ Ⓔ 40. Ⓐ Ⓑ Ⓒ Ⓓ Ⓔ 56. Ⓐ Ⓑ Ⓒ Ⓓ Ⓔ 72. Ⓐ Ⓑ Ⓒ Ⓓ Ⓔ

9. Ⓐ Ⓑ Ⓒ Ⓓ Ⓔ 25. Ⓐ Ⓑ Ⓒ Ⓓ Ⓔ 41. Ⓐ Ⓑ Ⓒ Ⓓ Ⓔ 57. Ⓐ Ⓑ Ⓒ Ⓓ Ⓔ 73. Ⓐ Ⓑ Ⓒ Ⓓ Ⓔ

10. Ⓐ Ⓑ Ⓒ Ⓓ Ⓔ 26. Ⓐ Ⓑ Ⓒ Ⓓ Ⓔ 42. Ⓐ Ⓑ Ⓒ Ⓓ Ⓔ 58. Ⓐ Ⓑ Ⓒ Ⓓ Ⓔ 74. Ⓐ Ⓑ Ⓒ Ⓓ Ⓔ

11. Ⓐ Ⓑ Ⓒ Ⓓ Ⓔ 27. Ⓐ Ⓑ Ⓒ Ⓓ Ⓔ 43. Ⓐ Ⓑ Ⓒ Ⓓ Ⓔ 59. Ⓐ Ⓑ Ⓒ Ⓓ Ⓔ 75. Ⓐ Ⓑ Ⓒ Ⓓ Ⓔ

12. Ⓐ Ⓑ Ⓒ Ⓓ Ⓔ 28. Ⓐ Ⓑ Ⓒ Ⓓ Ⓔ 44. Ⓐ Ⓑ Ⓒ Ⓓ Ⓔ 60. Ⓐ Ⓑ Ⓒ Ⓓ Ⓔ 76. Ⓐ Ⓑ Ⓒ Ⓓ Ⓔ

13. Ⓐ Ⓑ Ⓒ Ⓓ Ⓔ 29. Ⓐ Ⓑ Ⓒ Ⓓ Ⓔ 45. Ⓐ Ⓑ Ⓒ Ⓓ Ⓔ 61. Ⓐ Ⓑ Ⓒ Ⓓ Ⓔ 77. Ⓐ Ⓑ Ⓒ Ⓓ Ⓔ

14. Ⓐ Ⓑ Ⓒ Ⓓ Ⓔ 30. Ⓐ Ⓑ Ⓒ Ⓓ Ⓔ 46. Ⓐ Ⓑ Ⓒ Ⓓ Ⓔ 62. Ⓐ Ⓑ Ⓒ Ⓓ Ⓔ 78. Ⓐ Ⓑ Ⓒ Ⓓ Ⓔ

15. Ⓐ Ⓑ Ⓒ Ⓓ Ⓔ 31. Ⓐ Ⓑ Ⓒ Ⓓ Ⓔ 47. Ⓐ Ⓑ Ⓒ Ⓓ Ⓔ 63. Ⓐ Ⓑ Ⓒ Ⓓ Ⓔ 79. Ⓐ Ⓑ Ⓒ Ⓓ Ⓔ

16. Ⓐ Ⓑ Ⓒ Ⓓ Ⓔ 32. Ⓐ Ⓑ Ⓒ Ⓓ Ⓔ 48. Ⓐ Ⓑ Ⓒ Ⓓ Ⓔ 64. Ⓐ Ⓑ Ⓒ Ⓓ Ⓔ 80. Ⓐ Ⓑ Ⓒ Ⓓ Ⓔ

Master the AP European History Test

Practice Test 2

Section I of this examination contains 80 multiple-choice questions. Therefore, please be careful to fill in only the ovals that are preceded by numbers 1 through 80 on your answer sheet.

GENERAL INSTRUCTIONS

INDICATE ALL YOUR ANSWERS TO QUESTIONS IN SECTION I ON THE SEPARATE ANSWER SHEET. No credit will be given for anything written in this examination booklet, but you may use the booklet for notes or scratch work. After you have decided which of the suggested answers is best, COMPLETELY fill in the corresponding oval on the answer sheet. Give only one answer to each question. If you change an answer, be sure that the previous mark is erased completely.

<u>Example:</u>

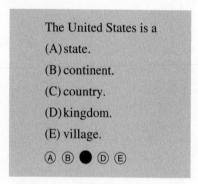

The United States is a
(A) state.
(B) continent.
(C) country.
(D) kingdom.
(E) village.

Ⓐ Ⓑ ● Ⓓ Ⓔ

Many students wonder whether or not to guess the answers to questions about which they are not certain. In this section of the examination, as a correction for haphazard guessing, one fourth of the number of questions you answer incorrectly will be subtracted from the number of questions you answer correctly. It is improbable, therefore, that mere guessing will increase your score significantly; it may even lower your score, and it does take time. If, however, you are not sure of the best answer but have some knowledge of the question and are able to eliminate one or more of the answer choices as wrong, your chance of getting the right answer is improved, and it may be to your advantage to answer such a question.

Use your time effectively, working as rapidly as you can without losing accuracy. Do not spend too much time on questions that are too difficult. Go on to other questions and come back to the difficult ones later if you have time. It is not expected that everyone will be able to answer all multiple-choice questions.

SECTION I—MULTIPLE CHOICE

80 Questions - Time—55 Minutes

<u>Directions:</u> Each of the questions or incomplete statements below is followed by five suggested answers or completions. Select the one that is best in each case, and then fill in the corresponding oval on the answer sheet.

1. The educational innovation of the Renaissance humanists was
   - (A) the use of classical primary sources.
   - (B) the study of modern languages.
   - (C) the return to traditional teaching methods.
   - (D) the focus on purely religious themes.
   - (E) the emphasis on theoretical instead of practical lessons.

2. During the sixteenth century, the Netherlands was known for
   - (A) religious tolerance and acceptance.
   - (B) strict adherence to Protestant tradition.
   - (C) strict obedience of papal orders.
   - (D) religious intolerance.
   - (E) persecution of all who were different and nonconformist.

3. The city once referred to as the Third Rome was
   - (A) Constantinople.
   - (B) Moscow.
   - (C) Prague.
   - (D) Belgrade.
   - (E) Venice.

4. Enlightenment thinkers considered themselves
   - (A) reformers.
   - (B) conservatives.
   - (C) anarchical.
   - (D) revolutionaries.
   - (E) equal to all men.

5. On the eve of the Revolution in France, the large debt could be partially, if not mostly, attributed to

   (A) the decrease in the value of French money in response to the collapse of the largest bank in Europe.

   (B) the huge army and navy built by Louis XV.

   (C) a significant loss of French sources of income.

   (D) the large war loans made to the American colonies.

   (E) the interest on loans borrowed from the American colonies.

6. The dark and sometimes horrifying Gothic literature, such as *Frankenstein*, was a manifestation of the intellectual movement known as

   (A) the Scientific Revolution.

   (B) the Enlightenment.

   (C) the Age of Reason.

   (D) the Age of Anxiety.

   (E) Romanticism.

7. At the height of the British Empire, the jewel of the British crown was

   (A) South Africa.

   (B) Kenya.

   (C) India.

   (D) Australia.

   (E) New Zealand.

8. In the 1960s, protests against the Vietnam War and the lack of decision making within the university system were most often employed by

   (A) socialists.

   (B) students.

   (C) homosexuals.

   (D) feminists.

   (E) writers and intellectuals.

9. In the map below, which depicts Europe c. 1550, the dark shaded area
   most likely represents

   (A) the regions most severely affected by the bubonic plague.

   (B) the regions most influenced by Gutenburg's printing press.

   (C) the regions under Catholic influence.

   (D) the regions under Protestant influence.

   (E) the regions hardest hit by the Inquisition.

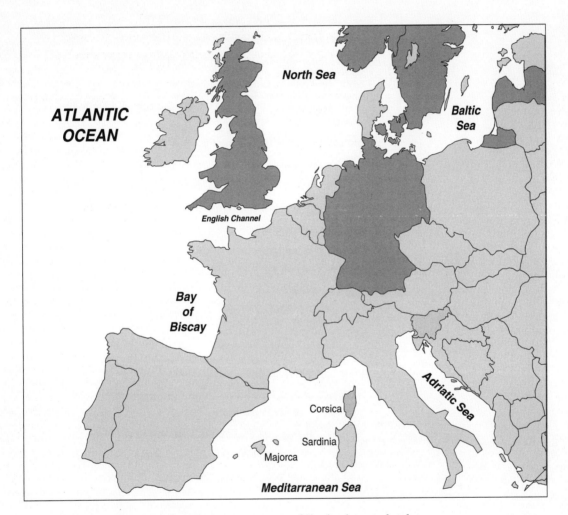

10. Under Oliver Cromwell, the government of England most closely
    resembled

    (A) a constitutional monarchy.

    (B) an absolute monarchy.

    (C) a democracy.

    (D) an oligarchy.

    (E) a military dictatorship.

11. The immediate cause of the Parisian women's march on Versailles was

    (A) the women's demands for suffrage.

    (B) the women's demands for an end to the violence.

    (C) a shortage of money in Paris.

    (D) a shortage of bread in Paris.

    (E) the amassing of troops in Paris.

12. The Declaration of Pillnitz was issued in 1791 to

    (A) support the revolutionaries in France.

    (B) spread the revolutionary spirit across Europe.

    (C) unite Europeans against Napoleon.

    (D) invite European monarchs to restore the French king to the throne.

    (E) demand the execution of the French king.

13. The diplomat who dominated the Congress of Vienna in 1815 was

    (A) Prince Klemens von Metternich.

    (B) Viscount Castlereagh.

    (C) Napoleon Bonaparte.

    (D) Prince Talleyrand.

    (E) Otto von Bismarck.

14. A unified Italy was achieved only after

    (A) a plebiscite in the Papal States and the Two Sicilies supported the union of the Italian states.

    (B) Garibaldi and his Red Shirts attacked Rome and forced the capitulation of the Papal States.

    (C) Victor Emmanuel III declared himself emperor of Italy.

    (D) Napoleon III defeated Austria and ceded the land to Cavour.

    (E) the Vatican had been granted sovereignty.

15. "Owing to this struggle (for existence), variations, however slight… will tend to the preservation of such individuals, and will generally be inherited by the offspring." This statement refers to Darwin's theory of

    (A) survival of the fittest.

    (B) origin of the species.

    (C) descent of man.

    (D) natural selection.

    (E) special relativity.

16. The elimination of the Jews by the Nazis was known as Hermann Göring's

    (A) answer to prayers.

    (B) *Kristallnacht.*

    (C) final solution to the Jewish problem.

    (D) *blitzkrieg.*

    (E) NEP.

17. "God, gold, and glory" best describes the motivations of

    (A) the papacy during the late nineteenth century concerning imperialism.

    (B) Louis XIV's military expansion.

    (C) Napoleon Bonaparte's military expansion.

    (D) Peter the Great's westernization of Russia.

    (E) expeditions to the New World during the Age of Exploration.

18. The Ptolemaic System, which was challenged by Copernicus,

    (A) placed the sun at the center of the universe.

    (B) did not take into account the existence of God and His place in the physical universe.

    (C) rejected the idea of epicycles of planetary objects.

    (D) was rejected by the Church.

    (E) was based upon a geocentric universe.

19. The *junkers* were

    (A) soldiers from the Ottoman Empire.

    (B) Russian peasants under Ivan IV.

    (C) Russian peasants during Stalin's rule.

    (D) aristocratic German landowners.

    (E) serfs on the Habsburg lands.

20. The Russians, to defeat Napoleon's Grand Army, used a military strategy known as

    (A) flanking maneuvers.

    (B) divide and conquer.

    (C) seek and destroy.

    (D) scorched earth.

    (E) slash and burn.

21. The Corn Laws

    (A) allowed for free trade of agricultural products in Great Britain.

    (B) reduced the price of bread in Great Britain.

    (C) were welcomed with open arms and sighs of relief by the British.

    (D) placed high tariffs on imported grain.

    (E) benefited the working class more than any other class.

22. The primary targets of Bismarck's *Kulturkampf* were

    (A) Communists.

    (B) Nationalists.

    (C) Catholics.

    (D) Protestants.

    (E) Conservatives.

23. The imperialism of the late nineteenth century was greatly impacted and even encouraged by the theory of

    (A) Social Darwinism.

    (B) Aryan superiority.

    (C) Communism.

    (D) Socialism.

    (E) Bolshevism.

24. The poster below most likely

    (A) was used to portray Russian women as manly and unattractive.

    (B) was used to show the effects of factory work on women.

    (C) depicted the way factories polluted the environment.

    (D) persuaded women to turn their backs on industrialization.

    (E) encouraged women to work in factories.

25. Luther would have most approved a woman

    (A) staying at home to be a wife and mother.

    (B) seeking election to a public office.

    (C) holding a leadership position in a church.

    (D) taking an active role in the leadership of a community.

    (E) leading a woman's suffrage movement.

26. Jethro Tull, Charles Townsend, and Robert Bakewell each played significant roles in the

    (A) Price Revolution.

    (B) Agricultural Revolution.

    (C) Industrial Revolution.

    (D) Glorious Revolution.

    (E) Russian Revolution.

27. During the new "Republic of Virtue" following the French Revolution, the renaming of the days of the week and the months of the year reflected
    (A) the desire to do away with traditions.
    (B) the attempt to disassociate France with the Church.
    (C) the attempt to return to classical Greek and Roman values.
    (D) the desire to institute Napoleonic ideals concerning time.
    (E) France's attempts to emulate the United States.

28. With regard to Industrialization, Britain differed from countries of the Continent in that
    (A) Britain practiced free trade and the countries of the Continent used protective tariffs.
    (B) the countries of the Continent practiced free trade and Britain used protective tariffs.
    (C) Britain lacked the capital of the other countries.
    (D) railroads first made their impact on the Continent.
    (E) Britain relied on an agrarian economy far longer than the Continent.

29. The Decembrists
    (A) were Russians who defended Nicholas I from revolutionaries in 1825.
    (B) sought woman suffrage in Russia and peacefully demonstrated for that cause in 1825.
    (C) led the revolt that overthrew Czar Nicholas I in 1825.
    (D) appealed to Czar Nicholas I for the preservation of serfdom in 1825.
    (E) revolted in 1825 and sought a constitutional monarchy and the abolition of serfdom in Russia.

30. Count Camillo Cavour hoped to unify Italy by means of
    (A) popular revolts against foreign rulers.
    (B) a military alliance with France against Austria.
    (C) a democratic plebiscite in all Italian-speaking areas.
    (D) conquest of the Papal States and the Kingdom of Naples.
    (E) a military alliance with Prussia against France.

31. The primary targets of Stalin's purges were
    (A) Catholics.
    (B) Jews.
    (C) Kulaks.
    (D) Old Bolsheviks.
    (E) Capitalists.

32. The European Economic Community, or Common Market, grew out of
    (A) the European Coal and Steel Community.
    (B) the North Atlantic Treaty Organization.
    (C) the Warsaw Pact.
    (D) the United Nations.
    (E) OPEC.

33. The Medici family, a wealthy banking family of Florence, exerted
    their influence during
    (A) the Renaissance.
    (B) the Catholic Reformation.
    (C) Italian Unification.
    (D) the rule of Mussolini.
    (E) the Cold War.

34. This statue of Peter the Great is most likely intended
    (A) to show his great military prowess.
    (B) to show his enormous physical stature.
    (C) to intimidate visitors.
    (D) to symbolize his greatness and his leadership of Russia in a new
        direction.
    (E) to commemorate his love of horses.

35. John Locke's idea of the human mind as a *tabula rasa* illustrated his belief that

    (A) man can never really know anything.

    (B) there are no innate ideas.

    (C) God can wipe the slate clean for any who ask.

    (D) the mind is resistant to influences from the external world.

    (E) only deductive reasoning produces true knowledge.

36. The main purpose of Napoleon's Continental System was

    (A) to cripple continental nations by cutting them off from other continental nations.

    (B) to cripple Britain by cutting them off from the continent.

    (C) to establish an elaborate system of trade routes on the continent.

    (D) to develop a system by which he could move his massive armies across the continent quickly.

    (E) to bring the continent under one law code.

37. Romantics criticized the *philosophes* for

    (A) the subjection of nature to endless rationalization and reason, thus suppressing emotion and feeling.

    (B) being too emotional and sentimental.

    (C) their fascination with all things medieval.

    (D) their support of the Catholic Church.

    (E) their fascination with things that seemed to exist beyond the reasonable, rational world.

38. Britain's Prince Albert said, "Man is approaching a more complete fulfillment of that great and sacred mission which he has to perform in this world… to conquer nature to his use." Prince Albert was referring to

    (A) the Scientific Revolution.

    (B) British Imperialism.

    (C) the discovery of the New World.

    (D) British conquest of Africa.

    (E) the Industrial Revolution.

39. The importance of Giuseppe Mazzini to Italian history was

    (A) his conservatism.

    (B) his resistance to the movement for Italian nationhood.

    (C) his zeal for Italian nationalism.

    (D) his resistance to Garibaldi and Cavour.

    (E) his overthrow of Austrian power in Italy.

40. At the onset of World War I, most people believed

   (A) that the war would be over very quickly.

   (B) that the war would eventually involve nearly all European nations.

   (C) that the war had the potential to be the bloodiest war of all time.

   (D) that the crisis in the Balkans would escalate to a worldwide conflict because of the volatility of the issues.

   (E) that Germany intentionally started the war with the aim of conquering all of Europe.

41. While the bankers and merchants were the art patrons during the Renaissance, during the Middle Ages, the leading patron(s) of the arts

   (A) were also the bankers and merchants.

   (B) was the aristocracy.

   (C) were the monarchs.

   (D) was the Church.

   (E) were the other artists.

42. The religious orders such as the Jesuits and the Ursuline Order were created

   (A) to combat the spread of Protestantism.

   (B) to find people who read books on the *Index of Prohibited Books.*

   (C) as a tool in the Inquisition.

   (D) to stop the spread of Nazism.

   (E) to convert the Jews to Protestantism.

43. Henry IV said, "Paris is worth a mass," referring to

   (A) his conversion from Catholicism to Protestantism.

   (B) his conversion from Protestantism.

   (C) the issuance of the Edict of Nantes.

   (D) his revocation of the Edict of Nantes.

   (E) his baptism at the Notre Dame cathedral in Paris.

44. German princes were made sovereign rulers according to the

   (A) Peace of Augsburg.

   (B) Edict of Nantes.

   (C) Peace of Westphalia.

   (D) Six Articles.

   (E) Council of Trent.

45. "The first principle to be followed by the monarchs, united as they are by the coincidence of their desires and opinions, should be that of maintaining the stability of political institutions against the disorganized excitement which has taken possession of men's minds..." This statement most likely could be attributed to

   (A) Napoleon Bonaparte.

   (B) Giuseppe Garibaldi.

   (C) Maximilien Robespierre.

   (D) Oliver Cromwell.

   (E) Klemens von Metternich.

46. Although the ostensible cause of the Crimean War was a dispute over the protection of certain Christian holy sites, the reason Britain and France entered the war was

   (A) to support Russia in its attempt to crush the Ottoman Empire.

   (B) to prevent Russia from upsetting the European balance of power.

   (C) to prevent Austria from becoming the dominant power in the Mediterranean.

   (D) to maintain the Concert of Europe.

   (E) to prevent the defeat of Russia by the combined forces of Austria and the Ottoman Empire.

47. During the Second Industrial Revolution, women

   (A) found many new job opportunities in factories.

   (B) were forced to work in sweatshops or as prostitutes.

   (C) were encouraged to give up domestic responsibilities in lieu of joining the work force.

   (D) experienced a new sense of equality because their wages were nearly equal to those of the men.

   (E) found lucrative new opportunities doing piecework in their homes.

48. The Soviet Union, after World War II,

   (A) experienced the Western Renaissance.

   (B) reinstated the totalitarian policies of the 1930s.

   (C) underwent extensive social and cultural transformations.

   (D) reinstated the political and economic policies of Lenin.

   (E) granted political freedom to the nations of eastern Europe.

49. The European contact with the Americas

   (A) led to cooperative efforts between European societies and Native American societies.

   (B) eventually led to deflation in Europe.

   (C) was primarily motivated by the desire to Christianize the inhabitants of the New World.

   (D) led to the destruction of several American civilizations.

   (E) relaxed tensions between such powers as Spain and Portugal.

50. For defending the sacraments against attacks by the likes of Sir Thomas More, Pope Leo X bestowed the title of Defender of the Faith upon

   (A) Martin Luther.

   (B) Ignatius of Loyola.

   (C) Mary Tudor.

   (D) William Tyndale.

   (E) Henry VIII.

51. One of the first great European novels was written during the Golden Age of Spain by

   (A) Dante Alighieri.

   (B) El Cid.

   (C) Miguel de Cervantes.

   (D) Sancho Panza.

   (E) Don Juan.

52. During the reign of Elizabeth I, England's main enemy was

   (A) France.

   (B) Spain.

   (C) Germany.

   (D) Portugal.

   (E) Scotland.

53. This painting, part of the realism movement, by Jean Francois Millet
   (A) depicts a scene that usually would have been unidealized by other artistic movements.
   (B) glorified women and the work they did in rural areas.
   (C) was one of the most famous of the Renaissance period.
   (D) was one of the most famous of the twentieth century.
   (E) depicts a scene of Russian serfs before they were emancipated.

54. "Christianity has taken the side of everything weak, base, ill-constituted, it has made an ideal out of opposition to the preservative instincts of strong life." This statement reflects the beliefs of
    (A) Sigmund Freud.
    (B) Adolf Hitler.
    (C) Elie Wiesel.
    (D) Friedrich Nietzsche.
    (E) Otto von Bismarck.

55. The increased influence of military leaders in European nations in the years before World War I resulted from
    (A) the nations' desires for a return to order.
    (B) the collapse of the parliamentary system in Europe.
    (C) the spread of Communism and the threat of a violent Communist revolution.
    (D) the desire for a new avenue for social mobility.
    (E) the increased size and importance of the militaries in European nations.

56. The Truman Doctrine was intended to
    (A) rebuild the nations that had been hardest hit by Allied bombs.
    (B) offer assistance to those nations that had been attacked by Germany.
    (C) offer economic assistance to nations who might need protection from Communism.
    (D) ease the suffering of the children in cities that were hit by the German blitzkrieg.
    (E) offer financial rewards to agents offering information about Communist governments.

57. The foundling hospitals in Paris and London were examples of
    (A) the increased emphasis on caring for the mentally ill.
    (B) the desire to care for unwanted children.
    (C) the mobile military hospitals created during the Crimean War.
    (D) the advances made by Pasteur and Lister.
    (E) the facilities used by Nazis during the holocaust.

58. Baron de Montesquieu's work *The Persian Letters* was typical of Enlightenment writings in that
    (A) the author was open and honest about his feelings.
    (B) the real, critical message of the book was hidden behind a satirical story.
    (C) the author personally addresses the reigning monarch and called for reform.
    (D) the content was considered pornographic.
    (E) the author defended contemporary religious institutions from attacks by secular critics.

59. One of the most important features of the Enlightenment was
    (A) the Jacobin clubs.
    (B) the Star Chamber.
    (C) the salons.
    (D) the court of Louis XIV.
    (E) the duma.

60. The Quadruple Alliance against Napoleon included all of the following EXCEPT
    (A) Great Britain.
    (B) Austria.
    (C) Spain.
    (D) Russia.
    (E) Prussia.

61. For Germany, one of the most dynamic results of the Franco-Prussian War was
    (A) the institution of social reforms throughout the German empire.
    (B) the institution of the *zemstvos*.
    (C) the institution of the *Zollverein*.
    (D) the rise of German nationalism.
    (E) the establishment of a standing army.

62. During the Victorian Age, the primary institution of the middle-class was
    (A) the Church.
    (B) the university.
    (C) the family.
    (D) the workplace.
    (E) the parlor.

63. The issue addressed in Rudyard Kipling's *White Man's Burden* is
    (A) socialism.
    (B) imperialism.
    (C) nationalism.
    (D) isolationism.
    (E) appeasement.

64. Hitler's motivations of space and race referred to
    (A) his desire to put the first astronaut in space and his desire to eliminate subhuman races.
    (B) his desire to advance technologically and his desire to eliminate all subhuman races.
    (C) his attempts to race the other world powers to be the first in space.
    (D) his dream of conquering both nature and man.
    (E) his dream of more land for Aryans and the elimination of subhu man races to create that living space.

65. "…The force of gravity towards the whole planet did arise from and was compounded of the forces of gravity towards all its parts, and towards every one part was in the inverse proportion of the squares of the distances from the part." This statement was made by

(A) Sir Isaac Newton.

(B) Jean Jacques Rousseau.

(C) René Descartes.

(D) Francis Bacon.

(E) Albert Einstein.

66. For René Descartes, existing things were related to either

(A) good or evil.

(B) government or anarchy.

(C) mind or body.

(D) classical ideas or contemporary ideas.

(E) man or woman.

67. The huge increase in Russia's population during the eighteenth century can be attributed to natural population increases and

(A) the agricultural revolution.

(B) the industrial revolution.

(C) the use of midwives in childbirth.

(D) territorial expansion.

(E) the reduction in the number of men who died in wars.

Increase in European Population, 1700s

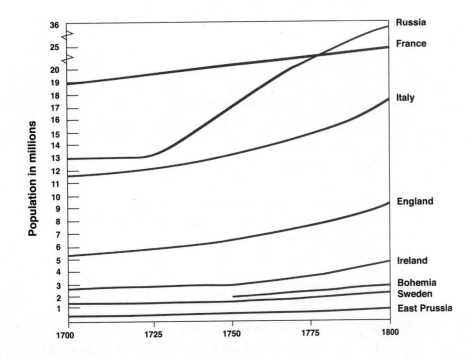

68. The open-field agricultural system was replaced by
    (A) crop rotation.
    (B) enclosure.
    (C) the three-field system.
    (D) the manorial system.
    (E) slash and burn farming.

69. The concordat between Napoleon and Pope Pius VII
    (A) gave the clergy the option to declare their loyalty to the state.
    (B) satisfied the pope's wishes for post-war France.
    (C) established the dominance of the Catholic Church in France.
    (D) required Rome to pay the salaries of the bishops.
    (E) stated that Catholicism was the religion of the majority of French citizens.

70. The *Zollverein*
    (A) was the lower house of the German parliament.
    (B) was a customs union that encouraged trade among German states.
    (C) was a Russian unit of local government dominated by the lower classes.
    (D) was a tariff that restricted trade among the German states.
    (E) was a tariff that restricted imports from non-German states.

71. The total war effort in World War I caused all of the following EXCEPT
    (A) the rise of the status of women.
    (B) the realization that socialism was a workable economy for European governments.
    (C) the increase in the destructive powers of the nations fighting the war.
    (D) the faster resolution of the conflict.
    (E) the increased profits for many businesses and industries.

72. In the Spanish Civil War of 1936, General Francisco Franco received assistance from
    (A) the United States.
    (B) Russia.
    (C) the pope.
    (D) Hitler and Mussolini.
    (E) Great Britain.

73. The time when Parliament ensured that no monarch would ever rule again without Parliament's assistance and guidance was

    (A) the Supremacy Act.

    (B) the Long Parliament.

    (C) the Short Parliament.

    (D) the Great Charter.

    (E) the Glorious Revolution.

74. Although Cardinal Richelieu and France were both Catholic, Richelieu supported Protestants elsewhere

    (A) because he secretly had converted to Protestantism.

    (B) because he felt sympathy for the Protestants who had suffered at the hands of Catholics.

    (C) because he tried to achieve a favorable balance of trade by doing business with Protestants.

    (D) because he conspired with foreign Protestants to overthrow Louis XIII.

    (E) because he pursued an anti-Habsburg foreign policy.

75. The revocation of the Edict of Nantes, originally intended to be a political and religious move, eventually turned out to be a military blunder because

    (A) the Catholics rose up against the French government.

    (B) the Huguenots rose up against the French government.

    (C) many of the exiled Huguenots joined other militaries and eventually fought against France.

    (D) England came to the defense of the Huguenots.

    (E) Spain attacked the French fleet that carried the Huguenots away from France.

76. The so-called print culture played a major role in the development and spread of

    (A) the Reformation.

    (B) the Scientific Revolution.

    (C) the Industrial Revolution.

    (D) the Enlightenment.

    (E) the Age of Anxiety.

77. The British Combination Acts of 1799 and 1800 outlawed

    (A) exploitation of children in the factories.

    (B) exploitation of women and children in the factories.

    (C) labor organizations.

    (D) protective tariffs.

    (E) free-trade practices.

78. Because of the restoration of the nobility and the Romantics' fascination with the Middle Ages,

    (A) people turned away from religion during the age of Romanticism.

    (B) Catholicism experienced a revival during the age of Romanticism.

    (C) Catholicism experienced a sharp decline during the age of Romanticism.

    (D) governments began outlawing religious worship during the age of Romanticism.

    (E) Protestant-Catholic wars of religion erupted in Western Europe.

79. The leader of Czechoslovakia when the Soviet Union invaded in 1968 was

    (A) Marshall Tito.

    (B) Lech Walesa.

    (C) Alexander Dubcek.

    (D) Gustav Husak.

    (E) Vaclav Havel.

80. The foundation of Mikhail Gorbachev's reforms was *perestroika*, or

    (A) the imposition of high tariffs on foreign goods in order to protect the Soviet economy.

    (B) the heating up of the arms race with the West.

    (C) the restructuring of the Soviet economy to allow for some private property and some free enterprise under a limited market economy.

    (D) the openness toward western culture and ideas.

    (E) free trade with all European nations.

SECTION II—FREE RESPONSE

Time—2 hours and 10 minutes

Percent of Total Grade—50

GENERAL INSTRUCTIONS

Reading Period - 15 minutes: All students should read and plan their answer to Part A, Question 1, the document-based essay question. If time permits, they may also read the essay questions in Part B.

Part A Suggested writing time - 45 minutes: All students must answer Question 1.

Part B Suggested planning and writing time - 35 minutes: Answer ONE question from Group 1; 35 minutes: Answer ONE question from Group 2

Section II of this examination requires answers in essay form. The supervisor will announce the time for starting and ending the reading period. To help you use your time efficiently, the supervisor will also announce the time that the writing for Part A should be completed. Be careful not to exceed the writing time suggested for Part A. If you do so, you may endanger your grade on the whole examination. If you finish writing Part A before time is announced, you may go on to plan and write Part B. If you finish the examination in less than the time allotted, you may go back and work on either Part A or Part B. Keep in mind that in an essay you should pay attention to the organization of your material, the validity and clarity of your general statements, and the intelligent and appropriate use of facts to support your generalizations.

You should write your answers with a pen, preferably one with black or dark blue ink. Be sure to write CLEARLY and LEGIBLY. Cross out any errors you make.

The questions for Section II are printed in the green insert. Use the green insert to organize your answers and for scratchwork, but *write your answers in the pink booklet*. Number each answer as the question is numbered in the examination. Do not skip lines. Begin each answer on a new page in the pink booklet.

After you have completed the examination, circle question 1 and the numbers of the two questions you have answered in Part B

PART A

Suggested Writing Time—45 minutes

Percent of Section II Score—45

Directions: The following question is based on the accompanying documents 1–11. (Some of the documents have been edited for the purpose of this exercise.) Write your answer on the lined pages of the pink essay booklet.

This question is designed to test your ability to work with historical documents. As you analyze the documents, *take into account both the sources of the documents and the authors' points of view*. Write an essay on the following topic that integrates your analysis of the documents. **Do not simply summarize the documents individually**. You may refer to relevant historical facts and developments not mentioned in the documents.

1. Describe and analyze the views of those involved in the women's suffrage movement in England in the late nineteenth and early twentieth centuries.

Historical Background: In the 1830s and 1840s, the Chartists unsuccessfully called for women's suffrage. Throughout the rest of the nineteenth century, other prominent individuals, such as John Stuart Mill, advocated women's suffrage, but leaders such as Queen Victoria, William Gladstone, and Benjamin Disraeli opposed a woman's right to vote. In 1897, the cause gained momentum when several suffrage groups merged to form the National Union of Woman Suffrage Societies.

Document 1

From a magazine article, *The Lancashire Factory Girl*, written by Selina Cooper in 1898

I have often heard the 'sarcastic' remark applied to the factory worker, "Oh she is only a factory girl," thus giving the impression to the World that we have no right to aspire to any other society but our own. I am sorry to say that we are not fully awakened to the facts that we contribute largely to the nation's wealth, and therefore demand respect and not insult. For in many a Lancashire home are to be found heroines whose names will never be handed down to posterity; yet it is consoling to know that we as a class contribute to the world.

Document 2

From the book *Women and Socialism* written by Isabella Ford in 1906

The Socialist movement, the Labour movement, call it which you will, and the Women's movement, are but different aspects of the same great force which has been, all through the ages, gradually pushing its way upwards, making for the reconstruction and regeneration of Society.

Document 3

From a speech given in 1913 by the Reverend Rupert Strong

The movement for women's suffrage was one of vital importance to the morality and welfare of the nation. I believe women should have some share in the government in order to promote clean living.

Document 4

An excerpt from a letter written to a newspaper in 1914

The impression is given that this and other countries are at war with one another. They are not. Their governments, composed of men and responsible only to the men of each country, and backed by the majority of men who have caught the war and glory fever, have declared war on one another. The women of all these countries have not been consulted as to whether they would have war or not. If men deliberately shut out women, the peace-loving sex, from their rightful share in ruling their countries, then all the appeals and sentiments and prayers will be of no avail in preventing hostilities.

Document 5

From a speech given by a woman suffragist and reported by The East Grinstead Observer in 1918

As an industrial worker, and since as a wife and mother, she realized how much legislation concerned her… women had expert knowledge to enable them to deal with great reform. Take the housing problem, a woman was far more likely to detect anything lacking in a house than a man was. They needed women's idea of economy and her grasp of detail.

Document 6

From the book *Unfinished Adventure* by Evelyn Sharp in 1933

At first, all I saw in the enfranchisement of women was a possible solution of much that subconsciously worried me from the time when, as a London child, I had seen ragged and barefoot children begging in the streets…

When the early sensational tactics of the militants focused my attention upon the political futility of the voteless reformer, I joined the nearest suffrage society, which happened ironically to be the non-militant London Society.

When militants and non-militants alike hastened to offer war service to the Government, no doubt many of them felt, if they thought about it at all, that this was the best way of helping their own cause. Certainly, by their four years' war work, they did prove the fallacy of the anti-suffragist' favorite argument, that women had no right to a voice in questions of peace and war because they took no part in it.

Document 7

A young girl from 1908

Document 8

A selection written by Mary Humphrey Ward and published in the February 1909 edition of *The Times*

Women's suffrage is a more dangerous leap in the dark than it was in the 1860s because of the vast growth of the Empire, the immense increase of England's imperial responsibilities, and there-with the increased complexity and risk of the problems which lie before our statesmen - constitutional, legal, financial, military, international problems - problems of men, only to be solved by the labour and special knowledge of men, and where the men who bear the burden ought to be left unhampered by the political inexperience of women.

Document 9

From a report of a meeting of published in May 1911

The speaker said that women had never possessed the right to vote for Members of Parliament in this country nor in any great country, and although the women's vote had been granted in one or two smaller countries, such as Australia and New Zealand, no great empire have given women's a voice in running the country. Women have not had the political experience that men had, and, on the whole, did not want the vote, and had little knowledge of, or interest in, politics. Politics would go on without the help of women, but the home wouldn't.

Document 10

A published summary of a statement made by Lady Musgrave, President of an Anti-Suffrage League in 1911

Lady Musgrave, President of the East Grinstead branch of the Anti-Suffragette League said she was strongly against the franchise being extended to women, for she did not think it would do any good whatsoever, and in sex interests, would do a lot of harm. She quoted the words of Lady Jersey: "Put not this additional burden upon us." Women were not equal to men in endurance or nervous energy, and she thought she might say, on the whole, in intellect.

Document 11

From a newspaper report of a 1911 Anti-Suffrage Society meeting

There was a large attendance – chiefly of ladies – at the Queen's Hall on Friday afternoon, where there was a debate on Women's Suffrage. Mr. Charles Everard presided. Mr. Maconochie spoke against the extension of the franchise to women. Mr. Maconochie was opposed to suffrage because there were too many women to make it safe. There were 1,300,000 more women than men in the country, and he objected to the political voting power being placed in the hands of women.

PART B

Suggested Planning and Writing Time—70 minutes

Percent of Section II Score—55

Directions: You are to answer TWO questions, one from each group of three questions below. Make your selections carefully, choosing the questions that you are best prepared to answer thoroughly in the time permitted. You should spend 5 minutes organizing or outlining each essay. In writing your essays, *use specific examples to support your answer*. Write your answers to the questions on the lined pages of the pink essay booklet. If time permits when you finish writing, check your work. Be certain to number your answers as the questions are numbered below.

Group 1

Choose ONE question from this group. The suggested writing time for this question is 30 minutes. *You are advised to spend 5 minutes planning your answer in the space provided.*

2.   "The Reformation was not only a religious movement but also a political and economic movement." Assess the validity of this statement.

3.   Evaluate the revolutionary nature of the Scientific Revolution in Europe.

4.   Analyze and discuss the origins of nationalism in Europe during the Napoleonic Era and the role of nationalism in the fate of Napoleon.

Group 2

Choose ONE question from this group. The suggested writing time for this question is 30 minutes. *You are advised to spend 5 minutes planning your answer in the space provided.*

5. Choose TWO of the following people and analyze their political goals, their methods, and the degree to which they succeeded in reaching those goals:

    Prince Klemens von Metternich

    Camillo de Cavour

    Otto von Bismarck

    Napoleon III

6. Discuss the extent to which music, art, and literature reflected the feelings and thoughts of Europe in the early twentieth century. Use specific examples to support your answer.

7. Analyze and discuss the steps taken by Western Europe toward economic recovery in the second half of the twentieth century.

Answers and Explanations

Quick-Score Answers

1. A	11. D	21. D	31. D	41. D	51. C	61. D	71. D
2. A	12. D	22. C	32. A	42. A	52. B	62. C	72. D
3. B	13. A	23. A	33. A	43. B	53. A	63. B	73. B
4. A	14. A	24. E	34. D	44. C	54. D	64. E	74. E
5. D	15. D	25. A	35. B	45. E	55. E	65. A	75. C
6. E	16. C	26. B	36. B	46. B	56. C	66. C	76. D
7. C	17. E	27. A	37. A	47. B	57. B	67. D	77. C
8. B	18. E	28. A	38. E	48. B	58. B	68. B	78. B
9. D	19. D	29. E	39. C	49. D	59. C	69. E	79. C
10. E	20. D	30. B	40. A	50. E	60. C	70. B	80. C

1. **The correct answer is (A).** Renaissance humanists advocated a liberal education, and they used many primary sources from Greece and Rome for their lessons.

2. **The correct answer is (A).** The people of the Netherlands were traditionally open-minded and tolerant of varying religious views.

3. **The correct answer is (B).** After the fall of Constantinople in 1453, the Russian Orthodox Church considered Moscow the Third Rome.

4. **The correct answer is (A).** The Enlightenment thinkers considered themselves reformers, not revolutionaries. They sought reform through writings and philosophy as opposed to violence and weapons.

5. **The correct answer is (D).** France loaned a great deal of money to the American colonies. In addition, France provided the colonies with men and supplies. This increased French debt exponentially.

6. **The correct answer is (E).** The Romantic Movement included such literature as that of Edgar Allan Poe and Mary Shelley. These and other authors seemed shockingly terrifying to many and simply bizarre to others.

7. **The correct answer is (C).** India was considered the jewel of the British crown. The British invested heavily in India and made Queen Victoria Empress of India.

8. **The correct answer is (B).** The students of Europe (and the United States) often took to the streets to protest war and other issues over which they felt they had little or no voice or influence. Participation in the youth movement dwindled in the 1970s.

9. **The correct answer is (D).** The dark shaded area is the land under the influence of Protestant thought around 1550.

10. **The correct answer is (E).** Oliver Cromwell used the military to take and keep control of England. He also used his military to enforce his many laws. Therefore, as Lord Protector, Cromwell acted as a dictator.

11. **The correct answer is (D).** In October 1789, about 7,000 angry women marched from Paris to Versailles to demand bread. They eventually forced the royal family to return to Paris from Versailles.

12. **The correct answer is (D).** Austria and Prussia issued the Declaration of Pillnitz as an invitation to other monarchs to offer support to the French monarchy in order to prevent revolutionary ideas from spreading to other European nations.

13. **The correct answer is (A).** Prince Klemens von Metternich, a staunch conservative, dominated the Congress of Vienna and ushered in the Age of Metternich.

14. **The correct answer is (A).** A plebiscite was held in the Papal States and in the Two Sicilies, and the people overwhelmingly voted to unite with Piedmont.

15. **The correct answer is (D).** Charles Darwin, in his theory of natural selection, argued that species that were fit would survive and their traits and attributes would be passed on to their offspring.

16. **The correct answer is (C).** Hermann Göring's final solution to the "Jewish problem" was the elimination of the Jews using labor and concentration camps.

17. **The correct answer is (E).** Historians often use the phrase "God, gold, and glory" to sum up the motivations of explorers during the fifteenth- and sixteenth-century expeditions to the New World.

18. **The correct answer is (E).** Ptolemy placed the earth at the center of the universe. Around it orbited crystalline spheres, and beyond those orbits were God and the angels.

19. **The correct answer is (D).** The *junkers* were German noble landowners and landlords.

20. **The correct answer is (D).** The Russians used the scorched earth strategy, which involves retreating and burning the land, food, and supplies along the way so that the pursuers are left with no resources.

21. **The correct answer is (D).** The Corn Laws added exceptionally high tariffs to imported grain, thus ending free trade of grain. The Corn Laws did not deal with British corn.

22. **The correct answer is (C).** Bismarck aimed his *Kulturkampf* at Catholics but later backed down from his original hard-line policies.

23. **The correct answer is (A).** The theory of Social Darwinism maintained that in the struggle for superiority between nations, stronger nations would inevitably consume the weaker nations.

24. **The correct answer is (E).** This Russian poster was used to portray the woman factory worker as a heroine during times of war. This encouraged Russian women to work in factories on the homefront.

25. **The correct answer is (A).** Luther believed that a woman should be a submissive yet supportive wife. He also believed that a woman should take an active role in the upbringing of children.

26. **The correct answer is (B).** Jethro Tull, Charles Townsend, and Robert Bakewell each made contributions to the field of agriculture that led to what historians have called the Agricultural Revolution.

27. **The correct answer is (B).** The leaders of the Republic of Virtue wanted to do away with all things Christian and Catholic, so they replaced the traditional month and day names with names relating to nature.

28. **The correct answer is (A).** Britain practiced free trade, but many countries on the Continent felt that the only way they could compete with Britain was through the use of protective tariffs.

29. **The correct answer is (E).** In December 1825, the Decembrists led an unsuccessful revolt against the czar in which they appealed for a constitutional monarchy and the abolition of serfdom.

30. **The correct answer is (B).** Count Cavour (1810–1861), prime minister of Piedmont-Sardinia, was a practical and realistic political man. His ambition was to unite Italy with King Victor Emmanuel and its leader. He knew the Italian states, divided as they were, could not rid themselves of Austrian domination without the help of a strong ally. He was willing to trade Nice and Savoy to France in return for her military assistance against Austria. In 1854, Cavour entered Piedmont into the Crimean War on the side of France and Britain in order to tie his country and France closer together. In the summer of 1858, Cavour managed to get Napoleon III's promise to help Piedmont in a war against Austria.

31. **The correct answer is (D).** Stalin arrested, tried, and executed many Old Bolsheviks in order to establish greater control of the party.

32. **The correct answer is (A).** The European Coal and Steel Community members created the EEC and eliminated trade barriers between the nations.

33. **The correct answer is (A).** The Medici family was one of the most influential families of Renaissance Italy.

34. **The correct answer is (D).** This statue of Peter the Great symbolically shows him leading Russia up a hill toward the west. It represents his greatness and his leadership of Russia toward a more Western culture.

35. **The correct answer is (B).** Locke believed that man was born with his mind as a clean slate and without innate ideas. He argued that knowledge is derived from experiences.

36. **The correct answer is (B).** Napoleon hoped to crush the British economy by cutting them off from their trade partners on the continent.

37. **The correct answer is (A).** The Romantics looked at nature in a much more organic, emotional, and sentimental way than the *philosophes,* who subjected things to reason and science.

38. **The correct answer is (E).** Prince Albert was referring to man's magnificent achievements, specifically Britain's achievements, in the Industrial Revolution.

39. **The correct answer is (C).** Giuseppe Mazzini founded a group called Young Italy, a group that advocated Italian nationalism in 1831.

40. **The correct answer is (A).** Most people initially believed that the war would be over within a matter of weeks or months and that their troops would be home by Christmas 1914.

41. **The correct answer is (D).** The Church sponsored many artists to do work on churches, abbeys, and other religious buildings.

42. **The correct answer is (A).** Created during the Catholic Reformation, the Jesuits and the Ursuline Order helped stop the spread of Protestantism and helped convert people to Catholicism.

43. **The correct answer is (B).** After he became king, Henry IV converted from Protestantism to Catholicism to appease the Catholic population of France.

44. **The correct answer is (C).** In 1648, the Peace of Westphalia reduced the power of the pope in Germany and granted the German princes sovereignty.

45. **The correct answer is (E).** Metternich made this statement after the threat of Napoleon had been eliminated. Metternich expressed his ultraconservatism by encouraging stability of the government and wariness of revolutionary and nationalistic ideas.

46. **The correct answer is (B).** Britain and France were concerned that Russia would upset the European balance of power by becoming the dominant nation of Eastern Europe and the Eastern Mediterranean.

47. **The correct answer is (B).** During the Second Industrial Revolution, women were deterred from working in the factories and mines and were encouraged to stay at home and raise children. Some women who needed to work to supplement the household income turned to prostitution or working in sweat-shops.

48. **The correct answer is (B).** After the war, Stalin reverted to his totalitarian methods of the prewar years.

49. **The correct answer is (D).** Europeans single-handedly destroyed such mighty civilizations as the Incas and Aztecs and forever altered the other societies they encountered.

50. **The correct answer is (E).** Henry VIII defended the sacraments from Luther's attacks and was rewarded by Pope Leo X. Of course, this was before Henry's relationship with Rome went sour.

51. **The correct answer is (C).** Cervantes wrote *Don Quixote* during the Golden Age of Spain. *Don Quixote* is considered one of the greatest European novels.

52. **The correct answer is (B).** England developed an intense rivalry with Spain under Elizabeth I, especially concerning naval power.

53. **The correct answer is (A).** Millet's painting *The Sower* depicts a typical rural scene, one that would have been unidealized by most other painters. This type of painting was often interpreted as a protest of poor conditions for rural inhabitants.

54. **The correct answer is (D).** Nietzsche believed that Christianity was a religion of pity and made everything weak. He believed that Christianity tended to crush the human spirit.

55. **The correct answer is (E).** The size of European militaries increased by leaps and bounds in the twenty or so years prior to World War I. With the increase in size came the increased influence of the military leaders in government affairs, especially in foreign policy.

56. **The correct answer is (C).** The Truman Doctrine pledged assistance to any nation that needed help escaping or avoiding Communism.

57. **The correct answer is (B).** The Paris and London Foundling Hospitals were created to care for unwanted children in the late seventeenth and early eighteenth centuries.

58. **The correct answer is (B).** *The Persian Letters* used fictitious letters written by Persians who had visited Europe to criticize various institutions and practices of Europeans. This style was typical of many Enlightenment writers.

59. **The correct answer is (C).** Hosted by prominent women, salons provided a safe environment for the *philosophes* to discuss intellectual and political matters without having to worry about being harassed by the government.

60. **The correct answer is (C).** Spain was not a member of the Quadruple Alliance against Napoleon's France.

61. **The correct answer is (D).** The Franco-Prussian War caused an unprecedented rise in German nationalism and patriotism.

62. **The correct answer is (C).** The middle class of the Victorian Age placed an unprecedented amount of importance upon the family and the development of children.

63. **The correct answer is (B).** Kipling's poem reflects the idea that the more civilized, superior nations have the burden of civilizing and bettering the inferior people of the world.

64. **The correct answer is (E).** Hitler wanted to create more living space for the superior races by eliminating the subhuman races and taking their land.

65. **The correct answer is (A).** This scientific statement is from Newton's work on gravitation.

66. **The correct answer is (C).** Descartes divided things into two categories: things thought, or of the mind, and things occupying space, or of the body.

67. **The correct answer is (D).** In addition to natural population increases, Russia's territorial expansion added vast numbers of people to its population.

68. **The correct answer is (B).** In the eighteenth century, landlords enclosed the land to consolidate it and increase their profits.

69. **The correct answer is (E).** The concordat merely stated that most French citizens were Catholic. It did not satisfy the pope, and it did not establish the dominance of Catholicism in France. Napoleon benefited the most from the signing of the concordat.

70. **The correct answer is (B).** The *Zollverein* was a customs union that stimulated trade among German states by eliminating tolls on roads and rivers.

71. **The correct answer is (D).** The total war effort did nothing to shorten the war. It simply increased the ability of each nation to inflict more damage upon the other nations.

72. **The correct answer is (D).** Hitler and Mussolini jointly offered assistance to General Franco in order to help him establish a fascist government in Spain.

73. **The correct answer is (B).** The Long Parliament made it illegal to collect ship money and taxes without parliamentary consent. Parliament also abolished the Star Chamber and required parliamentary sessions at least every three years.

74. **The correct answer is (E).** Cardinal Richelieu supported Protestants elsewhere to contain and check the power of the Habsburgs.

75. **The correct answer is (C).** A few hundred thousand people fled France, and many of them either joined the international efforts against France or joined the army of William of Orange.

76. **The correct answer is (D).** Although printed material played a role during the Reformation, the mass volume of books and pamphlets led to an unprecedented wave of reading and writing that resulted in an unprecedented dispersion of information and ideas across Europe during the Enlightenment.

77. **The correct answer is (C).** The Combination Acts outlawed labor organizations and worker associations. They did not outlaw trade unions, though.

78. **The correct answer is (B).** The Catholic Church experienced a great revival during the Age of Romanticism. Protestantism experienced a revival, or awakening, too.

79. **The correct answer is (C).** Alexander Dubcek attempted to create communism with a human face in Czechoslovakia, but his efforts were thwarted when the Soviets invaded in 1968.

80. **The correct answer is (C).** *Perestroika*, or restructuring, meant that Gorbachev wanted to relax the strict economic policies of the hard-line Communists and allow more free-trade and free-market economics.

FREE-RESPONSE QUESTIONS ANSWER GUIDE

1. Describe and analyze the views of those involved in the women's suffrage movement in England in the late nineteenth and early twentieth centuries.

Answer Guide:

Hopefully, you remembered to take notes on the documents and remembered to organize the documents using a chart. If you did, then writing this essay probably was not very difficult. The most important part of answering this question is the development of your thesis. Your thesis should be clear and concise. It should tell the reader exactly what you are going to say in your essay. In short, your thesis must clearly sum up your argument. For this particular question, your thesis should deal with the people who advocated women's suffrage and those who opposed it. In addition, your thesis should address a few of the reasons why each group felt the way they did. For example:

The women's suffrage advocates believed that women deserved the vote, that women had earned the vote, and that women could contribute to politics. Those that opposed woman suffrage believed that women had no place in politics, but rather women belonged at home.

The next step is the body of the essay. Your essay should offer a clear, organized argument that supports your thesis. The body of your essay should first include some historical background of the women's suffrage movement. Your essay could begin with either side of the issue of women's suffrage in England, either for it or against it. Your essay should include the reasons and arguments made on behalf of the suffrage movement.

Your essay should state that Documents 1 and 6 argue that women have contributed to society and therefore deserve the right to vote. Documents 2, 3, 4, and 6 advocate women's suffrage because women's suffrage would promote better living and a higher morality in society. Documents 5 and 7 argue that women are capable of understanding and contributing to the political system. Your essay should point out the authorship and the points of view of the authors of these documents, in particular Document 3, which was from a man. The remaining documents oppose women's suffrage. Document 8 portrays politics as a man's world better left to men alone. The document, along with Document 9, also implies that women would simply slow the process because of their political inexperience. Document 9 implies that no great empire had ever granted women's suffrage and that most women didn't want it anyway. In addition, Document 9 implied that women belonged in the home and not in politics. Document 10 warns of burdening the women with the vote. Document 11 argues that suffrage granted to so many women would be unsafe, also implying that women lack the political experience to vote, as did Documents 8 and 9.

Your essay could either present one side of the issue over the other or it could present one point and then a conflicting point from the opposition and so on. In this essay, it is very important that you discuss the points of view and biases of the authors. If your essay includes most or all of these points, you are well on your way to a good, solid essay. In addition, any extra historical information you can add to your essay will enhance the overall quality of your piece. Use the rubric in Chapter 2 to further evaluate your essay.

2. "The Reformation was not only a religious movement but also a political and economic movement." Assess the validity of this statement.

Answer Guide:

Your essay should begin with the historical background of the Reformation, including its causes and goals. Your essay should include a treatment of the economic effects that include the Protestant idea that all vocations are important and the justification of business classes. In addition, your essay should include a discussion of the Protestant work ethic. You should include in your essay the idea of a religiously homogenous state as decided by the prince, the decline of the intervention of the Church into affairs of the state, and the increasing identity of the Church within the state. An excellent essay would also include the legislation of England under Henry VIII as examples. You might also include a discussion of the religiously motivated military conflicts during and after the Reformation. Be sure your essay uses historical facts to support your argument. Finally, make sure your essay has a clear, organized thesis and an organized body that supports it.

3. Evaluate the revolutionary nature of the Scientific Revolution in Europe.

Answer Guide:

Your essay should argue that the Scientific Revolution either was or was not revolutionary and, if it was, to what extent. Regardless of your thesis, you should begin your essay with some historical background on the Scientific Revolution. Also regardless of your thesis, you should include a discussion of the move toward a new world view. You should include a treatment of the Copernican theory as opposed to the traditional Ptolemaic/Aristotelian theory of the universe, and discuss the extent to which this theory was accepted and rejected. An excellent essay would discuss the transition from focusing on the metaphysical to focusing on the physical during this time. An excellent essay would point out that the revolution occurred more in the way of thinking rather than in scientific and technological developments. Your essay should mention different thinkers of the Scientific Revolution and how they affected the new way of thinking. Be sure your essay uses historical facts to support your argument. Finally, make sure your essay has a clear, organized thesis and an organized body that supports your thesis.

4. Analyze and discuss the origins of nationalism in Europe during the Napoleonic Era and the role of nationalism in the fate of Napoleon.

Answer Guide:

Your essay should begin with some historical background on the French Revolution and the rise of Napoleon. You should also include a treatment of the rise of the nationalistic spirit during the French Revolution. You should discuss the extent to which the people of Europe did not want to be under the control of Napoleon but rather preferred to be united with others of a common history, culture, language, or geography. Your essay should include examples such as Spain and Prussia. Your essay should include a summary of the role nationalism played in the defeat of Napoleon. Be sure your essay uses historical facts to support your argument. Finally, make sure your essay has a clear, organized thesis and an organized body that supports your thesis.

5. Choose TWO of the following people and analyze their political goals, their methods, and the degree to which they succeeded in reaching those goals:

Prince Klemens von Metternich

Camillo de Cavour

Otto von Bismarck

Napoleon III

Answer Guide:

If your essay is about Metternich, you should include some historical background on Metternich, including his battle against liberalism and nationalism, his fight for a balance of power in Europe, his oppressive police force, the Carlsbad Decrees, and the fact that he was successful until 1848. If your essay is about Cavour, you should include the failed Revolutions of 1848, the emergence of Sardinia-Piedmont as the most influential Italian state, his diplomacy and wars, and his relationship with Garibaldi. You should include a discussion of the unification of Italy. If your essay is about Bismarck, your essay should include the struggles between Bismarck and the parliament, the Danish War, the Austro-Prussian War, and the Franco-Prussian War. You should also include the fact that Germany emerged as the most powerful nation in Europe under Bismarck. If your essay is about Napoleon III, your essay should include his rise to power, his control of the national elections, the political structure of the French government, and the governmental control of the French economy. You should also include a treatment of his success economically and politically in the Second Empire. Be sure your essay uses historical facts to support your argument. Finally, make sure your essay has a clear, organized thesis and an organized body that supports your thesis.

6. Discuss the extent to which music, art, and literature reflected the feelings and thoughts of Europe in the early twentieth century. Use specific examples to support your answer.

Answer Guide:

You should begin your essay with a discussion of the events of the early twentieth century and the feelings and emotions that accompanied and followed those events in Europe. Your essay should include a discussion of the musical changes that occurred in the early twentieth century along with some of the early twentieth-century musicians. You should also include a discussion of the major artistic movements of the time period and the way in which the art diverged from the traditional art that had gone before. An excellent essay would include several examples of both art and artist. Finally, your essay should include some of the writers who changed the face of literature in the early twentieth century and the methods of writing they employed. Again, an excellent essay would include several writers and examples of their work. Be sure your essay uses historical facts to support your argument, and make sure your essay has a clear, organized thesis and an organized body that supports your thesis.

7. Analyze and discuss the steps taken by Western Europe toward economic recovery in the second half of the twentieth century.

Answer Guide:

Your essay should begin with a discussion of the economic consequences of World War II on Western Europe. You should include the Truman Doctrine and the Marshall Plan. You could even include the Berlin Airlift. Your essay should emphasize the importance of the rise of capitalism and free trade in Western Europe, due mostly to the enormous economic success of the United States. You should also include a treatment of the move toward unity, particularly economic unity, in Western Europe. Good examples that need to be included in your essay are the European Coal and Steel Community and the Common Market. An excellent essay would include the elimination of colonies by some countries and the institution and the easing of socialist welfare programs in other countries. Be sure your essay uses historical facts to support your argument. Finally, make sure your essay has a clear, organized thesis and an organized body that supports it.

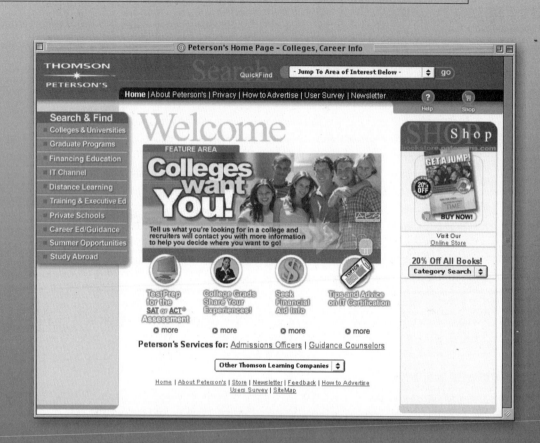